KU-495-954

Tim Hale

Smarter
Investing

Simpler decisions for better results

 Prentice Hall
FINANCIAL TIMES

An imprint of Pearson Education

Harlow, England ■ London ■ New York ■ Toronto Sydney ■ Tokyo ■ Singapore
Hong Kong ■ Cape Town ■ New Delhi ■ Madrid ■ Paris ■ Amsterdam ■ Munich ■ Milan

PEARSON EDUCATION LIMITED

Edinburgh Gate
Harlow CM20 2JE
Tel: +44 (0) 1279 623623
Fax: +44 (0) 1279 431059
Website: www.pearsoned.co.uk

First published in Great Britain in 2006
©Tim Hale 2006

The right of Tim Hale to be identified as author of this work has been asserted by him in
accordance with the Copyright, Designs and Patents Act 1988.

ISBN-13: 978-0-273-70800-1

British Library Cataloguing-in-Publication Data
A catalogue record for this book is available from the Library of Congress

Library of Congress Cataloging-in-Publication Data
Hale, Tim.
    Smarter Investing : simpler decisions for better results / Tim Hale.
    p. cm.
    Includes bibliographical references and index.
    ISBN-13: 978-0-273-70800-1 (alk. paper)
    ISBN-10: 0-273-70800-7 (alk. paper)
    1. Investments. I. Title

    HG4521.H228 2006
    332.6--dc22

                                                                            2006042334

All rights reserved. No part of this publication may be reproduced, stored in a retrieval system,
or transmitted in any form or by any means, electronic, mechanical, photocopying, recording
or otherwise, without either the prior written permission of the publisher or a licence
permitting restricted copying in the United Kingdom issued by the Copyright Licensing Agency
Ltd, 90 Tottenham Court Road, London W1T 4LP. This book may not be lent, resold, hired out
or otherwise disposed of by way of trade in any form of binding or cover other than that in
which it is published, without the prior consent of the Publishers.

10 9 8 7 6 5 4 3 2
10 09 08 07

Designed by Sue Lamble
Typeset in Stone Serif 9 point by 3
Printed and bound in Great Britain by Bell & Bain Ltd, Glasgow

The Publisher's policy is to use paper manufactured from sustainable forests.

Sheffield Hallam University
Learning and IT Services
Adsetts Centre City Campus
Sheffield S1 1WS

101 875 379 6

"An excelle [...] as the complexities, of personal investment. This book gives you what you need to plan your investment strategy with confidence and sleep easy at night."

Matthew Hunt, Chief Investment Officer and Principal of Prospect Wealth Management

"*Smarter Investing* reflects the uncomplicated yet innovative approach to understanding investing that Tim adopts in his consulting and training work – unlike many, this book will make a difference to you."

Cornelia Kiley, Former Managing Director, Head of Institutional Distribution, Columbia Management, Bank of America

"A lo
one-(
term:
finan

Willi(

"Prof(
inves1
and sl
proce

Ian O1

ONE WEEK LOAN

SHEFFIELD HALLAM UNIVERSITY
LEARNING CENTRE
WITHDRAWN FROM STOCK

FT Prentice Hall
FINANCIAL TIMES

In an increasingly competitive world, we believe it's quality of thinking that gives you the edge – an idea that opens new doors, a technique that solves a problem, or an insight that simply makes sense of it all. The more you know, the smarter and faster you can go.

That's why we work with the best minds in business and finance to bring cutting-edge thinking and best learning practice to a global market.

Under a range of leading imprints, including *Financial Times Prentice Hall*, we create world-class print publications and electronic products bringing our readers knowledge, skills and understanding, which can be applied whether studying or at work.

To find out more about Pearson Education publications, or tell us about the books you'd like to find, you can visit us at
www.pearsoned.co.uk

For Emma, Tilly and Betsy – my gorgeous girls
Sorry it wasn't just a pamphlet!

Contents

Preface

This book is written with a degree of frustration with investment management. As an industry, it plays an important part in our lives as we seek to secure our financial futures through sound investment programmes, yet much of the information and advice on investing in our daily lives, on the television, in the press and from cyberspace, is often confused by fuzzy thinking, frequently tainted by vested interests, and occasionally reeks of exploitation. This makes life difficult for anyone faced with making decisions about how they are going to invest. That, nowadays, means nearly all of us.

Not long after joining an investment management firm, quite a few years ago now, I began to suspect that something was up. I was studying a bar chart of the firm's less-than-stellar performance, where over each period our bar failed to match that of the markets, which was at odds with the glowing reports I had been sold during my interview. The market seemed the consistent winner. One of my more cynical colleagues came up to me and took hold of the chart I was looking at, turned it upside down and said 'Tim, I think that's what you are looking for!' I spent several years slowly becoming convinced that there had to be a better way, despite my colleagues' protestations: thus the genesis of this book.

The balance between what is best for the investor and what is best for the industry has become skewed in favour of the industry and we are regularly encouraged to act against our best interests and what the empirical evidence says we should be doing. Choice proliferation, a lack of investment education, selling scandals and information overload have resulted in an industry that appears confusing and confused, discouraging too many from investing or investing well. It's hard to know who to trust to provide advice and how to judge the value and appropriateness of advice given.

I have written this book to try and help you, as an individual investor, to overcome this dilemma and take your investing forwards, built on the confidence of knowing that what you are doing is the simplest and most effective way to go about things. It seeks to carve through the confusion and help you to develop a clear understanding of what good investing really is about. It takes into account the latest research and data that point us towards what we should all be doing, much of which is contrary to what the industry is telling us we should be doing. It will empower you to build an investment programme that you believe in and understand, that gives you a high degree of reassurance that your future financial goals will be met, and significantly reduces both the time demands and the stress that often seem to accompany investing. That's a lot to promise and it needs some effort from you. The key to investing is to do a few simple things exceptionally well, and this book tells you how.

Investment decisions are extremely important part of our lives and affect us profoundly. As such, you owe it to yourself to begin to put your investing in order. It can appear complicated out there, but if you have a few solid and simple rules to hand, you can use or discard information and advice as you see fit and make investing decisions with confidence. The investment power will then lie in your hands as opposed to others whose interests are not necessarily aligned with your own.

Looking beyond the Oxford English Dictionary's rather uninspiring first definition of 'invest' being 'to use (money) to buy stocks, shares, or property etc. in order to earn interest or bring profit for the buyer' one finds the second definition 'To spend money, time, or effort on something that will be useful'. Invest in your investing skills.

Tim Hale
Exeter
United Kingdom
2006

Publisher's acknowledgements

We are grateful to the following for permission to reproduce copyright material:

Figures 2.3, 2.4, 4.2, 8.1, 8.2, 8.3, 8.4, 8.5, 8.6, 8.8, 8.9, 8.10, 8.11, 8.12, 8.13, 8.16, 8.17, 9.2, 10.1, 10.2, 15.2, 15.3, 15.4, 15.5, 15.6, 15.7, 15.8, 15.9, 15.10, 16.5, 16.6, 16.7, 16.8, 16.9, 16.11, 17.2, 17.10, 18.1 and 18.2 and Tables 9.1, 9.2, and 15.1 use data from Elroy Dimson, Paul Marsh and Mike Staunton, *Triumph of the Optimists: 101 Years of Global Investment Returns*, Princeton University Press, 2002; Figure 6.1 from MASLOW, ABRAHAM, MOTIVATION & PERSONALITY, 1st Edition, © 1970. Adapted by permission of Pearson Education, Inc., Upper Saddle River, NJ; Table 4.4 and Figure 14.1 from WM Company (1999) *Comparison of Active and Passive Management of Unit Trust* with permission from WM Performance Services; Figure 9.3 from John Bogle, *Common sense on mutual funds* (1999) John Wiley & Sons, reprinted with permission of John Wiley & Sons, Inc; Table 13.2 and Figures 13.1, 13.2 and 13.3 from Lipper Fitzrovia; Table 14.1 from Standard & Poor's Indices Versus Active Funds Scorecard (SPIVA™): Fourth Quarter 2002; Figure 14.2 from Bernstein, William, *The Intelligent Asset Allocator* ©2001, McGraw-Hill, reproduced with permission of the McGraw-Hill Companies; Dilbert cartoons reproduced with permission from Knight Features.

In some instances we have been unable to trace the owners of copyright material, and we would appreciate any information that would enable us to do so.

Author's acknowledgements

'Writing is an adventure. To begin with, it is a toy and an amusement. Then it becomes a mistress, then it becomes a master, then it becomes a tyrant. The last phase is that just as you are about to be reconciled to your servitude, you kill the monster and fling him to the public.'

Winston Churchill

This book has been a long time in the making and my first thanks must go to all of those who have had to put up with me going on about it for so long. I apologise to those who asked me to write a pamphlet.

Special thanks to Emma, my wife, whose continuous encouragement and support helped me to get to the end. Also to my father, David Hale, who suffered my ramblings as I tried to unscramble the book inside my head, and who reviewed the preliminary drafts. As ever, his diplomatic skills, intelligence and encouragement helped me to reach this point.

I am particularly grateful to the team at Pearson Eduction: to Richard Stagg and Liz Gooster my editors, who backed the book and provided invaluable input into its structure and feel; and to Laura Brundell, my production editor, who kept me to schedule and had the patience to deal with my badly annotated proofs!

Special thanks to George Faherty and Matthew Hunt, both worthy active investment managers, who cast a critical eye over the drafts and provided a forum for debate and refinement of these ideas. I owe them both for their support both for this and throughout my career.

To Cornelia Kiley, Mark Chamieh, Bill Dessoffy, Kevin Norton, David DuRie, Taka Hashimoto and Kaoru Fukae, some of the best sales professionals in the business, whom I thank for their teamwork and friendship.

Thanks, too, to George Faherty again, Mitch Kessler, and Jimmy Sanchez, friends and money managers at Chase Manhattan Bank, who were a constant target for my ideas argued on numerous occasions over lunch at the

Cuban diner on 46th Street in Manhattan. All very knowledgeable active managers, but I like them none the less for it.

I have had the pleasure to work with a number of fund managers and thank them for their input in and influence in whatever forms it came. Special thanks go to Matthew Hunt, who gave me a chance and sowed the first seeds of my thinking. Thanks also to Hank Gooss, Lee Wortham, Dave McLean, Tim Haywood, Con Panayotou, John Simpson, Michelle Lusty and all those from the CGIL days, and to Debbie Duncan, Mark Richardson, Steve Prostano, Michael Boardman, Neil Ellerbeck, Gordon Ross, Rhydian Davies, Jo Kearins, Kim Wiehl, Craig Blessing, Vicky Preston, Dave Mace, Jerry Maravegias and Joe Desantis at Chase in New York, Hong Kong, Tokyo and London who made going to work fun.

Finally, a special thanks to some of the other fund managers I have worked with without whose egos, bull and lack of sustainable out-performance the angst to write this book would never have existed.

Foreword

When I was asked to write a few words to introduce this book before I had the opportunity to read it, I hesitated for a moment before agreeing for two reasons.

Firstly, having worked with the author for a number of years in the '90s and kept in close touch since, I knew the views that he was likely to express. Whilst this book is no attack on the investment industry, it certainly will not encourage too many readers to reach for the telephone to sign up with one of the many companies proffering their active investment management wares. Having been in the industry for 35 years, mainly creating, managing and promoting active products, I somehow felt that it might be disloyal to the business that has provided my livelihood all those years and that it would also be somewhat hypocritical.

Secondly, I felt that this might be a 'me too' book. The ground had to have been covered before. A few hours browsing the shelves of Waterstones and the Internet suggest that this is not the case. There are many books purporting to tell you how to pick the stocks that will make you a fortune but it is hard to find anything that stands back and puts equity investing into the context of a diversified portfolio. Those that do exist tend to focus on the US financial markets. I concluded that this is a book that needed to be written and the finished product does not disappoint.

Hardly a week goes by without the financial press reporting on yet another company closing its final salary pension scheme; most typically to replace it with a defined contribution scheme that will be unlikely on its own to meet the retirement aspirations of its members. When it is a large well-known company and other news is scarce, such reports will even make it to the front pages of the tabloids. Most defined contribution schemes require members to make some simple but crucial choices between different investment vehicles, whilst the prudent will supplement membership of such a scheme with additional contributions or their own investment portfolio. Those with SIPPs (self invested pension plans) will similarly have to make choices between different asset classes. We are all increasingly forced to make investment decisions, whether we like it or not, and only a small minority of people are properly equipped to make educated decisions relating to such asset allocation.

But asset allocation is only half the problem. When it comes to executing an investment strategy the pitfalls are almost as great. Unfortunately it is extremely difficult to get genuinely objective advice. Most investment companies derive at least part of their revenue from products that they manage in-house or share in the revenue of products managed by third parties. The professionals who work for them tend to be incentivised accordingly. Similarly, many IFAs (independent financial advisors) are con-flicted by the different financial arrangements that they have with the investment companies whose products they are recommending to their clients. Stockbrokers too are conflicted by the fact that they derive income from portfolio turnover. There is little incentive for an advisor, working for such companies to recommend a buy and hold strategy in low margin passive products.

The financial press is full of 'hard luck' stories of people who have lost a large proportion of their assets investing in totally inappropriate asset classes or investment vehicles, frequently having taken so-called 'pro-fessional' advice. Sometimes these people were just driven by greed but usually it was ignorance. My heart bleeds for (most of) them and if just a few are persuaded to spend some hours reading this book, Tim Hale will have done everyone a great service.

All investment professionals love recounting anecdotes, particularly when they 'get it right', and I am no exception. When I was working in the USA I purchased modest properties in Manhattan and on the north shore of Long Island. Like most British people I have a penchant for older properties and I managed to find two to refurbish. The building contractor, who helped me in this endeavour and who duly made a small fortune out of me, used to play the stock market and, knowing my profession, could not resist sharing the latest hot tips with me. With the strength of the US equity market in the late '90s, it was not too difficult to make money trading equi-ties. Nevertheless, you can imagine my surprise when he told me in late 1999 that he was giving up his thriving building business to be an equity day-trader. Stuart did me a huge favour. There is an old adage about it being time to get out of the market when the bell-hop in the elevator wants to discuss his share portfolio with you and this seemed to be a similar Damascene moment. I took appropriate action switching a significant proportion of my equity portfolio into hedge funds (a good idea) and art (less good but great fun). This book rightly argues against market timing but if you do feel compelled to indulge in it, just try and make sure that you sell after a major rise and not after a fall. You will not be surprised to hear that my friend is again a building contractor, at least for the moment.

Tim has the benefit of enormous knowledge and experience. He writes with a certain objectivity and detachment which arises from having the cold statistics to argue his case. He also conveys a passion, which comes from having seen just about every mistake in the book made by both clients and investment professionals. Critically he has absolutely no axe to grind. In my view, this book is a 'must read' for anyone with personal, trust or pension assets to invest.

Mark R. Richardson

Former CEO and CIO Chase Asset Management Inc.

Banbury
Oxfordshire
February 2006

Introduction

I.1 What should I do with my money?

Have you ever asked yourself this question? I bet you have, and quite right too. I would also wager that you probably feel a little uncomfortable that you haven't come up with an answer that you feel truly comfortable with either, or where to turn to for the help and advice that you need. Have you ever wondered how much you should be investing in for your future, or how big your pot needs to be to be able to take a good income from it, no matter how long you live? Even if you have these things in control, do you ever ask yourself what you should be doing with your investments today, to make the most of your money?

If you haven't asked yourself such questions, then you have the wealth of Bill Gates, or are already a smart investor, or have taken the ostrich approach to investing.

If you have asked such questions, and know that you really do need some help in answering what appear to be such simple questions, then this book is for you. You are not alone because nearly everyone is in the same boat. If you have taken the ostrich approach, this is a great chance to get your head out of the sand, and to take some easy positive steps towards unravelling the conundrum. Read on.

I.2 Ten eye-openers to get you thinking

A good place to start is by looking at ten facts that should make you sit up and take notice. If they don't, then either you are a very well informed investor, or you need to go away, drink a strong cup of coffee and start again. Don't despair though if you are shocked, because the solution to smarter investing is straightforward and this book shows you how. Smarter investing is simple investing – a mantra we will return to time and again. Perhaps now is the time to begin to commit to doing things differently and so avoiding some of the pitfalls that many investors fall into, including: failing to invest in the first place; investing too little to have any real chance of achieving your goals; asking too much from your portfolio; and chasing last year's best performing markets and managers – a fool's errand.

Eye-opener 1: The market will always beat the 'average' investor

Over the long term the market will beat a majority of investors, professional or otherwise. This is a mathematical fact not supposition. The market is made up of all investors; as such, the return of the average investor is by definition the return of the market before costs. After paying professionals to manage money, administration costs and costs associated with the buying and selling of shares, the average investor's return will inevitably be below that of the market. In the UK, investment professionals trying to beat the market represent the majority of investors, so for all of them to beat themselves is not possible. You might be surprised to hear that well over 80 per cent of all UK investors' money (90 per cent in the case of individual investors) is invested in strategies that try to beat the market. A lot of people will lose out – fact. Not everyone can be a winner.

Eye-opener 2: The average investor is terrible at investing

In the USA, the average individual investing in equity funds reduced $100 of spending power to around $90 over the nineteen-year period from 1984 to 2002 (Dalbar, 2003), most of which was during one of the greatest bull markets. This occurred because investors chased returns, moving from the funds they were in to those that seemed to be performing better, destroying their wealth with this buy-high and sell-low strategy. Such behaviour in all likelihood applies to investors around the world, not just those in the USA. During this time, the equity market itself turned $100 of spending power into a little under $500. Investors are simply throwing away wealth.

Eye-opener 3: The market beats most professionals

Over this same period the market beat the average professionally managed US equity fund by around 3 per cent a year (Bogle, 2003). An investor who started with $100 and remained invested in such a fund ended up with around $300 of purchasing power compared with around $500 generated by the market. That's a huge amount of your future wealth to give up by paying professionals to make decisions for you.

Eye-opener 4: Past performance tells you almost nothing

A track record of good past performance for a specific fund provides few clues as to whether performance in the future will be good or bad.

Performance in most cases appears to be random over time. As an investor, it's extremely hard continuously to outsmart all the other smart people trying to outsmart you. Some investors will get it right, either through luck or judgement, some of the time, but very rarely all of the time. You probably need fifteen to twenty years of performance data to be able to differentiate between the two. Yet for most investors, short-term past performance is the sole criterion for selecting a manager. How are you going to choose a good manager to manage your money without using performance data? If you find a way, let me know.

To be fair, a small handful of managers, such as Warren Buffett in the USA and Anthony Bolton in the UK, have excellent track records as a result of outstanding skills and investment processes. The challenge, as you will see, is picking them in advance.

Eye-opener 5: Others may take half or more of your returns

The average 'on the road' cost of a UK equity fund exceeds 3 per cent a year. In the long run equities have produced a real return, i.e. after inflation, of just over 5 per cent a year over the past 100 years or so (Dimson et al., 2002). In the long run, the industry croupier takes almost 60 per cent of your returns. Is that really fair or sensible? As the title to Fred Schwed's classic book about New York's Wall Street asks: *Where are the Customers' Yachts?*: (Schwed, 1995).

Eye-opener 6: Fewer than one in ten managers win based on skill

This is the investing equivalent of finding out that Father Christmas doesn't exist. As you saw above, most managers don't beat the market after costs, but to make matters worse, as an investor, it is disappointing to realise that not only do the majority of managers lose to the market, but of those who win in the short term, luck more than likely plays a big role. Probably fewer than one in ten managers succeed through skill rather than luck (Kosowski et al., 2001) and no one has yet come up with anything like a sure way of picking them in advance. Looking for a manager who will beat the market for you over the next 20 or more years is like looking for a needle in the proverbial investment universe haystack. With 3,000 funds managed by more than 100 firms, let alone managers, in the UK, and with the average investment manager hopping from one firm to the next every three to four years, you'll be kept busy trying!

Eye-opener 7: Much advice has only an even chance of being right

Most investors at some stage are given advice on what to invest in based on estimated future average rates of return for their suggested investment portfolio. This straight-line approach is not real life: by definition half of the possible return outcomes will be below the average return assumed. The unpredictability of the markets over the short term and sometimes long term means that your actual results will, in all likelihood, be nothing like the projections. In fact, if you take the advice, you have a high chance of failing to meet even your minimum goals. The advice process in the UK and elsewhere needs significant change to focus on your chances of being successful.

Eye-opener 8: Advice may not always be in your best interests

If that isn't bad enough, the business models of many advisors encourages them to sell you products that are better for them rather than for you. In the UK around 90 per cent of all equity funds sold to retail investors are funds trying to beat the market, managed by professionals. When investors make up their own minds, based on the evidence available, and buy funds directly without advice, the bulk of the funds they buy try and track the market as closely as possible, rather than trying to beat it – a route that makes better sense for most, as you will see. These index tracker funds keep fees as low as possible, and as a consequence, have little to share with advisors.

In addition, many advisors contribute to the return-chasing wealth destruction of hopping from fund to fund and between different investment choices by selling investments with a story that sounds, at least superficially, convincing, such as switching from equities into corporate bond funds in 2001–2003.

Eye-opener 9: Many people will be poor in their retirements

People in their twenties spend around £150 a month on booze and cigarettes yet only half save anything and of these half save less than £50 a month according to a Birmingham Midshires Bank survey (2004). *Carpe diem*. Forty per cent of UK workers told an AON survey in 2003 they didn't

think the state and company plans will provide them with a decent retirement yet only one in five is doing anything about it. The average annual
contribution rate into defined contribution pension plans, where the
employee makes the investment decisions, is only 6 per cent, when it
should be at least 15 per cent for a comfortable retirement (NAPF, 2003). A
recent report for the British government estimated that three-quarters of
these type of pension plan members have contribution rates 'below the
level likely to be required to provide adequate pensions' (Pensions
Commission, 2004). Half of all employees in the UK have no occupational
pension plan at all (TUC, 2002). That doesn't sound very encouraging. My
advice – don't be one of them.

Eye-opener 10: You can be smart and easily avoid these pitfalls

Hopefully, I now have your attention and we can focus on the task of
making sure that you avoid the many investment pit falls that lie in wait
for the unsuspecting investor, not by any complicated investing strategy,
but by doing a few plain, easy-to-understand things well. Please read on.

I.3 How this book will help you

Who are you?

It doesn't really matter because the fundamentals of investing are the same
whoever you might be, whatever you are hoping to achieve and however
much money you have to invest. Perhaps more contentiously, it shouldn't
matter how much you think you know about investing, because it's always
good to challenge your beliefs. If you are just starting out, excellent, this
book is for you too. Investors generally fall into three categories: those who
have no interest in doing anything themselves; those who want to be
involved but don't want to spend too much time or effort on it; and those
who are keen to run the entire show themselves. Whichever you are, the
one thing you need to do is at least understand the basics of what investing
is about.

Why did you pick this book up?

I imagine it's because you know that maybe all is not as good as it should
be in terms of getting your investment life in order. Maybe you feel that
you ought to start investing for your future, but feel at a loss where to start.

Perhaps you feel that your money should be working harder for you, but are unsure what to do, or are not sure how you should invest your pension contributions, surplus income, an inheritance or your bonuses. Read on if you have a suspicion that what you are doing at present is not optimal. It's an important business that deserves some of your time.

Most of us don't build our own houses or service our own cars, but increasingly we have to take on the responsibility for investing money without any formal training. You may well have some questions on your mind:

- Who should I turn to for advice?
- How do I know what is good advice and what is not?
- What type of investments should I make?
- How should I choose managers for my money?
- What type of products makes sense?
- How should I monitor my investments and manage them?

This book is a chance to arm yourself with what you need to know to answer these questions yourself.

Why is this book important?

This book is important because unless you develop a basic grounding in what investing really is about, as opposed to what you may be lead to believe it is about by others, you are at risk of giving up a significant proportion of your wealth, perhaps trading retirement in the Bahamas for Bognor. While this may sound dramatic, as you will see as you read on, it is not. When investing, seemingly small decisions make big differences because they get magnified by the long time periods involved.

What this book will not do for you

- Bore you, except where it is unavoidable, for which I apologise up-front.
- Pretend that I have the formula to miraculous wealth creation.
- Pretend that we are smarter than all the other smart people investing.
- Lecture you on investment instruments or macro-economics.
- Try and turn you into a professional bond or an equity analyst.
- Provide you with a detailed and all-encompassing financial plan.
- Give you detailed advice on tax planning, and investment products.

What this book will do for you

- Develop a simple set of rules to make your investment decisions by.
- Help you to control some of your demons that will tempt you into being a bad investor.
- Help you broadly to define what you want to achieve from your investing.
- Help you to construct a sensible portfolio of investments that you can live with.
- Suggest some practical ways of being an efficient, good investor.
- Provide some practical pointers about using managers and products.
- Help you to relax and enjoy your investing responsibilities.

Why is this book different?

This book will be different from anything you will have seen before for a number of reasons. First, it takes away the complexity of investing. Second, I am going to try and get to the points I want to make quickly and succinctly without boring you or being overly-academic. I am working on the reality that while most readers want to know more about investing, few want to study a degree course to get there. Third, it will be a more honest and modest book than most, avoiding the fads of the 'Stock-picking-your-way-to-£1million' and 'Retire-in-a-year-through-day-trading' genre. Some of what you hear will be surprisingly unexciting but far more valuable. Finally, this is a practical book that guides you through taking real investing action immediately.

I want to add a caveat here: while the tone may be light, this book will encompass a lot of serious issues and attempt to provide you with the foremost research and thinking in the industry.

Why am I qualified to write it?

While I am not a fund manager by trade (thank goodness), my career has revolved around the process of advising wealthy individuals and institutions on their investment strategies. I have probably heard most of the crazy notions that investors have about investing, discussed many of the old chestnuts they argue about, which we will throw around too, and had the privilege to meet and listen to some very smart and experienced investors.

Today, my company, Albion Strategic Consulting, focuses on helping wealth managers to provide valuable, clear and well-articulated advice to help clients meet their lifetime spending goals. I have spent many years thinking that there must be a better way to try and educate investors than the tools and books that the industry provides; in the end I decided to tackle the issue myself, both through my business and this book.

I.4 How this book works

The basic principle of this book is to provide a clear and balanced view of investing and some simple rules and practical tools to help you to make your own decisions. It will provide access to research, data, concepts and hotly contested debates that are central to the industry and from which good investing rules arise. It provides an understanding of investment ideas at a level that you decide and is broken down into five parts:

Part 1: Smarter investing basics

This is a foundation course on investing. It introduces some of the basic things that you need to understand before you go any further. Failing to take these basic concepts on board may prove to be very costly. If you are familiar with them, there is no harm in spending a few minutes in bringing them into the forefront of your thoughts. Even if you intend to employ an advisor to help you with your investment programme you should make sure that you understand the concepts that are raised. It is rounded off with twenty investing tips, although I urge you to read beyond this point!

Part 2: Smarter thinking

Here, you will build a simple and practical investment philosophy to develop rules that give you the highest chance of success in your investing, avoiding the many pitfalls set by the industry. It also provides an insight into the bad-investing demons that tempt you towards poor investment practices. Your emotions have the potential to destroy your wealth.

Part 3: Building smarter portfolios

Defining your goals is the first step to creating a suitable investment programme and you will find guidance and some useful tools to help you to work out what they are. The concept of building a smart but simple portfolio is covered and an insight into why equities and bonds form the structural core of this portfolio is provided. We'll take a refreshingly straightforward, novel and leading edge approach to finding the portfolio that is right for you including how and when to introduce other building blocks into the investment mix. You can even take a look at the more technical ways of deciding what mix of investment building blocks makes sense for you, covered in a simple and clear manner, if you have the interest and application to find out.

Part 4: Smarter implementation

It's no good getting to this stage of the book and failing to do anything because you are swamped by choice when you put the book down. This part of the book arms you with some down-to-earth advice and ideas about how to put into action what you have decided upon in Part 3, right down to website and product provider details.

Part 5: Smarter building block insights

Recognising that you do not necessarily want a degree in investing, a few useful and practical insights into the building blocks that you may be using is provided here. Really understanding what each element brings to your portfolio will make the choices you face, in terms of what to include in your portfolio, far easier.

I.5 A few points to note

UK and US bias to data

This book focuses on the UK marketplace using data from it and practical solutions that relate to it. Many of the better books on investing have a US orientation and I thought it was about time that UK investors got a chance to hear the story from their own perspective. You will see that much of the data and research is based on the UK and US markets. This is largely a consequence of availability of data and academic research. Experience in other markets such as Japan helps to bring added perspective and I have introduced facts from these places where I believe they add to the argument. Remember that the fundamentals of good investing are universal and as such it does not matter where you live.

Denomination

Throughout this book try and think about your own domestic perspective. I have used '£' and 'pounds' throughout this book frequently as the means of denominating units of currency rather than as a representation of a purely UK perspective.

An apology to active managers

Having worked with investment managers who try and beat the markets for a number of years, and now making a living as a consultant providing advice to them, I want to make clear that this book is not meant to be an assault on them or their efforts. There are some very smart and hard-working people in the industry, but that just raises the bar for all in a game of winners and losers. Rarely is an industry so brutally cruel on its skilled and dedicated participants, and rarely too are the chances of success (from an investment perspective) so stacked against them throughout their careers. As you will see, hard working and smart does not necessarily translate into outperformance of the market after costs, the measurement of success in this industry.

There are undoubtedly a few managers who outperform over long periods of time as a consequence of their superb skills, a name that comes to mind being Anthony Bolton of Fidelity. I congratulate them and hope to have the opportunity to work with them one day.

The central message of this book is that for an individual investor, without the time, focus and resources to dedicate to finding these managers, the default position should be that of playing the odds in their favour and choosing a strategy based on replicating, not beating, markets. I do not deny the significant benefit that accrues to an investor who finds a truly exceptional manager who is around for the period they need them to be, I just object to the odds of finding one with no sure way of narrowing these odds. The active route should not be considered the default position for individual investors and it is incumbent on active managers to demonstrate that they have the people, process and commitment to deliver exceptional returns into the future, when we need them. To all of my friends managing money, I apologise for all the years I have been blowing this trumpet, but I don't apologise for the tune.

References

Birmingham Midshires Bank survey (2004).

Bogle, J. C. (2003) The Emperor's New Mutual Funds, *The Wall Street Journal*, July 8, p. A16.

Dalbar, Inc. (2003) *Market chasing mutual fund investors earn less than inflation – Dalbar study shows* [online]. Available from: http://dalbarinc.com/content/printerfriendly.asp?page=2003071601.

Dimson, E., Marsh, P. R. and Staunton, M. (2002) *Triumph of the Optimists: 101 Years of Global Investment Data*. Princeton, NJ: Princeton University Press.

Kosowski, R., Timmerman, A. G., Wermers, R. R. and White, Jr., H. L. (2001) Can Mutual Fund 'stars' really pick stocks? New evidence from a bootstrap analysis. *Journal of Finance*, forthcoming: http://ssrn.com/abstract=855425.

NAPF (2003) *Annual survey commentary*, London: NAPF (National Association of Pension Funds), December.

Pensions Commission (2004) *The first report of the pensions: challenges and choices*. Norwich: TSO (The Stationery Office), October.

Schwed Jr., F. (1995) *Where are the customers' yachts?* 3rd ed. New York: Wiley.

TUC (2002) *Uncovered: workers without pensions*. London: TUC, July. Available from: http://www.tuc.org.uk/pensions/tuc–5429–f0.cfm

Smarter investing basics

A foundation course for the rest of the book. Understanding a few basic investment ideas and spending a few minutes thinking about them will give you the basis on which to move forward and design and implement your own portfolio. The chapters in this part of the book include:

Chapter 1: Simplifying the confusion

To many investors, the world of investment can seem both confusing and complicated; yet it can be reduced down to a simple process. Product proliferation and market noise are the culprits. Identifying and filtering out the industry's noise is a good place to start.

Chapter 2: Covering the basics

What is smarter investing actually about? Your understanding of a few simple concepts will allow you to focus on the really important issues. For some, this may seem trivial, but take a look anyway because it really is important stuff that you cannot afford to misunderstand or ignore.

Chapter 3: It only takes a minute

In recognition of the fact that some readers may not be able to find the time to read the whole book in one sitting, this chapter provides a summary of the rules, tips, hints and guidelines that you should be following. In fact, applying these ideas will put you at the forefront of investors, although you may well be doing the right things but without necessarily understanding why. I strongly urge you to read beyond this chapter.

1

Simplifying the confusion

It would not surprise me if the world of investing seems a confusing and complicated place; the number of investment choices is vast and making sense of it all may be daunting. Fortunately, it need not be so.

1.1 Choices, choices, choices

The menu of potential investments has the capacity to leave many new to the game mesmerised by choice; a little like when you go into a restaurant and have to choose what to eat from a menu ten pages long. Dishes on offer include bank deposits, corporate bonds, investing in China, UK companies, gold, property, commodities, the USA, Japan, stamps, wine and vintage cars to name a few. Your choice is as wide as it is confusing. Don't worry though; this book narrows down the menu to a sensible one-pager and give you help on what to choose!

In the UK there are around 3,200 funds (unit trusts or OEICs) registered for sale that you can choose from, managed by 260 investment management firms, of which 100 are based in the UK. It would take a year or so, reviewing ten funds a day, to cover them all, by which time about a third of the fund managers would have moved! That's a lot of choice. Add to this the fact that there are at least 150 private client investment managers, who would like to manage your money, three hundred investment trusts listed on the stock market that you can purchase, and forty authorised property unit trusts to consider. To make things worse, you face a constant barrage of noise and information from the industry, in its widest sense, trying to influence what you should be doing with your money.

This 'advice' comes from a wide range of sources. Journalists write articles in the Sunday papers along the lines of 'Is now the right time to be investing in [substitute the flavour of the month]?' creating a convincing spin on what to do with your money. Unfortunately it is usually just a return-chasing story encouraging you to jump out of one investment that is doing badly to one that is currently doing well – not a good strategy, as we saw in the Introduction. Fund managers advertise their spectacular market-beating returns over the past three years for a chosen fund, or laud their market-beating 'star' manager in the press. Financial advisers all seem to have their list of 'best performing managers'. Even the TV news gets in on the act with its valueless daily comments that the 'Footsie Index of the leading 100 shares was up 47 points today' or 'The pound fell by a cent against the dollar'. The magazine racks in the newsagents are full of investment magazines that provide stock and fund tips, the bookshelves groan with books on investing that try and teach you about how to pick stocks, day trade, make a million and time when to be in or out of markets, and your poor postman delivers sacks full of junk mail on what ISA to pick before April comes around again. Throw in the thousands of search results from a Google search on any investing topic, and if you weren't already confused, you are now!

The natural response to this confusion is to think about employing someone to unravel the mess and help make the decisions for you. This may well be a sound thing to do, provided you find the right person. Yet here too, uncertainty reigns: investors' confidence in the advice industry has taken a beating from a series of scandals and broken promises, from pension and endowment mortgage misselling to Equitable Life reneging on the payment of its annuity promises to some pensioners. It's not really surprising that many investors don't know which way to turn for advice they can trust.

Finally, let's not forget the stock market crash of 2000–2002 where the market fell by more than 40 per cent, which bruised a good few investors and brought real meaning to the term 'risk'. You can quickly understand the temptation to put investing in the 'I'll deal with that later' category; but face the problem you must and this book is a good starting point.

1.2 How did we get here?

A potted and generalised history provides an insight into how this complexity has arisen, and why the noise from the industry has been turned up so dramatically in the past few years. We can then work out how we can try and make your investing a calmer, simpler and more enjoyable process.

The best way to invest has shifted

This is really a story about the way in which the best means of investing has evolved. Many investors seem to believe that beating the market is the goal of their investment programme, somewhat ignorant or blind to the fact that the world of investing is one of winners and losers and that costs (in the form of fees, commissions and taxes) result in more losers than winners in aggregate. The active management industry has done a good job in encouraging them to do so, and will try to do the same to you. Today, the battle for investors' money rages around whether you should try and beat the markets through active decision-making, or simply try and be the markets as closely as possible, adopting a buy-and-hold strategy, as you will see. It is a question where the probabilities of success lie in your favour. This is how the story unfolds.

The stockbroking model is on its last legs

Before the early 1970s, investors had little option but to buy securities through stockbrokers, or employ a stockbroker to manage a portfolio for them, an optimal way of managing money at the time. Information about companies was disseminated largely in print, and portfolio reporting was commonly just a list of stocks showing their purchase and current prices. Online trading, powerful computers and financial software were still science fiction. Brokers usually made money based on transaction fees, thereby encouraging the churning of investors' portfolios. This was fine at the time, but is not the best option today. Most stockbrokers are moving towards annual fee-based models, as investors wise-up. Those who don't may be living on borrowed time.

Professional 'active' management of funds became a better option

Fortunately, the world has moved on. In the 1970s the mutual fund marketplace in the USA and other markets around the world, began to take off. Professional active managers looked after collective pools of money for a large number of investors, providing diversification by holding a wide number of securities, and a professional eye dedicated to watching over your money. Some managers provided individually managed investment services aimed at more wealthy clients.

Fund managers are remunerated via a management fee, calculated as a percentage of assets managed, so their interests are more closely aligned with their clients than the old stockbroking model. For many, this rightly became a better option than using a broker or investing on their own. These managers strove (and still do) to beat the markets and their peers by making active investment decisions – hence the term 'active managers'. With annual management fees of 1 per cent to 2 per cent and sales fees paid upfront of 5 per cent, this can be an expensive business, unless the manager is able to cover their costs and more. The problem with being paid good fees based on assets is that it has placed the gathering of assets as a higher objective than investment quality, in some firms.

The advent of the index fund challenges active management

A few visionaries in the USA began to question the blind belief that professionals could consistently outperform the markets and cover their increasing fees. They began to explore whether there was a better way of investing by simply replicating a market index rather than trying to beat it. Empirical research seemed to indicate that it made sense. The first index (tracker) funds were born in 1973 run by Wells Fargo and the American National Bank of Chicago. This happened a few years later in the UK, as seems the case with most investment developments.

In the 1970s and 1980s computers were a scarce resource and analysis of data from the money management industry was largely confined to academics. The advent of cheap processing power in the early 1990s provided the means to analyse large amounts of data, the means to run market-replicating portfolios efficiently, and via websites, disseminate information and monitor and administer a portfolio.

Index investing has slowly become mainstream, overcoming hurdles as extreme as the charge of being unpatriotic, levelled against it in the USA (no American should accept that they can't beat the markets!) and the vociferous attacks on them by the active management industry. Recognition in the institutional world, and increasingly by individuals in the USA and more slowly elsewhere, has created significant challenges for the active management industry. Today, a battle exists between the two camps.

1.3 Battling for investors' money

The great equity bull market from the early 1980s to 2000 created vast wealth and power for the active management industry, which captured the bulk of the inflows in the UK. In 2003, the UK fund management industry generated revenues from its clients of £7.5 billion from an asset base of £2.8 trillion (IFSL, 2004), a tenth of which is money invested for individuals either in funds or by private client portfolio managers. Not surprisingly, fund managers are reluctant to give this position up without a fight to the index usurper.

The active management industry works on the premise that the markets can be beaten, after costs, and over the long term. We will test the efficacy of this premise in some depth a little later on in the book, where you can make up your own mind. Each manager has to believe that they will be the winner and can persuade investors to believe the same. Unfortunately, the maths doesn't work. Market-replicating managers, on the other hand, defend their position on logic and abundant empirical evidence, as you will see.

Even so, the active management industry has been remarkably successful, remaining as the default choice for the majority of individual investors, often by default. It has five weapons that it uses remarkably effectively to maintain its dominant position, evidenced by the fact that today more than 90 per cent of individuals' money and still 80 per cent of institutional money remains in active beat-the-market strategies in the UK.

■ The first and most legitimate claim is that picking and investing with an active manager who beats the market can have a very substantial positive effect on your investment outcome, compared with just gathering the market return by owning an index fund. I whole-heartedly agree. Yet, this powerful claim that plays on the hopes and emotions of investors fails to point out the fact that your chances of identifying such a manager upfront are simply too long for most individual investors to consider as a core strategy.

■ Second, human beings tend to be impressed by short-term success and treat it as a proxy for long-term success, which makes them believe that they can pick the long-term winning managers by looking at two or three years of outperformance. Short-term performance tells you next to nothing, I'm afraid, as you will find out. Canny product selection by managers means that most firms have one or two good stories to sell.

■ Third, for investors who may be confused but are trying their best to be sensible, choosing a reputable firm to manage their money, which is staffed by bright people as most investment firms are, with a seemingly strong recent track record, appears like the safest thing to do and is a convenient way of passing on their investment responsibilities to someone else.

■ Fourth, the advice industry that many individuals turn to, which accounts for around three-quarters of all fund sales to individuals in the UK, runs on a business model that is driven by the need to sell actively managed products rather than index fund products, as only the former have upfront fees and high enough annual fees to share. Most advisers are acting in the best interests of their clients, as far as the constraints of self-survival allow. Paying hard cash purely for unconflicted advice is not yet a mainstream activity for investors or advisors.

■ Finally, the industry has incredible firepower to influence investors. Marketing and branding strategies are backed with big bucks. In the USA, in 2000, media advertising alone came to around $1 billion (Bogle, 2001).

1.4 Reducing confusion and complexity

Imagine that the top edge of the triangle in Figure 1.1 represents your current interface with the market. It is crowded, noisy, confusing and all based on the premise that if you are smart, and have access to enough information you can beat the market, or at least choose a manager who can. The lower layers give you an idea of the resources that are positioned in the

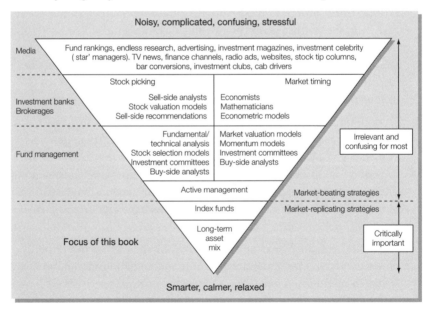

figure 1.1. Turning down the volume*

*Unless otherwise stated, all data analysis which appears in this book is by Albion Strategic Consulting

industry that is trying to beat the market – smart, hard-working, diligent, well-paid, but like alchemists of old trying to do the impossible, in aggregate. Remember that all the layers are being paid for by you, the investor, in one way or another.

The position this book takes

The premise of this book is that you can avoid most of the noise by focusing on the tip of the triangle. This is concerned with building and holding a sensible portfolio that gives you the greatest chance of success, not because you want an easier life, but because that is what the empirical evidence and logic tells you is the right thing to do.

In support of this position, a pertinent observation was made in the 2001 Myners Report commissioned by the government to look at pension plan management in the UK:

'A particular consequence of the present structure is that asset allocation – the selection of which markets [long term], as opposed to which individual stocks, to invest in – is an under-resourced activity. This is especially unfortunate given the weight of academic evidence suggesting that these decisions can be critical determinants of investment performance.'

That's why this book focuses on constructing the right mix of investments above all else, followed closely by making sure that you capture the bulk of the returns that are on offer from this mix. It's as simple as that.

Three unassailable benefits accrue if you take this route:

■ You dramatically reduce the noise and confusion associated with investing, which is predominantly focused on which stocks to invest in and whether to move your mix of investments around over time, with the hope of doing better than your long-term chosen mix.

■ Avoiding the noise as your default position, you provide yourself with the greatest chance of success in meeting your investment goals. You are stacking the odds in your favour and you can't ask for more than that. The alternative, active management, is a high pay-off proposition with a low chance of a successful outcome for most individuals.

■ You narrow the choices that you need to make dramatically, making it easier to identify products that have a very good chance of delivering what you want them to, and have little portfolio maintenance to do.

That sounds a lot easier, doesn't it?

References

Bogle, J. C. (2001) *After the fall: what's next for the stock market and the mutual fund industry?* Bogle Financial Markets Research Center. Available from: http://www.vanguard.com

IFSL (2004) *Fund management – City Business Series.* London: FSL, August.

Myners, P. (2001) *The Myners review of institutional investing in the UK.* HM Treasury.

2

Covering the basics

Let's start by getting some basic concepts straight. These form the foundations on which you will build an investment programme. While you may be familiar with some or all of them, it makes sense to cover the ground, because they are so important. Even if you feel that you are reasonably well versed in the basics, it's never a bad idea to refresh your thinking.

2.1 What is smarter investing?

As you saw from the ten Eye-openers in the Introduction, there is a lot of bad investing about, so it is important to make sure that you and I are on the same page when it comes to what we think smarter investing is about. For some, investing is about buying and selling investments through an online brokerage account, feeling that they are in control and enjoying the buzz from the excitement of the markets; for others it is about deciding where to put their money based on which markets will do better in the next year or two, often using funds to reflect their ideas. For a few, it means putting money into an interest-bearing account, because they are cautious and want to preserve the money that they have. Smarter investing is not any of these things.

Smarter investing is not about gambling with your money

When markets are going up, a combination of self-confidence and excitement encourages people to get involved in investing, particularly on their own – just witness the growth in online broking accounts in the late 1990s. The buzz and excitement of seeing your money growing every day you log into your account is a powerful drug, and reinforces people's self-confidence to play the markets. The bull market of the 1980s and 1990s influenced many people's perception of what good investing is about. Yet they conveniently forgot that a rising tide raises all boats. Many got caught up in the notion that it was about making significant money over the long term defined as two to three years, and if you had any nous, you could beat the market. Always remember short term is two to three years and long term is twenty-plus years.

Online trading, day trading and a plethora of expensive, complicated and ultimately wealth-destroying products rode on the back of the euphoria of the raging bull. That is gambling and end in tears for most, except for a few who get lucky. Gambling, unlike investing, is looking for long shots with high payouts and this includes: cards, horses and roulette; dipping in and out of the markets; trying to pick stocks that will outperform the market based on some sort of analysis, or guesswork; or picking professionals who you think will be able to beat the markets, and switching between them, as one falters and another shines. This may be a surprise, but as you will see in this book, you are entering a casino if you adopt such an approach, and one in which the croupier has a big fat hand in your pocket. The bank always wins in the long run. Few professionals manage to beat the bank and if they do, they fail to do so with any degree of consistency or predictability. So what chance do you have without the luxury of spending all day, every day analysing companies and markets, and watching screens like they do?

One of my favourite quotes on the problems that investors face when trying to decide what is investing as opposed to what is speculation (gambling) comes from Fred Schwed's book on the brokerage industry:

'Investment and speculation are said to be two different things, and the prudent man is advised to engage in one and avoid the other. This is something like explaining to the troubled adolescent that love and passion are two different things. He perceives that they are different but they don't seem quite different enough to clear up his problems.'

Throughout this book you will get plenty of guidance to clear up any problems you may have!

Smarter investing is not about saving

There is nothing wrong with saving, i.e. putting your money into a interest-bearing account if you either want to maintain a small contingency reserve for bad times or have a specific short-term goal that you need to accumulate cash for. However, if you have quite a few years until you need this money, one of the cardinal sins is to be recklessly prudent and 'save': placing your money on long-term deposit with a bank or building society if you do not need it for many years. The future spending power that you give up as a result is likely to be significant, as is the risk that unexpected inflation will eat up the spending power of your money.

In the UK, the government has promised to give each child born £250, which they can't get their hands on until they are eighteen. Yet nearly half of all parents in a recent survey said that they would put the money in an interest-bearing account rather than invest it. Why?

Some individuals, having spent considerable time and effort in accumulating wealth in their business lives, for example, may decide that simple wealth preservation is what they want to achieve. That's fine: however, they still face the erosion of their money by inflation if they don't act sensibly – long-term saving is simply not an intelligent option.

Smarter investing is a dull process

It is the boring process of deciding what you want your money to do for you in the future, putting your money into a mix of investment building blocks that has good chance of getting you there, using products that allow you to keep as much of the market returns you make in your pocket rather than giving it to the industry croupier, and sticking to your planned mix through thick and thin – no chasing last year's winning markets or managers please! In a nutshell that is it. How dull. Where's the excitement in that? My advice to you is that if it is excitement that you want, book a turn on the Cresta Run with some of the money you make from being a smarter investor.

As you can see in Figure 2.1, good investing is about aiming for pay-offs you can survive with chances of achieving them you can live with, not shooting

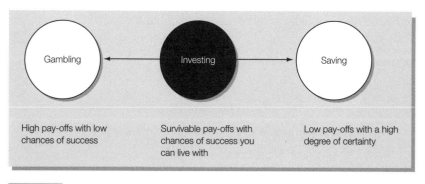

Gambling	Investing	Saving
High pay-offs with low chances of success	Survivable pay-offs with chances of success you can live with	Low pay-offs with a high degree of certainty

figure 2.1   **Focus on the middle ground**

the lights out with a wild bet or being certain of an unacceptably poor outcome.

Good investing is about playing the probabilities in your favour for every investment decision that you take. To know where the favourable probabilities lie requires a basic knowledge of the markets, an insight into the research that has been done, and a good dose of common sense. This book summarises the evidence and knowledge that you need to make these choices. By the end of Part 3: Smarter portfolios, you should feel confident that you could identify which path gives you the greatest chance of success, whenever you face an investment decision.

2.2 Ten points of focus for smarter investors

One of the things that I have noticed about the smart investors that I have met is that they all have a very firm grasp of the game they are playing, and I don't mean about understanding economics, or how to read a company's balance-sheet. What I am talking about is that they understand the basic concepts that drive success: they understand first and foremost that this is about playing the probabilities in your favour: that time is your friend; the power of compounding is immense; that using history and research are valuable tools in raising their chances of success. They realise too that inflation, emotions and giving away too much to the industry croupier savage wealth creation. Let's take a closer look at the things they focus on.

Focus 1: Smart investors make decisions that improve their chances

Smart investors make investment choices that give them the greatest chance of achieving survivable outcomes.

Smart investing involves three key decisions

Perhaps somewhat surprisingly, you only have three big decisions to make on how you should be investing:

- What mix of blocks should you own?
- Should you alter this mix over time to try and improve returns?
- Should you implement it using a strategy that seeks to beat each market or be each market, as near as possible?

Figure 2.2 illustrates the three main decisions you face and what your choices are. As you will see, one of the paths provides a greater chance of

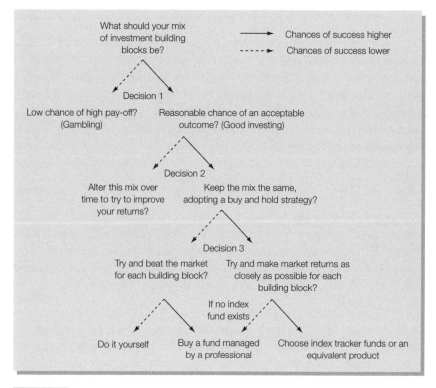

figure 2.2   **Smarter investors only have a few decisions to make**

success than the other. This book provides you with the knowledge and evidence to see why. At this stage just take my word for it.

Focus 2: Smart investors know that higher returns come with more risk

This is one of the inescapable facts of investing. In a capitalist society, capital and labour should be allocated to achieve the best returns for the risk being taken. Investments that incur higher risks will be required by investors to deliver higher expected returns. If they did not, no one would invest in them. Smart investors question any product or opportunity where high returns apparently come with low risks. They also avoid risks for which they are not rewarded adequately.

Focus 3: Smart investors spread their investments around

Diversification, diversification, diversification – a central tenet of the smarter investor. Realising that markets could go pear-shaped is at the forefront of their minds. They build portfolios that will hopefully help to protect their wealth if some markets do not go in their favour. As such, spreading risks between different building blocks to provide a portfolio for all seasons, and making sure that within each building block your money is well diversified between securities, is critical.

Focus 4: Smart investors use history and research wisely

Knowing how different investment building blocks, such as equities and bonds, have performed in the past provides both guidance and warnings. Studying their behaviour over the past one hundred years or so helps you to understand why such generalisations as 'equities for the long run' are made and, as importantly, to understand the magnitude and longevity of the exceptions.

Some advisors and investors claim that using history is 'investing by looking in the rear view mirror'. I've always thought that is nonsense. Of course, blind use of data from shorter-term periods without placing it in the context of the long-term, or using generalisations as being true all the time,

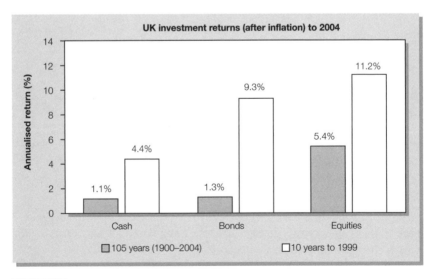

figure 2.3 **Use returns in the context of history**

Source: DMS Global Data (Ibbotson) © 2006 E Dimson, P Marsh and M Staunton

are likely to land you in investing trouble. Look at Figure 2.3 below and compare the long-term (105 years) data against that for the ten-year period ending 1999. If you used the ten-year data to 1999 blindly as a means of extrapolating into the future, with no reference to the long-run averages, then you would be likely grossly to overstate the returns that you are expecting and as a result would be sorely disappointed with the outcome of your investment.

However, use history wisely and you will find that there is much to be gained. This book allows you to take a good look at the history of different investments and to draw your own conclusions. Reviewing data from several markets helps you to explore a wider range of circumstances than just those in your domestic market. Always bear in mind that the unobserved may occur, hence the need to own a diverse portfolio.

Using research helps to get through to the truth of what investing is about and provides the foundation on which to make decisions. Research also illustrates that some issues remain unresolved. This book has distilled some of the most pertinent research that affects the decisions that you face. Reviewing its conclusions allows you to make up your own mind.

Focus 5: Smart investors know what they are letting themselves in for

Knowing how your investment portfolio could behave is extremely valuable, particularly the consequences of being wrong about your expectations. It's no good resorting to a 'no one ever told me that could happen' defence – by then it is too late. Good investors understand what their hoped-for outcome is, but as importantly what the risks are they will not be successful, and just how bumpy their investment journey will be along the way. Being sprung surprises is the surest way of invoking an emotional (and probably wealth-destroying) response. Understanding history and anticipating the magnitude of market crises you could face is essential, before you start. This book provides plenty of opportunity to discover what you are letting yourself in for.

Focus 6: Smart investors obsessively seek to minimise costs

As will become apparent later, keeping your costs low, or in other words keeping as much of the returns generated as possible for yourself, contributes more to investing success than you may, at this point, realise.

Always remember that the success of investing is shared out between you, the people who manage your money the people who buy and sell shares for the people who manage your money, and the Chancellor of the Exchequer. It is your money and you should be obsessive about keeping as much of it as you can. As such, understanding and controlling costs will be a significant contributor to your investing success. Investing in a way that minimises costs, including the potential cost of manager underperformance, is the second most important decision in investing after defining the mix of your investments.

Good investing should not cost more than 0.5 per cent to 0.75 per cent a year at most, as you will see – and hopefully even less in the future.

Focus 7: Smart investors try and keep emotions in check

If you are able to keep your emotions in control, you have a good chance of becoming a good investor. Understanding the emotional demons that divert you from the path of good investing is a good starting point. If you understand and are convinced that the way you invest and the mix of investments that you hold is right, then you have a base on which to stand firm when the markets get tough, as they inevitably will. Without this footing you will be sucked into the world of 'maybe I should have done that instead' and begin the fateful return chase. Understanding the characteristics of your portfolio allows you to prepare yourself for short-term and long-term outcomes and avoid being surprised by them. In doing so, you will create defences against being swayed by your emotions when markets get either very depressing or very exciting.

Focus 8: Smart investors plan for inflation

Inflation eats away relentlessly at your investments and on occasion in the past, such as the 1970s and early 1980s, voraciously. As a long-term investor, you need to protect your purchasing power by investing in ways that provide a strong hedge against inflation. To get some jargon out of the way, returns that are calculated after the effects of inflation are called *real returns* and relate to how your purchasing power (spending power) grows. Returns calculated before inflation is taken into account are *nominal returns*.

Look at the serious effect inflation can have over time: Table 2.1 shows you how much inflation leaves you with if you hide £100 under the bed instead of investing it.

table 2.1	Sticking £100 under the bed is not a good strategy						
Inflation	5 years	10 years	15 years	20 years	25 years	30 years	35 years	40 years
1%	£95	£90	£86	£82	£78	£74	£70	£67
2%	£90	£82	£74	£67	£60	£55	£49	£45
3%	£86	£74	£63	£54	£47	£40	£34	£30
4%	£82	£66	£54	£44	£36	£29	£24	£20
5%	£77	£60	£46	£36	£28	£21	£17	£13
10%	£59	£35	£21	£12	£7	£4	£3	£1

table 2.2	Your £ is worth less every year			
Shopping Item	1980	2004	Annual price increase	Buying power End 2004 (£100 = 1980)
Pint of beer	£0.55	£2.35	6%	£21
Pint of milk	£0.17	£0.35	3%	£47
Sliced white bread	£0.34	£0.55	2%	£61
Average house price in SE England	£31,670	£276,698	9%	£9

Source: Housing OPDM, 1980. FT 1 July 2003. End 2004: Land Registry

In a low-inflation environment, like today, the temptation is to ignore inflation. Do so at your peril. Five per cent inflation over thirty years leaves you with only £21 spending money out of £100 at the start. Table 2.2 illustrates some common purchases in the UK comparing 1980 prices with those in 2004, which gives you a feel for the effect of inflation on your daily life.

Many investors suffer from 'money illusion', a mental state that fails to take inflation into account. A return of 17 per cent sounds far better than a return of –1 per cent. However, if inflation is 20 per cent in the former case and 2 per cent in the latter, these returns are the same from the perspective of purchasing power. Figure 2.4 illustrates the dangers of looking at investment returns in nominal terms rather than real terms.

In this book, the focus is on real returns because this avoids the money illusion trap. By thinking in this way, you can understand clearly the increase in purchasing power your money may generate. Put simply, there is not much value in knowing that your nominal money has doubled but then

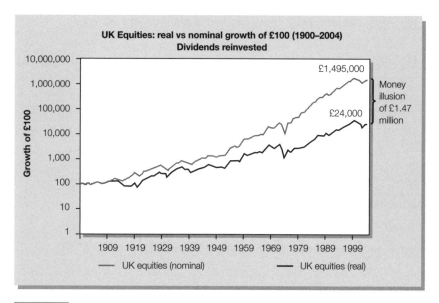

figure 2.4 The money illusion trap catches many investors

Source: DMS Global Data (Ibbotson) © 2006 E Dimson, P Marsh and M Staunton

discover that the prices of the goods you want to buy have tripled. By using real returns, you don't have to worry about scaling up income and capital amounts to reflect tomorrow's debased money.

Focus 9: Smart investors understand the power of time

A common attitude among the young is that the future is too far off to worry about and it is boring to be thinking about pensions and investments, so the thought is buried in the 'to-be-dealt-with-later' pile. Yet that is the time to begin to plan your investing, as time is a powerful ally. Some older investors adopt a similar head-in-the-sand strategy because the consequences of their lack of investing action to date are too dreadful to think about, and they believe it is too late to rectify the problem. It's never too late or too early to begin investing. Start now. The point to remember is that longer is better for three reasons.

First, time goes hand-in-hand with compounding, which is explored below. The longer you can give yourself to reach your goals, the greater the effect of the mathematical phenomenon of compounding.

Second, each investment building block exhibits certain characteristics that are often turned into generalised statements such as 'equities have higher returns than bonds'. From studying and understanding the history of the markets, it is evident that there are exceptions, and at times rather harsh exceptions that go against this generality: bonds have, for some prolonged periods, outperformed equities. The longer you have to invest, the higher the probability that your investments will behave like their generalisations, rather than like their exceptions. Time gives you the opportunity to work through the difficult, yet not unexpected periods when these exceptions to the rule arise.

Third, time moderates the range of returns that investments exhibit. Over short periods, some investments have very wide ranges of returns. However, over many years, these more extreme returns, generally but not always, tend to cancel each other out, generating much narrower ranges of returns and thus investing outcomes.

Focus 10: Smart investors harness the power of compounding

Compounding, as I am sure you are aware, is the effect of interest-on-interest. For example, a portfolio of £100 that compounds by 10 per cent a year rises to £110 in year one to £121 in year two, £133 in year three and so on. The effect of compounding returns is central to investing success and goes hand-in-hand with time. Its effects are exponential. Albert Einstein is commonly credited with the often-quoted statement that:

'[Compounding] is the greatest mathematical discovery of all time.'

You may be familiar with the ancient story where, in return for a favour, a wise man asked a young sultan for one grain of wheat on the first square of a chessboard to be doubled each square, to two on the second, four on the third and so on. The sultan acceded, bankrupting the kingdom well before the sixty-fourth square on which the wise man was owed 9,223,372,036,854,780,000 grains or about 165 times the world's annual harvest today! However, many investors will not have sat down and worked out the parallels when it comes to investing. Table 2.3 illustrates some simple rates of return compounded over different periods of time.

As you can see, compounding and time make a significant difference. While the difference between £100 compounded at 8 per cent versus 10 per cent over five years is only small (£147 versus £161), over forty years you would lose out on over half of your potential future wealth, i.e. £2,172 instead of £4,526. You may think forty years is a long time but if you start your investing at twenty-five and retire at sixty-five you have clocked up forty years. A favourite quote of mine about time and compounding comes

| table 2.3. | Value of £100 with compound interest rate over time |

Interest rate	5 years	10 years	20 years	30 years	40 years
2%	£110	£122	£149	£181	£221
4%	£122	£148	£219	£324	£480
6%	£134	£179	£321	£574	£1,029
8%	£147	£216	£466	£1,006	£2,172
10%	£161	£259	£673	£1,745	£4,526

from Sidney Homer in *A History of Interest Rates*, a book far more interesting than it sounds.

'One thousand dollars left to earn interest at 8 per cent a year will grow to $43 quadrillion in 400 years, but the first hundred years are the hardest.'

Good investors always try and keep money in their portfolios for as long as possible. You should always be aware that any money that you withdraw, any income you receive from your investments and spend instead of reinvesting, pay out in tax, or in management fees, brokerage commissions, initial fees, etc., is going to cost you dearly in the long run because it will not benefit from compounding over time. Seemingly small differences make big differences in the long run.

In summary: Smart investors do these few things exceptionally well

Smart investors realise that investing is not about trying to be an economist, or knowing how to read a company balance sheet, or having the ability to pick and choose when to be in or out of markets, or what stocks to buy or sell. What they do know is that their mix of assets has a good chance of delivering them a successful outcome and will not lose them too much if things do not go as planned. They ruthlessly pursue options that increase the chances of success: they stick with their mix, avoid chasing returns, try and be rather than beat the market, and eliminate costs in whatever form they take to keep their money in their pockets. They focus ruthlessly in pursuing these few things exceptionally well. That's all there is to it! Now read the rest of the book to make sure that you too become a smarter investor.

2.3 The two distinct phases of investing

Having quickly highlighted where smart investors focus their time and effort, it is important that you take a quick look at the two phases that all investing falls into. The ultimate goal of investing is to build the purchasing power of your wealth to a level that allows you to fulfil your lifestyle plans, which usually involves either the distribution of income or the disbursement of capital at some time in the future. As such, most investors can break down their investing into two main phases: the accumulation of wealth and the distribution of financial benefits from this pool of accumulated wealth. Which phase your investments fall into at the moment will be unique to your own personal circumstances.

A thirty-year-old investing for retirement still has thirty years or more of the accumulation phase left and will be concerned with maximising the chances of accumulating enough in his or her investment pot to generate a decent income in the future. On the other hand, retirees no longer pay into a pension plan but draw an income from their investment pool: they are primarily concerned with maintaining the purchasing power of their income, and avoiding running out of money before they die, although some may be seeking to grow their money if the risks are acceptable. Figure 2.5 below provides a generic representation of the two phases of investment.

For each pool of money that you have, representing a specific future goal, you will have to decide which phase of investing you are in and how long you have to go before you reach the transition point between the two. An example of this transition point comes at the time of retirement where occupational income stops and investment income takes over.

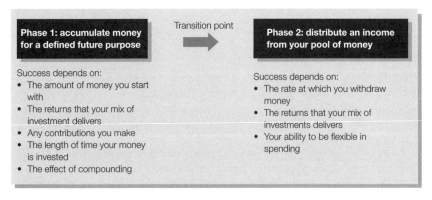

figure 2.5 **Are you accumulating wealth or distributing wealth?**

A quick look at the accumulation phase

Let's look at the accumulation phase of investing in a little more detail. The generic process of accumulating wealth is a simple one: you start by choosing a mix of investments that has a good chance of delivering a rate of return that, in conjunction with any contributions you may make, and the time you have available, will deliver a pool of assets that is sufficient to meet either your requirement for capital, or deliver an acceptable level of income to you. Figure 2.6 below helps to highlight some of the issues that you need to think about.

In reality, your investment life is not going to generate straight-line returns, but fluctuating returns that at times will leave you wondering whether you are doing the right thing when markets take a beating (as they will at some stage) and the outlook looks bleak. Your final pool of money will depend on what the actual returns have been like in your investing lifetime. The real risk is that they are disappointing, despite the fact that the chances of success were in your favour. You need to decide what the lowest acceptable outcome is for you, and make sure that the combination between the mix of assets you choose and the contributions you make, offers you a high enough chance of achieving a successful outcome. The accumulation stage of investing begs answers to the following questions:

■ How much capital or income do you need at the end of your accumulation period to achieve the things you want to do?

■ How long have you got to achieve this growth in your wealth?

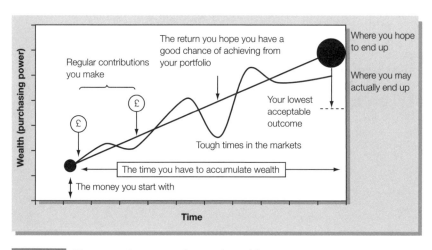

figure 2.6   **The generic accumulator of wealth**

■ What is the lowest acceptable outcome you can stomach?

■ What combination of portfolio returns and contributions will provide you with a high chance of successfully meeting your target, or at least your minimum?

■ What mix of assets will generate these sorts of returns with a high degree of comfort?

■ What are the worst-case times in the market that you could suffer with such a mix of investments and can you stomach it?

Part 3: Building Smarter Portfolios leads you step-by-step through the process of unravelling these issues. With the right tools, it is easier to do than you may think.

A quick look at the distribution phase

The distribution phase of investing is generally concerned with wealth and income preservation rather than wealth accumulation. The commonest example is that of retirees who have accumulated a pool of assets to live off in retirement. The risk they face, if this income is critical to them, is running out of money before they die. The goal of the distribution phase is to find the combination of portfolio investment mix (and thus returns) and rate of income withdrawal that preserves the spending power of the pool of money and thus the spending power of the income derived from it. This is generically represented in Figure 2.7.

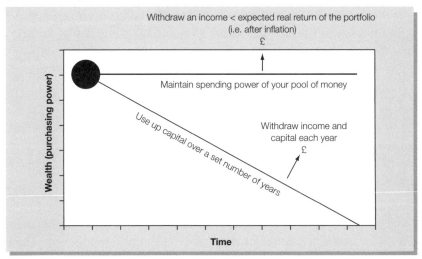

figure 2.7 **The distribution phase is commonly about preserving spending power**

When you reach the distribution phase of your investment life, there are really only two important questions that you need to answer:

- How much can I sensibly take out of my portfolio every year?
- What mix of assets will allow me to do this a) without eroding my capital or b) using up my capital over a defined period of time?

These questions can be answered in terms that you can understand by asking and answering questions such as 'If I am invested with mix A and withdraw 5 per cent of the value of my portfolio each year, what chance do I have that I will run out of money before I die?' Finding the balance between maintaining your capital, or decreasing it at a prescribed rate, and generating a suitable income is critical.

2.4 There are no perfect answers

Finally, let me tell you that there are no perfect answers to investing and this book does not seek to provide any. Instead, it aims to provide enough insight to allow you to understand the trade-offs and risks that investing entails, and to build yourself an investment portfolio that gives you what you believe is the highest chance of success to achieve your goals and should protect your wealth in poor markets.

We can't see into the future, yet we have to make assumptions about a range of events; many of the measurements that we make and use in coming to decisions vary depending on the time periods we are looking at; and the process of forecasting is littered with the bodies of those who have tried. Add to this the fact that we are all emotionally different as investors and the science of investing quickly becomes the art of common sense.

What we do have on our side is the ability to learn from history, to read and evaluate the empirical research that exists, to maximise the use of all the things that we know to be proven and minimise uncertainties that we know have the power to divert us from achieving our goals. This book pulls all these together to allow you to make your own decisions with confidence. Just remember that common sense and rational thinking are your friends and that emotions and spurious accuracy are your enemies.

The marketplace abounds with software that will spew out pie-charts saying what you should invest in; risk questionnaires to evaluate your tolerance for losses; and investment calculators for retirement or school fees. These will all claim to tell you how much you should save and provide what seem like definitive solutions to how you should invest down to three decimal places. Just remember that these are all just estimates made by someone else, embedded with their own assumptions and imperfections – useful guides, no more. In addition, most of them don't tell you what chance you have of succeeding, which is what you really want to know. At the end of the day it is your money and you need to understand how you arrived at the investment strategy that you do.

In this book you will find few complicated algorithms, calculations, forecasts or models for allocating assets between building blocks – just the application of standard investment rules, common-sense and a determination to keep things simple not for simplicity sake, but because that is fortunately what the empirical evidence tells us we should be doing.

2.5 Summary: smarter investing basics

■ Investing is about playing a game that has long-term high probability of success, not about long shots and get-rich-quick strategies.

■ Focus on the few things that good investors do: make sure you take decisions that improve your chances of success; use history and research wisely to help you do so; understand what you are letting yourself in for; keep the croupier's hand out of your wallet; control your emotions; be aware of and plan for inflation; and use the powerful effects of time and compounding to your benefit.

■ As an investor you are in one of two phases: the accumulation phase or the distribution phase. As you plan your investment strategy, you will be trying to find answers to questions relevant to each stage – bear these in mind as we move forwards.

■ Remember there are no perfect answers, only some that have a greater chance of success than others.

References

Homer, S. and Syllar, R. (2005) *A history of interest rates*. 4th ed. New York: Wiley.

Schwed, Jr. F. (1995) *Where are the customers' yachts?* 3rd ed. New York: Wiley.

3

It only takes a minute

When I talked to friends and colleagues about my plan to write a book the unanimous response was: 'Great, but please make it a pamphlet'. They are to a large extent right. The 80/20 rule applies in investing – you gain 80 per cent of what you need to know from only 20 per cent of the effort. To that end, the summary below provides a brief list of some of the guidelines commonly used in the investment industry when giving advice.

These tips can help you to become a better investor by way of a kind of investing by numbers, without a real understanding of why or the consequences of the actions you take. They may help you to avoid some of the pitfalls that lie in wait. Some use gross oversimplifications and assumptions about your personal circumstances, but, by and large, they will put you in the right ballpark.

I hope that the list at least makes you ask yourself whether this is how you are currently investing. But only by truly understanding what you are doing and why will you be able to bear the emotional pressures that force many investors to destroy their wealth. I encourage you to use this section as an aide-memoire for later.

3.1 Twenty tips for smarter investing

First of all . . .

1 **Start investing now** If you haven't begun investing yet, then better late than never. The effect of time will be hugely beneficial to you through the power of compounding, i.e. the effect of interest-on-interest. The longer you give it the more powerful it becomes. Time also gives you a greater chance that the investments you choose will act as you hope they will rather than as the exceptions to the rule that inevitably occur over the shorter term, from time to time. Invest whenever you have the cash to do so, regularly if possible.

Choosing your mix of investments

2 *Investment period* Decide how long you can invest for each pool of money, whether it be pension, nest egg or school fees. Getting this right is very important. A mismatch between your mix of investments and your investment period could result in either having to sell investments when markets are down to meet your obligations, or giving up potentially higher levels of future money by being too conservative if your investment period is actually longer than you say it is.

3 *The mix of investments is the most critical decision you will make* At the end of the day, it is the mix of investments that you own that drives your portfolio returns (along with keeping as much of this as you can by keeping other people's hands out of your pockets). Messing around with this mix and trying to pick market-beating investments or managers will add little, for most. Choosing this mix carefully is the first step towards smarter investing.

4 *Rules of thumb for defining your mix* A couple of simple rules provide a sensible starting point for deciding the appropriate mix between equities and bonds, the building blocks of your portfolio. Both provide similar outcomes. Think about them carefully.

Rule 1 Own 4 per cent in equities for each year until you need the money as defined by your investment period above and own bonds for the rest.

Rule 2 If this money represents general funds to support your future lifestyle, own your age in bonds and the rest in equities. Own more in equities if you are more aggressive and able to weather market falls, or more in bonds if you want more certainty of your outcome.

These mixes are based on the probabilities that equities and bonds will perform something like they have over the long run. You could, however, be one of the unlucky investing generations for whom markets stink; it is a possibility. Only you can decide whether you can tolerate such an outcome. If not, you may need to be less aggressive (by owning more bonds), save more, invest longer or scale down your expectations.

5 *Be conservative in your estimates of future returns* It is far better to be conservative about the returns your portfolio will generate, than to be overly optimistic. If you pay in more and expect less, most surprises will be on the upside – a far more pleasant place to be than the flip side.

Practical investing

6 ***Diversify using funds or equivalent baskets of investments***
Own your bonds and equities through some sort of pooled fund
vehicle, such as a unit trust in the UK. This allows you to own a large
number of securities to spread the risk of any one security being a
duffer and damaging the value of your investments. A benefit of
using funds is that capital gains are only payable on the sale of the
fund (in the UK) and not as gains on individual investments in it are
crystallised.

7 ***Don't try and beat the market, be the market*** Buy index
funds, known as tracker funds in the UK, that seek to track the
market as closely as possible, or similar products such as exchange
traded funds. Don't try and move in and out of different building
blocks just because the story for one sounds bad and for another
good. Accept that trying to beat the market is a mug's game for most
investors.

8 ***Own the broad (total) equity market*** Your equity fund should
reflect the broad base of companies that make up the market as a
whole and not one or a few sectors of it. In the UK this would be the
FTSE All-Share index, which covers the whole market. In the USA
this may be an index such as the Wilshire 5000. Look for words like
total market or *broad market* when selecting products.

9 ***Own high-quality domestic bonds*** Your bond investments
should be high quality. Look for the words 'investment grade'. If you
see the words 'high yield', 'high income', 'extra income', 'sub-
investment grade' or 'junk' avoid them. The safest bonds are issued
by the government and are called gilts in the UK and treasuries in
the USA. Corporate bonds should be investment-grade only and
generally rated AA or above on average. If the threat of inflation
worries you, allocate some of your bond holding to index-linked
(inflation proof) bonds issued by the government.

10 ***Reduce costs at all times*** As costs, which include initial fees,
management fees and brokerage charges, destroy your wealth, always
buy cheaper product equivalents. Never buy any product until you
are sure of the stated and hidden costs. Never pay an initial fee for
investments. Understand what a *total expense ratio* is and always
check what it is for each investment.

11 ***Don't buy products you don't understand*** If products are
confusing or opaque, which includes most insurance-wrapped

products such as with-profits endowments, and guaranteed or principal-protected products, avoid them. If you can't understand it, don't invest in it.

12 *Beat the taxman – legally of course* Make use of all legal tax breaks. In the UK, like many other countries, there are breaks on contributions you make to your pension, tax-free investment wrappers, such as ISAs and previous schemes such as PEPs, and capital gains tax allowances. Make sure you are using these to the best effect and get independent advice if you need to learn how best to do so. However, make your investment decisions first and then seek to maximise the tax advantages.

On investing for retirement

13 *How much to contribute* You need to save regularly to build a suitable pot and it may surprise you just how much this is for a half-decent retirement. Start early.

Rule 1: Save £1 in £6 for retirement If you are saving for your retirement invest 15 per cent to 20 per cent of your gross salary every year of your working life. If you don't, be prepared to have a quiet retirement. You need to balance the pleasurable and gratifying feeling of spending today with what feels like the nebulous and remote comforts of investing for tomorrow. In effect, you are buying all of your future fun today, with a little help from the markets and compounding to get you there.

Rule 2 Your *age less twenty-five*: If you are starting later in life then your contributions, as a percentage of your gross salary, should be equivalent to your age less twenty-five years, for an income in retirement that is half to two-thirds your final salary – a scary thought for many! Alternatively, invest half your age as a percentage of your gross salary in your retirement savings pot.

These all come out to a similar level of contributions. The resounding message is the same: saving fifty quid here or there is not going to do it for you; retirement investing needs to be a systematic and financially significant process.

14 *Lifecycle investing* As you approach retirement make sure that you take the investment mix (point 3) into consideration. If you really want to protect your wealth from equity market falls and inflation as you approach retirement, own *index-linked bonds* and hold them to

maturity, this being the date you need the money as cash, which may be when you retire or when you buy an *annuity*.

15 ***Taking an income from your portfolio*** If you need to take an income from your portfolio and you don't want to run out of money before you die, withdraw a maximum of 4 per cent per year from your portfolio. A portfolio that is half bonds and half equities over the long term has a good chance of returning inflation plus 3 per cent to 4 per cent. So, withdrawing 4 per cent should, if you are lucky, allow you to maintain the purchasing power of your capital and thus your income. Be sensible; if you have a sustained run of bad markets you may need to rein in your spending. To up your chances, only withdraw 3 per cent.

Ongoing maintenance

16 ***Maintain the mix*** Rebalance the proportion of equities and bonds back to your plan (points 3 and 4, above) if they are out of line by more than a tenth of the value of your total portfolio. If you are a regular investor you could redirect new cash flow to the underweight investment to rebalance the portfolio. Check that the bond and equity investments have performed in line with the broad markets they reflect. If they have not, find out why. If the answer is unsatisfactory, then replace them with a similar option.

Controlling your emotions

17 ***Stick with your mix through thick and thin and avoid chasing returns*** One of the greatest risks to good investing is you. Hold tight when markets get bumpy, as they inevitably will. Remember buying high and selling low is the worst, but most popular investment strategy. Never chase what seems like better performance with another type of investment or manager. Investors tend to be prone to emotional excesses that cloud their judgement both as markets go up and as they inevitably come down. Staying calm and staying the course is easier said than done, but is critical.

18 ***Don't look at your portfolio too often*** Try to avoid looking at the value of your investments more than once a year. Any more than that and you will begin to get short-termist and jumpy about irrelevant short-term market movements.

19 *Avoid the noise* Do not be taken in by articles that begin 'Is now the right time to be investing in . . .?' Ignore most of what you hear and read about the state of the markets, as most of it is nonsense and fluff – interesting but unimportant. Much of it is telling you to be happy or distraught at the wrong time. Generally it makes you covet investment products that have already gone up in price. A bizarre, yet real emotion. Also, remember that if a product or idea looks too good to be true, it is too good to be true. If you get offered any sort of product that provides high returns for no or low risk to your capital, then look very carefully and reject it. Free lunches like this just don't exist in investing.

And finally

20 *Pay for truly independent advice if you need it* If any of this confuses you, get independent advice. Pay by the hour as you would if you were meeting an accountant or lawyer. It may seem expensive but in the long run good advice will pay for itself many times over. Don't give up your future lifestyle for the cost of good advice upfront. Question it if it is markedly different from the points above. Check that the advice is truly independent before you commit. Ensure you know that this is their only remuneration – no kickbacks, no commissions, and no other hidden fees or charges. Never pay upfront fees on funds (sales fees, commissions, etc.) – it is not necessary.

Ask questions of your adviser that relate to your chances of meeting your goals such as: 'What are the chances of me not running out of money before I die if I withdraw £50,000 a year from my portfolio?' If they can't give you a satisfactory answer, go elsewhere.

If you need more meat on these bones, then read on – after all that is why you bought the book.

Smarter thinking

Perhaps one of the biggest mistakes that investors make is focusing on 'doing' rather than 'thinking' about investing or their own behaviour in relation to it. Before we talk about *what* you should invest in, it is critical that you formulate some simple rules about *how* you should invest. To that end, the following two chapters provide an insight so you can come up with some guiding principles to help you make decisions and curb your emotions on your investing journey.

Chapter 4: Get smart – find your philosophy

Defining and believing in a set of investing rules lies at the heart of successful investing. Although you can't control how the markets will perform during your investment lifetime, you can stop throwing money away needlessly. Much of the industry noise, either directly or indirectly, encourages you to do just that. Having some clear guidelines through which to filter the nonsense from the valuable is the key. By the end of this chapter you will have formed a clear set of rules to live your investment life by.

Chapter 5: Get smart – have a word with yourself

Without doubt, one of the hardest aspects of investing is having the courage to stick with an investment plan when times get tough, as they undoubtedly will from time to time. Failing to curb your emotions will be costly – one of the few things you can truly guarantee as an investor. This chapter helps to identify some of the pitfalls that you face. Understanding them is the first step to avoiding them. Take a long, hard, look at yourself.

4

Get smart – find your philosophy

Too often, investors fail to spend enough time trying to sort out what will work and what will not work, but instead dive into the markets and end up being thrown around, chasing returns and damaging their wealth. To avoid being one of them, you need to determine a set of guiding rules and beliefs that will provide the basis for making astute investment decisions. These rules form your investment philosophy. This will become the central perspective from which you evaluate all investment options and ideas, providing a filter to eliminate the industry noise and help focus on what is truly important. By the end of this chapter you should have a pretty good idea of what it should be. This book can guide you, but at the end of the day you need to convince yourself, based on the evidence.

4.1 Without a smart investment philosophy you are lost

The following scenario reflects the way in which many people go about their philosophy-free investing. It uses the late 1990s and early 2000s as the backdrop.

It is 1998 and James, a corporate banker in the City, is keen to put some of his hard-earned cash to better use than just sitting in a bank account. He is fully aware of the clamour surrounding the rising stock market and decides that he should think about investing a lump sum in equities. In the weekend money pages of a respected broadsheet, three things catch his eye: an article about the outstanding returns being made from the market; an advertisement expounding the excellent market-beating performance of an equity fund managed by

▶

Top Wealth Investors; and a small column on the fact that index tracker funds have tended to outperform professionally managed funds over time. He rips out and sends off the coupon for some literature on the stellar performing fund.

Over a beer after work the following week, James is given the name of a financial advisor that one of his colleagues uses. At home, in the glossy pile of literature that arrives, he is impressed with Top Wealth Investor's sophisticated process, global resources of over a hundred analysts and fund managers and a UK equity fund that has done really well over the past three years, pasting the market and its peers.

He sets up a meeting with the advisor his colleague recommended to ask for some advice on how to go about things – he really doesn't want all the fuss and bother of doing it himself. The advisor agrees that investing in equities makes sense, as James doesn't need the money in the foreseeable future and concurs that equities have a strong positive outlook, both long and short term. James shows him the literature about the stellar performing fund and his advisor agrees that it is a reputable firm, but suggests that he should also look at a couple of other funds on his recommended fund list, which have good track records of beating the market over the past couple of years. James doesn't ask how much the advisor will get paid for selling them to him.

James raises the story about index tracker funds, but the advisor suggests that he should give himself the chance of beating the market by picking a good actively managed fund rather than accepting the inevitable defeat of an index tracker fund. He also adds that active managers, who seek to beat the market, have the chance of protecting his money in down markets by holding cash or defensive stocks, and picking better-performing stocks when markets are rising, which sounds good. James should get the upside of beating the markets when times are good and some protection in down markets. He feels that this seems reasonable.

He decides to split his investment between Top Wealth Advisor's fund and a fund his advisor suggests. He writes the cheque then and there, thankful that he doesn't need to waste any more time dealing with his investments. Within a few days, his account is set up and he has access to his portfolio online. The first thing he does each morning is to check how much he is worth, and feels elated watching his money grow.

▶

All goes well for the first year and James adds his annual bonus into the funds, which have both outperformed the market. However, shortly into 2000, the market begins to fall and before long he has lost an amount equivalent to a few months' salary. James hangs in there, assured by a friend that the market bounced back quickly after the crash in 1987. But in 2001 the market falls by more than 10 per cent, and further at the start of 2002. At this point he is beginning to panic as he has lost more than 30 per cent of his wealth and both his funds have done significantly worse than the market.

Two articles catch his eye in Sunday's money section: 'Is this the death of the equity cult?' and 'Is now the time to be investing in corporate bonds?' James feels unnerved at the losses on his portfolio and he doesn't want to lose any more money. He decides that it may make sense to get out of the equity market and perhaps buy corporate bonds instead: these have performed well and are being touted as a safe, income-producing haven from the turbulence of the equity markets, with good future return prospects.

He doesn't feel he can hold out any longer: why stay in equities that may well go down further when he could be in something that is doing well? He rings his advisor, who concurs that the outlook for equities looks poor but that for bonds looks good. He sells most of his equities and switches his portfolio into bonds. His advisor is happy with the additional commission.

James initially feels happier as the market falls further. But in 2003 the equity market rallies by 30 per cent and bond returns have been flat; there is talk that the bond market rally has run out of steam. A nagging doubt exists as to what you should do next. He calls his advisor . . .

Without a sound investment philosophy the dangers of James destroying his future wealth are exceedingly high. He has made a number of fundamental mistakes, because he has no guiding principles to help him to manage his investment. Our hypothetical investor James has:

■ Not thought about what he really wants to achieve with his money.

■ Not set up a long-term plan for the mix of investments that he will use. Investing is a journey, which needs to be planned.

■ Chased returns and entered a cycle of buying high and selling low, which is a certain recipe for wealth destruction, based on short-term market and emotional pressures.

■ Paid fees upfront for advice based on the value of his assets, has bought high-cost products and has incurred switching costs by moving funds.

■ A remarkable belief in his ability to pick an outstanding manager. For some reason he believes that he has the skills to select one of the very few managers who will outperform the markets consistently over the years by looking at an advertisement.

■ Chosen a manager who has a low probability of beating the market in the long term and a high probability of losing out to an index fund tracking the market.

■ A pretty good chance of destroying a significant part of his wealth in the long run like the Dalbar study referred to in Eye-opener 2 at the start of the book so clearly shows.

All in all his investment programme is a mess. Fortunately, he is only a hypothetical investor and not you!

4.2 The foundations of your philosophy

The time has come to build yourself a smart philosophy that gives you the highest chance of achieving your investment goals. This is not a difficult process. It is a matter of looking at the evidence and weighing up where you have the greatest probability of success and acting accordingly. Your resulting investment philosophy is the set of rules that you can use to guide you through the decisions you face.

Establishing your philosophical mindset

The best place to start as you begin to establish your philosophy is with the central message in Charles D. Ellis's superb book *Winning the Losers Game* (Ellis, 2002) as it provides the mindset that you will need to adopt in all the decisions that you face through your investing lifetime: it is that the ultimate outcome of investing is determined by who can lose the fewest points, not win them. It is as simple as that!

I cannot stress how important and central this subtle statement is to your future wealth and financial security. When you look at investment success in this light, it becomes a lot easier to devise a set of rules that will give you a high chance of success – actions that revolve around minimising the chances of eroding the returns that your portfolio mix as a whole can generate for you. If you persist with the view that success comes with winning points by beating the market you are on a very complex, angst ridden road to likely failure, as you will see. In the pages ahead, you will be able to review for yourself the evidence that will hopefully make you believe in this simple statement as well.

Throughout this book we will ruthlessly apply this philosophy. First, though, we need to see why it is this philosophy, alone, that forms the basis of smarter investing.

Your starting point is your long-term mix of assets

As an investor, the choices include cash, bonds, equities, property, hedge funds, gold, art, commodities and stamps, each of which has its own returns characteristics and risks. Depending upon what you are trying to achieve with your money, and the time frame you can invest for, you can put together a sensible mix of investment building blocks that will provide you with a reasonable probability of achieving your goals.

The mix that you choose will determine the level of potential returns of your investment programme, the chances that an acceptable outcome will be achieved, such as having enough income in your retirement, and how bumpy the investment road that you take is likely to be. Getting this mix right is critical.

The chosen mix is often referred to as your long-term *investment policy* or *strategic asset allocation*. All sophisticated investors have investment policy statements that set out exactly what this long-term strategy is – you need to do the same. We will not try and answer what this mix is for you until we reach Part 3 of the book, where we will explore the process you need to go through to decide what it is in some depth. Let's explore instead the fundamental philosophical questions that all investors face.

Should you try to beat the returns from your long-term mix?

The central tenet that will underlie the investment philosophy is whether or not you believe that you have a *reasonably high chance* of beating the returns that your long-term investment policy portfolio will generate (simply through buying and then holding it), by making investment decisions during your investment lifetime that move your portfolio away from this long-term mix of investments and securities.

Ultimately you face a choice: either try and identify an active manager, who through either personal skill or a robust investment process, add returns relative to the market, which in the long term could be highly beneficial; or simply make sure that you capture the bulk of the market returns on offer. It comes down to your chances of success. Smart investors always make decisions that maximise their chances of being successful. Make up your own mind where you stand by the end of this chapter. Three potential ways exist to beat your investment policy mix.

1. Improving returns by moving between different investments or markets

The biggest decision you face and the one that is most likely to govern the success of your investment programme is whether you always keep your investment policy mix constant or whether you move money around to take advantage of investments that are performing, or appear likely to perform, well and sell those that are or are anticipated to perform poorly.

Moving your mix around to try and beat the returns from a static mix is called *tactical asset allocation, investment strategy,* or *market timing.* Proponents of this approach are *market-timers.* Seeking to add returns over and above those expected from your long-term investment policy from market timing is often referred to as being a *top-down approach.* Such a strategy 'looks down' on the portfolio and moves chunks of it around either at the asset class level, for example between bonds and equities, between countries or at the sector level by preferring, say, the oil sector of the economy over the financial sector. The jargon is worth remembering, as it is the common language of managers and advisors. Much of what you read in the papers is about market timing decisions such as: 'Should you be investing in Japan (or read: oil, timber, art, wine, etc.) at this time?'

2. Improving returns by picking better securities

Irrespective of your answer to market timing, you also need to decide whether or not you believe if it is possible consistently to pick (or ignore) individual stocks or bonds, generically referred to as securities, that will beat those that make up the market as a whole. This process is known as *stock selection* for equities, or *security selection* in generic terms. Proponents of this approach are referred to as *stock-pickers.* Because it focuses on the smallest element of decision-making, stock-picking is referred to as a *bottom-up approach.* TV pundits, stock-tip columns and investment magazines and stockbrokers are the conduits of stock-picking noise.

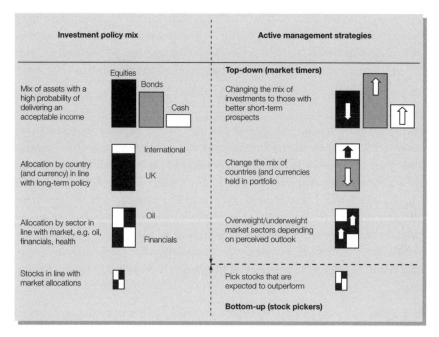

figure 4.1 **Ways to try and beat a long-term buy-and-hold investment policy**

3. Improving returns by picking market-beating managers

You may feel that you cannot achieve the first two options above yourself, as you have neither the expertise nor the time to do so, but you may feel that you have a good chance of selecting a manager who does, or finding an advisor who can find one that can. It is tempting to be drawn into the comfort of passing the responsibility over to the professionals, who after all should be best placed to beat the market, as they spend their lives working with valuation models, work with bright colleagues, meet and analyse companies, and have good access to information. Surely if anyone can beat the markets, they can?

Figure 4.1 illustrates how active managers attempt to beat the returns from a long-term investment policy mix of investments.

The route you choose is a question of probabilities

Managers who believe that they can beat your investment policy mix returns by market timing and security selection are known as *active managers*. The funds they manage are known as *actively managed* funds.

Investors who do not believe that they can improve upon investment policy returns through market timing or security selection are referred to as *passive* or *index investors*. Using the word passive is a misnomer, at least when it comes to managing funds that try and replicate, rather than beat, markets i.e. index tracker funds, as you will see later.

The difference between an active and a passive approach is actually about the probability of success, not skill, intelligence or hard work of those involved. Passive managers believe that the odds of success, through capturing as much of each market's available gain as possible, for your given mix, and thus losing the fewest points, lie in their favour. Active managers on the other hand believe that they can win points because they have superior insight and the ability to use information better than others in the market, and their process and people will allow this superiority to be sustained into the future. As you will see shortly, the probability of being successful is higher through avoiding losing points than trying to win them.

The attraction of active management is similar to that of smoking. It lies in a hope of beating the odds and enjoying a lifetime of rewards, despite that fact that the probabilities of financial and physical ill-health are high in both cases, in aggregate. As human beings, we seem to have an innate sense that we will escape the probabilities and be the lucky winners. After all, many people gamble on the lottery, despite the odds that a thirty-five-year-old man buying a lottery ticket on a Monday has a greater chance of dying than winning the jackpot!

For some reason, we hate to be considered average. We seem to aspire to want to be winners, which is fine if it is winning an egg and spoon race, but dangerous in the less-than-zero-sum game that we play as investors. In investing, there is nothing wrong with being average if by average you mean achieving the market return for your buy-and-hold portfolio, as you will see.

The problem with many investors is that they are attracted to active management because they have not thought through the issues clearly, and have not seen or read the evidence that exists that helps them to decide which course of action is likely to be best for their investing health. Others see the evidence, which is now widely available, but still can't stop themselves from being attracted to trying to beat the markets and a buy-and-hold portfolio strategy. This is compounded by our propensity erroneously to value short-term success as a good proxy for long-term success, abrogate investing responsibility to others, and to be influenced by the apparent absolute (as opposed to relative) levels of expertise that reside in investment firms. Fortunately, you have the opportunity to see the evidence and weigh up the probabilities yourself.

Before we begin the process of establishing which approach has the greatest chance of success, you need to be aware of the zero-sum game that investing represents in aggregate.

Understanding the zero-sum game

As we unravel the chances of success from adopting either a passive or an active approach to your investing, you need to make sure that you understand the game that is being played by all investors in aggregate. It is a zero-sum game, assuming that we ignore for the moment the significant issue of costs, where one investor's gain is another investor's loss. For every winning position, there has to be a corresponding losing position, relative to the market. Factoring in the costs of investing, it becomes a significantly less-than-zero-sum game.

If you buy a share at a certain price believing it will rise faster than the market, and it does, you win and the person who sold it to you loses – you cannot both be right. Take a look at the simple market in Table 4.1, which consists of just two investors, me and you, and two shares, ABC plc and XYZ plc. As you can see, the combined returns over one year of our two-stock market must be the market return. You win and I lose relative to the market.

table 4.1 **We can't both be winners**

	My portfolio	*Your portfolio*
Start of year	ABC plc (1 share)	XYZ plc (1 share)
Price	£100 per share	£100 per share
Trade	I buy XYZ plc from you for £100	You buy ABC plc from me for £100
Performance during year	XYZ plc up 10%	ABC plc up 20%
Portfolio value at end of year	£110 = **10%** (absolute)	£120 = **20%** (absolute)
Market performance	Total market value now £230 instead of £200 = **15%**	
Relative to market	Loser with −**5%**	Winner with +**5%**

The same applies for all investments. So, if you sell equities and buy bonds, again it has to be a zero-sum game before costs. Only one of the seller or buyer of the bonds can win in the short term. In order to believe that you can be one of the few who can consistently win over time at someone else's expense, you have to believe the following:

■ You are superior to the average investor, and are able to access and interpret information in a way that others can't, in order to make market-beating decisions.

■ There are enough consistently dumb investors to be the losers funding your wins.

It should therefore come as no surprise that the investment management industry has more than its fair share of overly confident and prima-donna fund managers throwing tantrums, computers and phones around the trading desk (all of which I have seen). To believe that they have the key to above-average wealth generation is a powerful drug, particularly given the talent of their peers in competitor firms. Not to believe it means that your professional worth is meaningless.

Who are the losers that make winning possible?

That's a good question, given that in the UK professional active investment managers make up around 80 per cent – 90 per cent of investors, the losers by definition are likely to include a fair number of this group! Perhaps it's the small minority of individual investors, who are providing the huge market beating opportunities for all the professionals. Don't bank on it.

A study of 60,000 individual investors in the US trading their own brokerage accounts, a group that is at most risk of being persistent zero-sum-game losers, found that the average gross return, i.e. returns before costs, was more or less in line with the market return (Barber et al., 1998). So, as a group, these individuals are not being fleeced by the institutional managers, who you would expect to be the consistent winners.

4.3 The path to establishing your philosophy

Whether active management can beat the markets with a reasonably high chance of success over the long term, and is thus a philosophy worth adopting, depends on resolving three questions:

■ Can active managers beat the markets after costs?

■ If so, do some managers beat the markets consistently over time?

■ Third, do you have a reasonable chance of identifying them in advance?

Remember that we are not trying to answer these questions with specific examples where a forecast has been right, or a particular manager who has performed well over the past few years. What you need to decide for yourself is whether you can be *reasonably confident* that there is a *high chance* that you can identify and exploit anomalies consistently over time, or find a manager who can. If you believe that this is a tough thing to achieve, then you need to adopt a 'lose the least number of points' strategy. As simple as that! The rest of this chapter deals with answering these three questions, the outcome of which will drive your core beliefs and the rules by which you will manage your money.

4.4 Can active managers beat the markets after costs?

To answer this question, we need to review some of the evidence on the active management industry's success or otherwise. First, though, consider the following logical argument that immediately puts the active managers case on the back foot, with the probabilities favouring a passive (index) approach.

Passive investors will beat the majority of active investors

As we have discovered in the zero-sum game above, all investors are the market. So, the average investor will generate the market return before fees, transaction costs and taxes. In the real world these costs cannot be avoided so the average investor must inevitably be below the market by the amount of these costs. If index funds have lower costs than the average investor, which is the case, then they will beat the average active manager by the difference between these costs. Index funds will thus beat the majority of active funds over the long run. As Professor William Sharpe, a Nobel Prize winning stock market economist, puts it:

'The laws of arithmetic have been suspended for the convenience of those who pursue their careers as active managers.'

Opportunities abound for the active manager

Active managers have a wide range of opportunities to deliver above-market returns: many asset classes to switch between; the choice of domestic and non-domestic markets and currencies; and a very wide number of securities to pick from. On the face of it, the scope is there for them to outperform. The question is whether they can do so after costs, with a high chance of success from an individual investor's perspective.

The allure of market timing as a route to active returns is easily apparent. Let's look at a simple scenario. In Figure 4.2, the annual return for UK cash, bonds and equities over the past twenty years or so are ranked from highest to lowest. The first thing you see is that, over this short period, the rankings of each jump all over the place. Surely it can't be that difficult to work out which investments are likely to do well and which are likely to do badly? Surely paying a professional manager with their access to market information, economists, analysts, MBAs, etc., should be able to work it out?

To a believer in market timing, this is great news. Their superior skills and insight should provide them with the opportunity to move into and out of these investments to the benefit of their clients. To be able to do so successfully implies success in forecasting future asset prices.

As a simple exercise, let's look at what the consequences are of being right and being wrong. Take two market timers, Ms Lucky and Mr Unlucky, who both have £100,000 to invest at the start of 1990. The former calls the market right, investing all of her funds in cash in 1990. On New's Year's Eve 1990 she decides to move all of her money into equities and so on, receiving the full returns of the top line. Mr Unlucky on the other hand chooses the loser's line each time. Ms Lucky would have ended up with over £1 million (18 per cent a year) and Mr Unlucky would have lost money and ended up with around £90,000 (−1 per cent per year) of his original £100,000 before the effects of inflation are factored in. So, the rewards are there if you can get it right and the trade-off looks good. Can you get it right though? It seems so tempting to give it a go but research points strongly towards a conclusion that even most professionals struggle to do so.

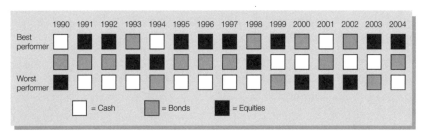

figure 4.2 **Annual winners and losers – UK cash, bonds and equity returns**   *Source: DMS Global Data (Ibbotson) © 2006 E Dimson, P Marsh and M Staunton.*

Winning points from market timing is very tricky

In the next few pages you should be acting like a jury and asking yourself whether beyond reasonable doubt, active management can beat the markets consistently. If you believe it can, then active management is for you, and good luck to you. If there is a level of reasonable doubt in your mind then you need to drop any notion of a points-winning philosophy and adopt a lose-the-fewest points philosophy. Here are some of the hurdles that you face:

Forecasting is notoriously difficult to get right, consistently

As economic forecasts are the basis for making forecasts about markets and securities, an active investor needs to be able to make consistently above-average forecasts to win. Wide scepticism by many acknowledged investors, backed up by empirical evidence, tells us this is so. Here are a couple of sceptical quotes about economists and forecasting to set the tone. The first I have always loved, its source unknown to me:

'An economist is an expert who will know tomorrow why the things he predicted yesterday didn't happen today.'

The second is attributed to Ray Marshall, a former US labour secretary, and is an example of the healthy scepticism that we all would do well to adopt.

'When it comes to forecasting, there are only two kinds of economist, those who don't know, and those who don't know they don't know.'

Your forecasting batting average needs to be Don Bradman-esque.

A study in the USA (Sharpe, 1975) using data from 1929 to 1972 (and others since) estimated that if you employed a market-timing approach, moving your money between equities and short-term bonds, you needed to call the up markets and down markets over 70 per cent right throughout this period just to make the same return as buying and holding equities. That's a steep hurdle to set. In addition, the study calculated that even if an investor managed to avoid all declining markets and to get back into half of the rising markets, they still would not have beaten the return of the market. In reality the hurdle is higher because no tax or transaction costs were included in these numbers.

Each decision you make actually requires two decisions

As the research above indicates, you need to be smart enough to make the call when to get out of the markets and to make the call when to get back in. If you have even a 50 per cent chance of getting one decision right, you only have a 25 per cent chance of getting two consecutive decisions right and so on. You need to be pretty consistently good at forecasting to be successful.

You need to act very quickly to win

To make matters tougher, many investors underestimate the rapidity and magnitude of the movements that markets make. Look at Table 4.2, which uses the Dow Jones index in the USA as a source of data. It demonstrates that if you miss the best ten days, in over twenty-two years of trading, you miss out on 40 per cent of returns. Miss the best fifty days, which is still less than 1 per cent of days, and you lose out on over 85 per cent of all the returns of the market. In this simple analysis, costs and taxes are ignored, which would only make the picture worse. As you can see, not only do you have to make two decisions as to when to move out of the market and back again, but also the exact timing of each move is critical.

Being right is quite a challenge. Being wrong can be very costly. The odds of success are beginning to stack up against you.

Alternatively, you need to be lucky

Napoleon's response of 'send me lucky generals' when asked what type of generals he needed to turn things round against the British, could apply to the type of market-beating strategy to adopt when choosing active fund managers.

In the past decade or so, particularly with the rapid expansion of the financial media, the cult of the star investment manager has grown. In fact it probably takes less than three years of market, or peer-beating perform-

table 4.2   **Missing just a fraction of good days can be very costly**

Nominal returns for Dow Jones Industrial Average (start Q1 1981, end Q2 2003)			
	Value of $100	Annualised return %	Contribution of missed days	Days missed %
Invested at all times	$932	10.4%	n/a	n/a
Top 10 days missed	$536	7.7%	42%	0.2%
Top 20 days missed	$353	5.8%	62%	0.4%
Top 50 days missed	$134	1.3%	86%	0.9%

Total number of trading days = 5679
Source: Dow Jones Industrial Average

ance and some good public relations to make a star manager and be pushed into the limelight as the new 'guru'. Yet how can we tell whether this performance is down to skill or judgement?

A lucky run is probably what you get more often than not when you employ an active manager on just a good short-term track record. There are 300 funds investing in the UK equity market and each manager at the start of each of the past three years had made a decision to allocate a portion of the fund into cash or not – a market-timing decision. Just by flipping a coin you would expect around forty of them to get the correct answer (300 × 50% × 50% × 50%). That's more than 10 per cent right. Marketing departments can now use these 'exceptional' results to push product and support the case for active management. Sure. Some may be geniuses but most will just be lucky over a short period. The problem is, can you tell which is which?

In summary – the hurdles faced by active managers are significant

To be a successful active manager, you need to be able to forecast well, get a high percentage of your forecasts right, get your timing spot on as markets move so rapidly and with such great magnitude, or just be one of the lucky few. The hurdles to success are high, but that does not matter if you or managers out there have the ability to overcome these hurdles consistently and you can identify who they are in advance. So, do they exist and can that be done?

This is nicely summed up in the comments made by John Bogle (2003), one of the patriarchs of losing-the-fewest points investing. He founded Vanguard, one of the USA's largest managers, which focuses on index investing to replicate the market.

'A lifetime of experience in this business makes me profoundly sceptical of market timing. I don't know anyone who can do it successfully, nor any one who has done so in the past. Heck, I don't even know anyone who knows anyone who has timed the market with consistent, successful, replicable results.'

Winning points through security selection is no easier

Quite a few active managers would happily go along with the proposition that trying to time markets is difficult, and put little effort into trying. They do, though, believe that they can beat markets by picking stocks. They are, however, up against a concept known as market efficiency. The concept is a simple one. It suggests that all known relevant information is incorporated in the current price of a security. Collectively, all the individual shares aggregate to form the market, which as a consequence is efficiently priced. Intuitively, the more analysts, journalists, brokers and lenders digging around companies, the more likely that all information is known about them. Some research estimates that new information is fully priced in within sixty minutes (Chordia et al, 2002). As such, in an efficient market it is hard to find securities that are anomalously priced. The price of the security will only move again on any news that is unanticipated. Price movements are therefore random in their nature.

You would, in this case, not expect to achieve continuing superior profits from investment decisions that you make because any short-term market-beating investment ideas, reflecting the mispricing of assets, would be quickly spotted by all the other smart professionals and the misalignment between price and value would disappear. If a market is efficient, you would conclude that it should be difficult to beat it, particularly after all costs are taken into account. Rex Sinquefield, an economist and proponent of index investing, provides his own humorous slant on the debate:

'So who still believes that markets don't work? Apparently it is only the North Koreans, the Cubans and the active managers.'

This theory is known as the Efficient Market Hypothesis or EMH and is eloquently described as the seminal text *A Random Walk Down Wall Street* by Burton G. Malkiel, which I would recommend you to read if you want to pursue this topic further.

Academics and professional investors argue endlessly about the degree to which markets are efficient. Some mine data for anomalies, which others seek to disprove. They are fortunate to have the luxury of time to do so. Burton Malkiel's overall conclusion, as you will see from active manager returns illustrated later, is hard to disagree with (Malkiel, 2000).

'I remain sceptical that markets are systematically irrational and that knowledge of such irrationalities can lead to profitable trading strategies. Indeed, the more potentially profitable a discoverable pattern is, the less likely it is to survive. This is the logical reason one should be cautious not to overemphasize the apparent departures from efficiency.'

For the rest of us, we don't have to prove whether markets are efficient or not. What we should be interested in is whether after all the costs incurred in investing are accounted for, can any inefficiencies that exist be exploited by active managers to generate market-beating returns consistently over time? To draw a conclusion we need to look at the track record of active managers as a collective group, to see if they do. We study the evidence a little later. Signs of efficiency include a narrow dispersion of longer-term returns between the top and bottom managers, as no one has a truly sustainable advantage or disadvantage. On this basis, the fixed income markets are reasonably efficient, as are equity markets such as the USA and the UK.

Active managers invariably claim that their market-beating approach will work better in less-efficient markets, such as small company stocks or small overseas equity markets, as they theoretically have the ability to exploit these inefficiencies. However, always remember that even in markets where information is deemed to be less than perfect, if the anomalies cannot be exploited to exceed the transaction costs involved with investing in them, then active management for you or me is worthless. Transaction costs are significantly higher in smaller, less efficient, markets, negating much of the benefit. Remember that they are still playing in a zero-sum game, but with higher costs.

What does the research tell us?

The reality is that research suggests that few investors outperform the market portfolio consistently over time, especially after transaction costs and taxes are taken into account. The magnitude and consistency of this research, from a wide number of angles, supports this emphatically. Let's look at the case more closely.

Even major investors have failed the active test

Some of the world's most renowned market timers have failed the test of time. The story of George Soros, perhaps the best known and, a very successful international market timer for a long time, provides a sobering indication of what a tough game it is. Commonly known as the man who broke the Bank of England, betting against the UK's ability to stay in the failed Exchange Rate Mechanism in the early 1990s, he was a major market timer. His investment firm, which managed $14 bn at the start of 2000 lost $5 bn of this before the year was out. The activities of the firm were dramatically reorganised thereafter. Ironically, Victor Niederhoffer, a protégé of George Soros, set up and ran his own fund, until that closed in 1997 after large losses.

Other notable examples of just how difficult it is exist: Julian Robertson's Tiger Funds were highly revered until they closed down; John Meriwether's Long Term Capital Managements, complete with two Nobel Prize winning economists, threatened to drag down the global financial system with it

$100 bn balance sheet when it got its view on Russia wrong and markets behaved out of line with expected, at least in their eyes, norms.

Then there was Jeff Vinik, formerly of Fidelity, who made one of the largest market timing mistakes recorded on the largest mutual fund in the world, The Magellan Fund. The latter's demise was recorded in BusinessWeek.

'When Jeffrey N. Vinik ran Fidelity Investment's huge Magellan Mutual Fund, he was known for his large – and often short-term – bets on stocks and sectors. Vinik's record was stellar – until the end of 1995, when he shifted a big chunk of the $50-plus billion portfolio into bonds. Not smart. Rates rose, returns collapsed, and he departed in June, 1996.'

In aggregate, active management deducts value from investors

Research by John Bogle compared the performance of the average, actively managed balanced fund, where investors could market time between the mix of bonds and equities and select securities, with an index fund that invests in bonds and equities at a fixed mix, replicating as closely as possible the underlying markets and rebalancing its mix back to the original proportions regularly (Bogle, 2002). Table 4.3 illustrates the results of this study looking at US-based balanced funds over the period from 1970 to 2002.

The difference in return between the two can largely be accounted for by the likely difference in fees between them. However, the active funds must be making active market timing and/or stock selection decisions as the volatility of their returns, otherwise known as risk, is higher than the index fund that merely tries to replicate the balance and the markets as closely as possible. The explicit conclusion is that the average balanced-fund manager has not only failed to add value through the active management techniques of market timing and stock selection, but also did so with greater

table 4.3   **Average active balanced fund vs. average balanced index fund (1970–2002)**

	Average annualised return %	Growth of $1	Level of risk
Index funds (no market timing)	10.2%	$22.1	12.2%
Active funds (scope for market timing)	9.4%	$17.2	14.1%

Source: Bogle (2002)

fluctuations in returns. The implicit conclusion is that these smart and dedicated professional managers were, as a group, no smarter than other participants in the markets.

Similarly, the majority of active UK equity funds were beaten by the market

We can come at this from another angle, by looking at how many actively managed UK equity funds beat the market. WM Company, a research company, compared actively managed unit trusts in the UK all-companies sector against the FTSE All-Share index, a broad market equity index, for the 20-year period to the end of 2000.

The main findings were that the market return was in the top quarter of unit trust returns and 44 out of 55 unit trusts with a 20-year record, failed to beat the market over this period. The first index tracker funds were established by the start of 1989. Over the subsequent twelve-year period, 80 out of 115 active funds failed to beat the index tracker funds and index funds themselves underperformed the market by 1 per cent a year due to costs. This study was updated in 2003 and looked at twenty-year data to the end of 2002. Of forty-eight trusts with a twenty-year history over this period only ten outperformed the index. Similarly, in the USA, over the twenty years to the end of 2003, more than 80 per cent of active managers failed to beat the market (fewer still over 30 years) and the average index fund beat the average active fund by 2 per cent, or so (Malkiel, 2004).

Investment policy outweighs investment strategy

A classic study (Brinson et al., 1986) relating to actively managed US pension plans and the role of long-term policy versus short-term active management decisions concludes that:

'Investment policy dominates investment strategy, explaining on average 93.6 per cent of the variation in total plan returns.'

This has also become one of the most misquoted pieces of research in investment academia. When I started work in the industry, I too was led to believe that an investor's total return was therefore about 90 per cent due to asset allocation and 10 per cent due to active decisions. Nonsense! What it refers to is the variation, i.e. changes, in returns over time, not what proportion of total return, is attributable to investment policy. You'd be amazed how many people still misquote this study.

The relevance of this study is that it implies that even sophisticated players implicitly accept that it is difficult to beat markets and constrain their active decision-making. A similar study was undertaken in the UK looking at 300 pension funds (Blake et al., 1999). It concluded that:

'Strategic asset allocation accounts for most of the time-series variation in portfolio returns, while market timing and asset selection appear to have been less important.'

They also concurred that this was probably due to the lack of active decision-making by managers rather than any measure of the economic role of asset allocation decisions. Their lack of activity, however, implies their acceptance that they probably don't have the ability to add value through active decision-making, and don't want to risk being out of line with their competitors.

Active management adds nothing to total return, in aggregate

Roger Ibbotson and Paul Kaplan (2000) undertook some research to clear up the general misunderstanding of the original research by Brinson et al., to estimate just how much of a typical actively managed fund's return was due to investment policy. Their conclusion was that the long-term mix of building blocks used, i.e. the investment policy of the funds under review, basically accounted for the entire portfolio return that was generated.

This implies that active management deducted a small amount of return after costs from the returns that would have been generated by the investment policy mix alone. To get this figure, the compound annual return of the policy portfolio, i.e. investment policy mix of assets, was divided by the actual compound return of the portfolio. In plain English this means that your passive policy mix of investments is likely to be the crucial determinant of your portfolio's return, not moving this around, to try and win points.

Where do you stand now?

The evidence against using active management as a high probability points-winning philosophy is mounting up: markets are competitive and probably reasonably efficient; forecasting has some serious hurdles to success, few active managers appear able to do it consistently; and research studies show that the majority of managers fail to outperform the index (and index funds) over the longer term. In its favour there appear to be a few managers who do. As a rational investor the probability of success lies in favour of an index approach over active management at this point.

4.5 Do a few managers outperform consistently?

If, however, some managers do have exceptional skills that allow them to beat markets, rather than luck, and they can consistently use these skills to generate outperformance (after all costs) of the markets over long periods of time, then employing them to manage your money would make sense as each incremental point is extremely valuable, when compounded over time. A few do, and the UK's most celebrated manager is Anthony Bolton, with a remarkable track record (see the box at the end of this chapter). Perhaps you could do this by picking funds with persistent past performance, as a guide to future performance. Let's see whether this is the case.

Testing whether performance persists

Significant amounts of research have been undertaken to test whether investment managers' performance does persist over time. In other words: are the few who outperform over one time frame the same managers who outperform over subsequent time frames? If performance persistence exists, then you could act on that information. Two recent and comprehensive reviews of the literature on performance persistence have been published. The conclusions of which are laid out below. The first was a paper commissioned by the Financial Services Authority, the UK's industry regulatory body (Rhodes, 2000). The conclusion that was reached was as follows:

'The literature on the performance of UK funds has failed to find evidence that information on past investment performance can be used to good effect by retail investors in choosing funds. The general pattern is one in which investment performance does not persist. Small groups of funds may show some repeat performance over a short period of time. However, the size of this effect and the fact that it is only short-lived means there is no investment strategy for retail investors that could be usefully employed. The results of the US literature are similar.'

This is further indication that the UK market is pretty efficient, or that any inefficiency cannot be profitably exploited. If it were not, some managers would have been able to generate long-term persistent records of performance due to their superior skills. Bear this in mind the next time you see an advertisement in the paper for a stellar fund.

The UK study undertaken by WM Company, which is in the full text of the FSA paper, illustrates the general conclusion nicely. The methodology was

| table 4.4 | Performance persistence – what persistence? | | | |

		Quartile position in period 2			
		1	*2*	*3*	*4*
Quartile	**1**	22.2%	22.2%	33.3%	22.2%
position	**2**	19.1%	34.0%	17.0%	29.8%
in period	**3**	13.0%	17.4%	32.6%	37.0%
1	**4**	43.8%	25.0%	16.7%	14.6%

Source: WM Company (2001)

to take the period 1979–1998 and track the performance of the top quartile of funds in one five-year period and record which quartile they ended up in the subsequent period. If performance persistence were in evidence, then a high proportion of top-quartile funds would remain there. Even distributions across quartiles would indicate that performance was random. Table 4.4 shows that the evidence fails to indicate performance persistence. It seems that those at the top of the pile rotate and, as a result, a consistent performer, relative to the market, such as good index fund, will, over time slowly float towards the top of the pile. As you will see in a moment, the evidence seems to support this.

The report concluded:

'Over the entire period of the study the probability of selecting a top quartile performer based on historic top quartile performance was no better than would be expected by chance.'

Another paper was commissioned by the Australian Securities and Investment Commission (Allan et al., 2002). The study again took the form of a review of the literature in the USA, the UK and Australia. Three of its general conclusions were:

'Good performance seems to be, at best, a weak and unreliable predictor of good performance over the medium to long term. About half the studies found no correlation at all between good past and good future performance. Where persistence was found, this was more frequently in the shorter term (one to two years) than in the longer term.'

'More studies seem to find that bad past performance increased the probability of future bad performance.'

And:

'Where persistence was found, the 'outperformance' margin tended to be small.

Where studies found persistence, some specifically reported that frequent swapping to best performing funds would not be an effective strategy, due to the cost of swapping.'

Again, as a rational investor, you have to admit that the weight of evidence backs the claim that 'past performance is no guide to future returns' always quoted as a disclaimer on investment literature.

Are longer-term outperformers lucky or skilful?

Earlier you saw that luck might well play a part in short-term market beating track records of some managers. A skilled active manager should be able to generate returns in excess of the level of returns expected from a portfolio of equivalent market risk. The risk that the manager takes over and above that inherent in the general market, for example by choosing a few specific equities to hold in the portfolio, can be measured. If you work out the ratio of the excess return (known in the industry as *alpha*) to the excess risk taken on (known as *residual risk*), you can get a measure of how well an active manager manages money. In plain English, it describes the active bang of return they get for their active buck of risk they take. This is known as the *information ratio*.

A number of studies have calculated the information ratio of top quartile managers, tends to be around 0.5 on a gross basis. After fees and costs this is likely to be considerably lower. The point I am getting to is that for an information ratio of 0.5 you need sixteen years of data for you to be 95 per cent sure that the returns are due to skill rather than luck. At 0.33, which may be nearer reality for these 'top' managers after costs, you would need thirty-six years of data. At 0.2 you need one hundred years. The reality is that you rarely get more than five years of data, let alone twenty.

Who can tell as managers move around so frequently?

As food for thought, you may want to ponder on recent data in the UK relating to fund manager turnover on unit trusts, which is quite staggering: In the UK, a quarter of fund managers have been in their current role less than one year, half have been with their present funds for under two years, only a third have been with the same fund for three years or more and alarmingly fewer than one in five for more than five years! Few have served twenty years. Just whose track record are you looking at?

In fact a few truly talented managers do exist

This part of the book may sound like a bit of an indictment of the active management industry. It is not meant to be. It is just meant to convince you that as an average investor, like me, you are unlikely to have the time, inclination, data or skills to evaluate active managers, or try to invest actively yourself. As a rational investor you need to make decisions based on the likelihood of long-term success, and therefore should adopt a lose-the-fewest points strategy.

There are some exceptional managers in the investment business, some of whom have moved to hedge funds or continue to manage funds or investor portfolios. An example of a long-term outperforming manager in the UK is Anthony Bolton who runs the Special Situations fund at Fidelity – but now you've found him, unfortunately he is just about to retire! Take a look at the box at the end of this chapter to see just what a remarkable job he has done and to see what challenges investors faced sticking through the tougher periods the fund suffered along the way. It took a brave investor to reap the benefits.

4.6 Can you identify them in advance?

At this point you have the answers to the first two questions posed. You know that your mix of investments drives your portfolio returns, and the probability of capturing most of these returns lies in favour of a passive strategy rather than using active managers. You also now know that you cannot use past performance as a guide to picking future winners. As a result, you now have little to go on if you still want to use active managers.

Even if we can find a manager who can demonstrate fifteen years of outperformance, based on skill, and/or a robust investment process rather than luck, the problem is that it is highly unlikely that they will be around for the next twenty years or more that *you* need them. They will be long gone to their beach houses in the Bahamas. If you can't use something simple such as past performance to choose managers, you have a problem. Waring and Siegel (2003) sum this problem of manager selection up well in a recent paper where they state:

'Each investor has to develop his or her own methodology for forecasting manager alphas . . . if you don't think that you can do this, maybe you should not hire active managers.'

Even some of the world's largest and most sophisticated pension plans are index investors for at least some of their assests, such as the California Public

Employees' Retirement System (CalPERS), who oversee more than $200 billion of assets. A few successful institutional investors such as the Yale University Endowment managed by David Swensen and his team, use their proprietary insight, access to information and managers, and evaluation skills (combined with much hard work) to build an entire portfolio of high quality active managers. That may be fine for them, as they are some of the most astute investors around, but for you and me, we should stick where the probabilities favour us i.e. indexing of long-term investment policy mix and sticking with it.

4.7 Leading active managers endorse index investing

So, having probably reached the conclusion that a passive index approach rather than an active approach makes most sense in terms of maximising your probability of long-term success, you are now with the 10 per cent of investors that think like you. The other 90 per cent of investors, both individuals and institutions, are still trying to pursue a points-winning strategy. However, you may be surprised by who has advocated the use of index investing as a sensible way to invest for most investors. Let me name a few, all of whom have made reputations for themselves as leading active managers or proponents of active management. You can rest assured that adopting a lose-the-fewest-points strategy is the only way for you to manage your own investing.

Warren Buffet (the Sage of Omaha), widely regarded as one of the greatest active investors of our time, has been described by John Bogle (Targett, 2001) as follows:

'He thinks like an index investor: he buys a few large stocks, holds them for a good holding period – forever – and it's worked quite brilliantly.'

In further support of index funds, Warren Buffet himself stated in one of the annual letters to shareholders (1997) of the investment firm Berkshire Hathaway that he and Charlie Munger run:

'Most investors, both institutional and individual, will find the best way to own common stocks is through an index fund that charges minimal fees. Those following this path are sure to beat the net results (after fees and expenses) delivered by the great majority of investment professionals.'

Peter Lynch: One-time manager of Fidelity Investment's Magellan

Fund, the world's largest actively managed fund and highly respected active manager states of most investors that (Anon, 1990):

'They'd be better off in an index fund.'

Charles Schwab: The pioneer of online brokerage in the USA actively supports indexing as the core of an optimal long-term portfolio states: (Schwab, 1998):

'Most of the mutual fund investments I have are in index funds, approximately 75 per cent.'

Fidelity Investments: One of the world's largest active management companies, and familiar to UK investors, implicitly supports the concept of index investing through the addition of an index range of funds to their active fund stable.

What better testimonials could you ask for than those?

4.8 Summarising what you now know

So, given all of the arguments put forward in this chapter, you now need to condense this down into a simple investment philosophy that will provide you with a set of rules to guide you in investment decisions. I am assuming that you have been suitably convinced by the arguments put forward to adopt a lose the fewest points strategy. Let's summarise what you now know:

- Investors play a less-than-zero sum cost game (after costs and taxes).

- Opportunities may exist for some managers to beat the markets if they have superior skills and/or access to information or ability to interpret information.

- Most professional investors tend to take only small active decisions, such as market timing or security selection, and long-term investment policy thus overrides active strategies as the main contributor to the variation in returns over time. This implies that they believe it is hard to do.

- In fact, professional managers tend marginally to underperform their investment policy portfolio mix due to their active decisions and costs.

■ This may be because markets are efficient. Forecasts are hard to make, decisions are in fact two decisions, and markets move very rapidly and with magnitude.

■ Even where markets are less efficient, costs tend to be higher and exploiting the inefficiencies that exist after costs remains challenging.

■ Logic tells us that as all investors are the market, the average investor will be the market before costs. The average investor after costs will underperform the market by these costs. As index fund costs are lower than active costs, the average index fund will outperform the average active fund.

■ In practice, an index fund will outperform 60 per cent to maybe 80 per cent of comparable active funds over the long term.

■ That would be fine if the market beaters of the future were easy to identify by their past performance record.

■ However, active funds' outperformance does not persist to any degree that is useful. Underperformance may be an indicator of future poor results in some cases. This means you cannot use past performance, profitably, to select managers.

■ Some exceptionally skilful managers may out there waiting for your money, but you have a tough job trying to find them in advance. Those few who have already performed through skill are unlikely to be around for the period you will need them, or are inaccessible to you.

■ At least fifteen years of data is generally required to validate statistically that good outperformance is due to skill rather than luck.

■ Most managers have been in their current roles for fewer than three years.

■ If you don't have a proprietary method for selecting these outperforming managers, along with the skill, time, resources and appetite to screen hundreds if not thousands of managers, then don't try to. Your chances of success are very poor.

4.9 In conclusion

So, without any hesitation I suggest to you that you choose, as your default, index-replicating vehicles to create your long-term investment policy portfolio. Avoid trying to add returns by moving your mix of investment around or trying to pick winning stocks or managers. The chances are slim that you will be able to do it consistently. I know it's tempting to get swayed by the supposed evidence of short-term performance of markets and managers but you will not be being rational if you are. Play the highest probability game. The rationale for adopting a passive approach to investing is made succinctly by Professor Keane (2000):

'The significance of the empirical evidence is not that passive investment will always outperform active investment, but that, at the time of decision-making, the balance of probabilities is always in favour of passive investment.'

4.10 A personal philosophy

Hopefully at this point you will have a pretty clear picture of what your personal investment philosophy should look as a rational investor. I will now share with you my personal investment philosophy. Some of the concepts referred to are introduced later in the book.

My philosophy

On goals: I want to achieve my investment goals, which I think of in terms of lifetime purchasing power goals: sending the kids to school, paying off my mortgage and retiring early with a good standard of living until I die. Success or failure should be measured against these goals.

On being rational: I realise that I do not have a crystal ball that I can foresee the future with and will therefore try and act as rationally as possible to allow myself the greatest chance of achieving these goals, in an environment of uncertainty. If I let emotions sway my reason, I know that it will cost me dearly.

On probabilities: There are many things that I know for sure when I invest. I know that time and compounding are on my side and that inflation and all sorts of costs always work against me. I will maximise the forces that work in my favour and minimise or eliminate those that work against me.

The one thing I don't know for sure is how the markets will perform over my investing lifetime. I therefore need to diversify my portfolio well, and try and make the best estimates that I can that I have a reasonable chance of obtaining an acceptable investment outcome.

▶

Research, analysis and empirical evidence provide me with the opportunity to improve my chances of making good investment decisions, and thus reaching my goals.

On my portfolio mix: I understand that choosing and maintaining the long-term structure of my portfolio is the most important decision that I face and all other decisions are secondary to it and revolve around capturing as much of the available return from this mix of portfolio building blocks as is practicably possible.

The choice between holding equities to drive returns from my portfolio and buying 'market trauma protection' by owning bonds is the primary decision I need to make. In building my investment programme, I include a rational assumption that over time different building blocks will generate returns and volatility of returns in the approximate ranges that have been shown historically in the long run. I understand that they are only a guide and I am aware that over the shorter term, and possibly over the longer term, they will be different from what has historically been the case. I should therefore be prudent in any assumptions that I make and use. I realise that the longer I have to invest, the more likely the building blocks in my portfolio will act like their generalisations than like their exceptions.

I will use the tools that are available to all investors, including diversification, to create the best portfolio that I can within practical reason. I will also seek to add other building blocks to my portfolio, either to increase returns or to diversify my portfolio further in an attempt make my investment journey smoother without giving up too much return potential. I will only use these other portfolio building blocks when I understand and feel happy with the risks that I am taking on by including them.

On costs Small differences in returns e.g. caused by bad performance relative to other comparable investment options combined with costs, when compounded over time, can dramatically reduce the effectiveness of my investing and may force me to change my hoped for goals and suffer the consequences that I would rather avoid.

In a practical sense, capturing as much of the market return possible should be my aim. Index-replicating strategies, with low costs, will be my base position for obtaining these returns, based on the logic, research and evidence that is available. Index (passive) management is the winning strategy because it minimises the risk of losing points. I choose it relative to active strategies for my portfolio. I realise that some portfolio building blocks such as real estate, hedge funds and private equity cannot be indexed. If I include them in my portfolio it will be as a diversified group, probably through a fund of funds structure, to eliminate excessive manager and strategy risk.

I will always be alert to the fact that the investment management and brokerage industry, whilst providing me with assistance, is always seeking to maximise its own shareholder value. I understand that there will always be some costs associated with investing but I will ensure that I always fully understand all of the costs involved, that I will not pay for advice that I do not receive or is unnecessary, and will not pay for investment professionals that can not prove, on terms that I set, that they personally, or the investment process they adopt, can consistently generate long-term value for my portfolio. The onus lies with them to convince me to move away from index products and pay higher costs.

I will always think about the tax consequences of how I invest any funds that I will need to pay tax on. I will look at returns after tax. I will maximise the use of all legal tax shelters and breaks available to me, and will make sure that my investment strategy allows me to maximise the benefit of legitimately paying the tax man later rather than sooner through the reduction of turnover and active efforts to manage my tax position.

On technology: I will use technology to my advantage to monitor, manage and administer my investments, taking advantage of the technology provided at very low costs by some online brokers, banks and investment companies.

On managing my investments over time: As part of the portfolio maintenance process I will rebalance my portfolio regularly, not driven by some hope of benefiting from selling overperforming assets and buying underperforming assets, but driven by the desire to maintain the risk of my portfolio at a level that I can live with, which I worked out upfront before embarking on my investment programme.

On sticking with it: All of these objectives, assumptions, constraints and intentions I will write down in a simple statement of my investment programme. When times get tough, as they inevitably will, I will take out this document and remind myself just why my portfolio is invested the way it is. I will also refresh my memory to the fact that severe bumpiness on the way to meeting my lifetime purchasing power goals is to be expected.

On a personal note: I will try to keep up-to-date with developments, avoid being tempted into making emotional decisions, which I know can severely damage my wealth accumulation, have the courage to stick to my strategy when times get tough as they will from time to time, avoid looking at my portfolio too often, avoid listening to financial news programmes and believing what I hear, and try and enjoy my investment responsibilities.

4.11 Your investment philosophy rules

1 *Set an appropriate investment policy mix of assets and stick to it at all times.* This will be the most crucial decision that you will make. How you get to the right mix is explored in Part 3.

2 Remember at all times the wise words of Charles Ellis, particularly if you have any investment decision to make:

   'The ultimate outcome is determined by who can lose the fewest points not win them.'

3 A penny saved is a penny earned; become obsessed with reducing the actual or potential loss of points in all aspects of your investing programme, as losing the least number of (return) points is your ultimate philosophical goal. Keep other people's hands out of your investment pie, which includes advisors, active managers, badly structured and managed index funds, brokers and the taxman.

4 Active management is a tough game for all but the few most brilliant or lucky. You have a low chance of winning points and a high chance of losing points if you go this route.

5 Avoid trying to time markets and being tempted to jump between asset classes, countries, sectors or managers. Chasing returns is a road to wealth destruction.

6   Don't try and pick stocks. Too much evidence demonstrates that after all costs, fees and taxes are taken into account it is a game you won't win.

7   You will lose if you try and pick a manager by their performance record. Be sensible and pick a fund that has a 60–80 per cent chance of beating all active funds over the long run, i.e. an index tracker fund.

8   However bright you think you are, or however confident you are, or how convincing a story, sales patter, brochure of performance record is, do not be tempted either to change your investment policy mix or become an active investor yourself.

9   Index all bond and equity market investments wherever possible.

10 If you decide to invest in markets that are less efficient and that have no index alternatives, e.g. UK property and hedge funds, you need to be pretty confident that you have the resources, time and skill to pick the best managers or manager of managers.

11 Sticking with a passive buy-and-hold index funds approach to investing not only reduces your chances of losing points, but it provides you with a much more straightforward approach to investing at a number of levels, as you will see.

Anthony Bolton – The exception that proves the rule

In the introduction, I made an apology to the cohort, be it a small one, of fund managers who truly have something special – the ability consistently to beat the market over long periods of time, either through their exceptional individual skills, a unique investment process, or a combination of the two.

Anthony Bolton is a fund manager at Fidelity, one of the world's largest and most respected active fund management firms. He is an exceptional manager: he has been managing his Special Situations fund for more than 25 years (few others can match his longevity); he is truly dedicated to making money for the investors who place their faith in him; and he is very much a contrarian at heart (unlike some), being prepared to manage his money in quite a different manner from most of his peers and the market benchmark. In his words (Davis, 2004):

▶

'If you want to outperform other people, you have got to hold something different from other people. If you want to outperform the market, as everyone expects you to do, the one thing you mustn't hold is the market itself.'

His UK-focused Special Situations fund has done just that; exhibiting a focus on smaller to medium-sized companies and value stocks, although that masks the flexibility of his approach to the companies he invests in; and his track record has been exceptional. With his impending retirement, he has firmly placed himself in the pantheon of active investment greats, alongside the likes of Warren Buffett and Peter Lynch, one of his former colleagues at Fidelity.

For investors who put £1,000 into his fund at its launch in 1979, their money in December 2004 would be worth about £90,000, whereas the market would only have made you just over £20,000. That is 6 per cent every year, on average, better than the market and twice his nearest rival. One of his exceptional feats was to make a positive return of around 4 per cent in the bear market of March 2000 to March 2003, when the market itself was down almost 40 per cent – only a handful of other managers made positive returns in this period. This is a truly remarkable record.

Active management can really pay, if you get it right, because compounding outperformance over time makes a big difference to the money in your pocket. No one in this case would begrudge paying a 1.5 per cent annual fee and all the other associated fund costs! I don't deny the fact; all I am trying to do is help you face the realities when you invest your money and try and make the best decisions you can to increase your chances of success. In that sense, and somewhat disappointingly, going the active route in search of the truly talented is a gamble – a low chance of a high payout, in this case an exceptionally high payout.

Ironically, Anthony Bolton's exceptional track record helps to highlight the very real challenge you are up against. Forgetting the notion that you can invest directly in the markets yourself successfully, finding true talent like Anthony Bolton is not easy and you need to ask yourself if you have the skills and the time to try and do so.

First of all, it is very hard to pick a manager in advance of the twenty to thirty years that you will need them to manage your money. Who in

1979 knew that Anthony Bolton would be one of the best fund managers yet? It's made no easier by the fact that managers hop from job to job so quickly. Bolton is one of only 17 managers who have managed their fund for more than 15 years, out of more than 300 funds.

Here's an illustration of the dilemma you face. Imagine you had £10,000 to invest at the start of 1989. You open the paper and see that his Special Situations fund has beaten the market by a remarkable 8 per cent a year for nine years. You (rightly as it turns out, of course) decide that he is the man to look after your money. You invest. Three years later you find yourself a whopping 45 per cent or so behind the market, turning your £10,000 into £9,700 against the market's £14,300. What do you do? Hold? Sell? The problem is that you simply don't know, at that point in 1991, if he is brilliant or whether his luck has just run out. Even Ned Johnson, the head of Fidelity, seemed to have his doubts, calling him in to talk about the fund's performance.

In 1996 you almost get back in line with the market but 1997 and 1998 see you drop back by about 20 per cent against the market. Still going to hold? In fact, it would have taken you until 2000 to get back ahead of the market. Eleven years of uncertainty – would you really have had the stomach to see this through? I doubt it and I can understand why. If you had, though, you would have ended up with almost twice what the market delivered by the end of 2004! Very few investors have held the fund since inception and over half of today's 250,000 investors have invested in the last five years.

That brings us back to the issue of needing to find a manager now who will be around for the period of time you need them, i.e. from today. New investors in this particular fund won't have Anthony Bolton managing their money. Do you believe his replacement will replicate his unique talent and insight? Who else out there is the next Anthony Bolton? And how can you pick them now, given that past performance is a weak indicator of future success in most cases? That's your dilemma. As a smarter investor you should accept that you may have to give up an outside chance of a very substantial upside of tomorrow's Anthony Bolton and simply accept that the market return, as near as possible, is a worthy ambition, if a somewhat boring one.

Congratulations to Mr Bolton, and to those other managers who in a few years' time we will look back on and say, 'Boy, they were good!' while secretly wishing we had found them today.

References

Allan, D., Brailsford, T., Bird, R. and Faff, R. (2002) *A review of research on the past performance of managed funds*, Funds Management Research Centre.

Anon (1990) Is there life after Babe Ruth? Peter Lynch talks about why he's quitting Magellan, *Barron's*, April 2, p.15.

Barber, B. M. and Odean, T. (1998) 'Trading is hazardous to your wealth: the common stock investment performance of individuals', *The Journal of Finance*, vol. LV, no. 2, 773–806.

Blake, D., Lehman, B. N. and Timmerman, A. (1999), 'Asset allocation dynamics and pension fund performance', *The Journal of Business*, vol. 72, no.4, 429–461.

Bogle, J. C. (2002), 'The investment dilemma of the philanthropic investor', Bogle Financial Markets Research Center. Available from: http://www.vanguard.com

Bogle, J. C. (2003) 'The policy portfolio in an era of subdued returns', Bogle Financial Markets Research Center. Available from: http://www.vanguard.com

Brinson, G. P., Hood, L. R. and Beebower G.L. (1986) Determinants of portfolio performance, *Financial Analysts Journal*, vol. 42, no. 4, 40–48.

Buffett, W. (1997) *Annual Report 1996: Chairman's Letter*. Berkshire Hathaway Inc. Available from http:// www.berkshirehathaway.com/1996ar/1996.html

Chordia, T., Roll, R. and Subrahmanyan, A., (2003) Evidence on the speed of convergence to market efficiency, UCLA Working Paper, November 3.

Davis, J. (2004) *Investing with Anthony Bolton*, UK: Harriman House, p. 18.

Ellis, C. D. (2002) *Winning the losers game* 4th ed. New York: McGraw Hill, 3–7.

Ibbotson, R. G. and Kaplan, P. D., (2000) Does asset allocation policy explain 40%, 90% or 100% of performance? *Financial Analysts Journal*, vol. 56, no.1, 26–33.

Keane, S. (2000) *Index funds in a bear market*, A monograph published by Glasgow University in association with Virgin Direct.

Malkiel, B. G. (2000) Are markets efficient? Yes even if they make errors, *The Wall Street Journal*, December 28, p. A10.

Malkiel, B. G. (2004) Three decades of indexing: What have we learned about indexing and index construction? *In: The handbook of world stock, derivative and commodity exchanges 2004 edition*. London: Mondo Visione. Available from: http://www.exchange-handbook.co.uk.

Rhodes, M. *Past imperfect? The performance of UK equity managed funds*. London: FSA, FSA Occasional Paper Series 9. Available from: http://www.fas.gov.uk/pubs.occpapers/op09.pdf.

Schwab, C. (1999) *Charles Schwab's guide to financial independence: simple solutions for busy people*. New York: Three Rivers Press, p.90.

Sharpe, W. F., (1975) 'Are gains likely from market timing?'. *The Financial Analysts Journal*, vol. 31, no. 2, (March/April): pp. 60–69.

Sharpe, W. F. (1991) The arithmetic of active management. *The Financial Analysts Journal*, January/February, vol. 47, no. 1, 7–9.

Sinquefield, R. (1995) *Opening address: Schwab Institutional Conference, San Francisco, CA, October 12.*

Targett, S. (2001), Survey – index-based investing: An industry enjoying life in the fast track. *Financial Times*, Jul 18.

Waring, M. B. and Siegel, L. B., (2003) The dimensions of active management', *The Journal of Portfolio Management*, vol. 29, no 3, 35–51.

WM Company (2001), *A comparison of active and passive management of unit trust*. A report produced for Virgin Direct Financial Services.

5

Get smart – have a word with yourself

While we all like to think that we are capable of making rational decisions, it appears that when it comes to investing, a switch inside even the most sensible person seems to flick and rationality disappears in a cloud of emotion. It is impossible for me simply to tell you to be rational in the decisions that you face, but what I can do is point out the consequences of emotional behaviour on your wealth accumulation and some of the demons that drive it.

5.1 You are your own worst enemy

Being an investor is not easy. You have to contend not only with the erratic and unpredictable nature of markets but also the sometimes erratic and irrational way in which you will be tempted to think and behave. This book encourages you to do your best to make rational decisions and to make your head rule your heart in all matters relating to investing. Yet for most, while understanding that being rational makes sense, putting it into practice can be exceedingly difficult. Benjamin Graham, one of the great investment minds of the twentieth century, famously stated:

'The investor's chief problem – and even his worst enemy – is likely to be himself.'

Irrational investing manifests itself in many different ways: chopping and changing your investment plan influenced by what has just happened to the markets; trading shares in an online brokerage account; trying to pick market turning points, i.e. when to be in or out of different markets; being tempted into buying flavour of the month investment ideas or products; or chasing performance. The list of irrational decision-making opportunities is long and distinguished. John Bogle summed this up perfectly in an address to the Investment Analysts Society of Chicago (2003):

'*If I have learned anything in my 52 years in this marvellous field, it is that, for a given individual or institution, the emotions of investing have destroyed far more potential investment returns than the economics of investing have ever dreamed of destroying.*'

Reflect on this for a moment

Eye-opener 2 at the start of this book looked at the performance record of individual investors in the USA over the period from 1984 to 2002. The staggering results of the study showed that because investors are all tempted by the media, their own research, or their advisors, to chop and change their investment strategy and chase last year's returns, the average equity investor earned just 2.6 per cent annually over this period, when inflation was 3.1 per cent. That is a bad result.

The market, as measured by the S&P500 index, a commonly used proxy for the US market, returned 12.2 per cent a year. If you assume that an investor could have replicated the market at a 0.2 per cent cost, which is not unreasonable in the USA, you can calculate what the true difference in purchasing power would have been over this period. Figure 5.1 displays the results. Remember it every time you make an investment decision. As you can see from the right hand chart, investors are their 'own worst enemy' and cost themselves a lot of money through their decision-making.

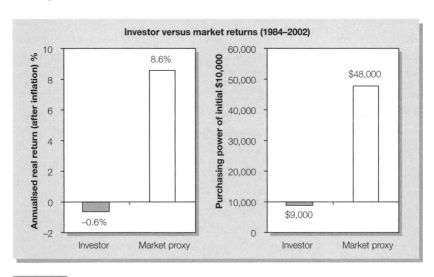

figure 5.1   **You may be highly dangerous to your wealth**

Source: Dalbar

Get a grip on yourself

Unfortunately emotional demons affect the way in which you make your investment decisions. Understanding these demons may help you to identify how you can try to keep them in control. The times when most investors become irrational are generally periods of market trauma or market exuberance. As Warren Buffett said (2001):

'The line separating investment and speculation, which is never bright and clear, becomes blurred still further when most market participants have recently enjoyed triumphs. Nothing sedates rationality like large doses of effortless money.'

Buy high, sell low – the common recipe for wealth destruction

Figure 5.2 shows how many people invest, allowing their emotions and lack of market knowledge to drive the type of wealth destruction that you saw in the research above. This is the sort of investing that our hypothetical investor, James, undertook in the previous chapter. While most investors can understand the simple concept of buy-low-sell-high, the very nature of their behaviour results in exactly the opposite. Investors tend to be influenced by what is going on in the markets over the short term. This makes them vulnerable to what the industry refers to as being 'whip-sawed'

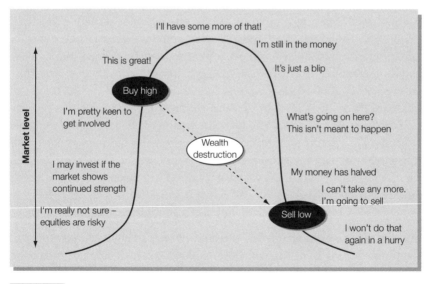

figure 5.2   **Generic wealth-destroying behaviour**

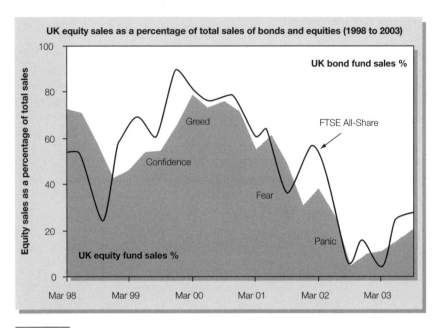

figure 5.3   **Buy high, sell low – the road to wealth destruction**

Source: Investment Management Association; Thomson Datastream

as they move from last year's bad performing investment to this year's best performer.

Let's take a look at this behaviour in practice in the UK. Figure 5.3 shows the net retail sales by unit trusts and open-ended investment companies (OEICs) to UK investors. Rationally, you would expect that after the UK equity market had fallen by 40 per cent or so, new fund flows into equities would increase as investors were getting better value for their money than at the start of 2000 when the market was at a high. Yet it is clear that fund sales are driven by short-term market sentiment, where investors become increasingly eager to enter the market when markets have performed well recently, i.e. when they are relatively expensive, and tend to cut back their investment when they fall, i.e. when they are cheaper. This is ironic given that in all other walks of life we have no trouble in being attracted to goods and services which are cheap, yet when it comes to investing we seem to lose not only our rational selves, but also a good deal of common sense.

As you can see from Figure 5.3, the level of sales of equity funds rises and falls almost exactly in line with the market. As equity markets fall, bond sales increase in proportion. Given that the vast majority of sales are made through advisors of some description, it begs the question as to just how valuable and costly this advice is. It appears to constitute selling last quarter's best performer, or am I being too sceptical? Decide for yourself. It is a good illustration of emotions taking over, and bad advice encouraging them.

Ironically, many investors were willing to buy into the equity markets in the late 1990s with 'irrational exuberance' not because it was part of a long-term strategic plan, but because they thought there was a quick buck to be made, as markets powered ahead. When the UK equity market reached its highest point in 2000 where the FTSE 100 Index, which represents the largest one hundred, listed companies, reached almost 7,000, there was an almost hysterical urge to invest in equities. When it fell to 3,500 in mid-2002, few investors wanted to invest money in equities. Corporate bond funds became the flavour of the day as strongly performing havens for investors, or so the salespeople said.

This is perverse and is best described Warren Buffett, who has a habit of speaking common sense (1998). He poses a short quiz to his shareholders:

'If you plan to eat hamburgers throughout your life and are not a cattle producer, should you wish for higher or lower prices for beef? Likewise, if you are going to buy a car from time to time but are not an auto manufacturer, should you prefer higher or lower prices? These, questions of course, answer themselves.'

He follows on with the paradox of investors:

'But now for the final exam: if you expect to be a net saver during the next five years, should you hope for a higher or lower net stock market during that period? Many investors get this one wrong. Even though they are going to be net buyers of stocks for many years to come, they are elated when prices rise and are depressed when they fall. In effect, they rejoice because prices have risen for the 'hamburgers' they will soon be buying. This reaction makes no sense. Only those who will be sellers of equities in the near future should be happy at seeing stocks rise. Prospective purchasers should much prefer sinking prices.'

The problem is that these sentiments persuade some investors to change tack when market trauma events occur and often act precisely against their own best interest. To be a good investor at times is a bit like playing a game of poker with yourself, pitching your logical-self against your emotional-self and seeing who blinks first.

5.2 Challenges to decision-making

Many investors act irrationally, rather than rationally as economic theory demands; this irrational behaviour is a relatively new and interesting area of academic study. A whole industry has grown up in the past couple of decades studying it called 'behavioural finance'.

The next few pages is not meant to be a review of the psychology of investment decision-making as espoused by these academics, but a practical guide to how you can avoid being tempted into becoming irrational. If you understand a little more about who you are and importantly how, where and when you may be tempted into being irrational then you will have made some useful progress. It is based in part on the general ideas of behavioural economists, in large part on my experience of dealing with a wide number of investors over the past few years, and will probably seem to you like just a dose of common sense.

Making investment decisions

As you make investment decisions, you go through a mental process of trying to evaluate the wealth outcomes that you can expect and trying to assess the likelihood that they will happen. You have a wide choice of options and you need to weigh up one against the other. It is hard trying to process all the information that is available in any ordered and value-

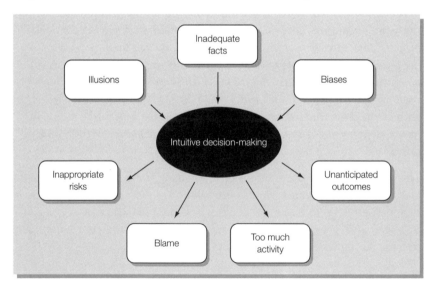

figure 5.4   **Intuitive decision-making can be costly**

added way and in the end you generate some sort of intuitive feel for what the answer is for you.

A lack of knowledge, combined with a number of illusions and biases can lead to errors in making decisions that may damage your chances of making the most from your money. These include: the likelihood that you take on an inappropriate and usually higher level of risk than you might have considered sensible if your assessment of the effect had been more realistic; the possibility that the outcome you get is not one you considered, but should have done; the greater likelihood that you will continue to make decisions rather than leaving your investments alone; and the common and sometimes ugly outcome of blaming your advisor or yourself when your luck runs out (Kahneman et al., 1998).

All in all, not being aware of and not curbing your inner biases and illusions is likely to be painful, upsetting, and from a wealth perspective grossly sub-optimal. Figure 5.4 summarises the decision-making process.

5.3 Thirteen questions for you to answer – unlucky for some?

A number of emotional demons regularly influence investors, advisors and fund managers; the degree to which they will affect you, only you will know. Think hard about yourself and be honest, because cheating will only lead to bad decisions and cost you money.

1. Are you interested in investing?

I am sure you will have a pretty good feel for this!

No: You probably know that you should be doing something with your money; perhaps improving your retirement planning, sensibly investing the proceeds from the sale of a business, or making provision for education fees, but have little interest in sorting it out yourself. That's understandable. Not everyone needs to have an avid interest in investing, but everyone needs to be an investor. What you probably want is to get everything sorted out, simply and efficiently so you can get on with life. This book will help you to do that. The danger lies in avoiding the issue altogether, because tackle it you must.

Yes: Good for you. Just make sure that your interest and enthusiasm does not cloud your judgement and make you too aggressive with new ideas and overly complex in your portfolio structure.

2. Are you knowledgeable about investing?

This is perhaps a good place to start. By knowledge I mean understanding the basic rules that guide simple, good investing, not how much you know about a certain stock, or economics, bond mathematics, or derivative pricing. If you know why these are irrelevant then you have a reasonable knowledge of the basics. Hopefully you will, because they were covered in Chapter 2.

No: Don't worry about it, just don't stay there. Investing is not part of most people's education, even though it inescapably plays a major part in their lives. Picking up this book indicates that you are trying to improve things. You'd be surprised at just how many self-acclaimed knowledgeable investors actually know less than they think. In my experience this group includes many pension fund trustees, private bankers, corporate treasurers and journalists of otherwise respectable papers and journals.

Yes: Extremely knowledgeable investors are few and far between and here sit the likes of Charles Ellis, John Bogle, Burton Malkiel, Warren Buffett and David Swensen, to name a few of the truly inspirational investment minds. Fortunately, we can all exploit their wisdom and knowledge to our own advantage. Most have written books and much of their thinking underpins this book. What they have in common is that they have thought hard about the effects and probabilities of the decisions that they make and the theories of investing that they support. They have established their own consistent philosophy, which they apply ruthlessly to keep them on their rational path, and keep their emotions in control. You too should have put in place a sensible philosophy of losing-the-fewest points.

3. Are you confident in your investing abilities?

As a general rule, most of us are innately overconfident in our own abilities in most things. Many studies demonstrate this in all sorts of different areas and professions. A classic study is based on giving people a scenario such as 'How high will the FTSE 100 Index (a key UK equity market index) be at the end of the year?' and asking them to set a range that this end point will fall within, which they are 98 per cent confident in but no more. In many studies the surprise rate, i.e. the number of times that the result falls outside of the range, is 15–20 per cent, demonstrating considerable overconfidence in our own abilities.

Overconfidence also breeds a state of mind that attributes positive out-comes to skill and poor outcomes to bad luck. I've sat in many meetings with fund managers who have proudly crowed about the great stocks they have picked when they have beaten the markets, yet the next quarter they blame underperformance on unforeseen and random events. Amusingly, every active fund manager is confident of beating the market – a mathematical impossibility but nonetheless a certainty in the minds of all of them. Ask yourself if you are a better than average driver. More than 80 per cent of us think we are, apparently.

No: You may not feel confident that you have the appropriate understanding or knowledge to make investment decisions for yourself, but don't worry. The danger for you is that you turn to industry professionals for advice and abrogate almost the entire decision-making process to them. Advice is frequently costly and, even if it is good advice, may strip away too much of your wealth. With a little time spent understanding the fundamentals, you can quickly build your confidence level to allow you to discuss what you want from your investments sensibly and rationally with an advisor, if you choose to hire one.

Yes: Take care, as this is one of the main danger areas for you. Overconfidence can tempt you to make ill-judged decisions, often based on a lack of hard facts, hearsay, or simply a lack of thought. Overconfidence can manifest itself in a number of many ways. You may believe that you can pick outperforming managers, pick market-turning points, or believe that you understand a company stock well enough to own it, to name a few. The major detrimental consequence is usually excessive trading of the investments in your portfolio.

4.   Do you have trouble controlling your emotions?

Investors often have trouble keeping a grip on their emotions, resulting in overly optimistic or pessimistic outlooks relative to reality. Emotions nearly always affect wealth creation, driving a buy-high-sell-low strategy, illustrated earlier.

No: You are one of the lucky few. As an investor you are playing a probability game, trying to maximise the chances of success by looking at the evidence that you have, evaluating it in realistic and unemotional terms and acting upon it. Taking emotion out of investing is the best, yet probably hardest, thing to do. Being a stoic, getting neither too optimistic nor too pessimistic about what is happening to the markets, is a significant plus. The chances that you will be a successful and astute investor are high.

Yes: Beware. Emotional investors tend to become overly optimistic in good times and overly pessimistic in bad times leading to a 'fear and greed' syndrome, synonymous with a buy-high-sell-low strategy. The difficulty for you is that you may feel rational when sitting in the calm oak-panelled offices of your private banker or fund manager, and agree wholeheartedly with the rational investment plan you draw up. However, when the markets begin to tumble, as they inevitably will from time to time, or rise dramatically, the emotions take over and rash heart-driven decisions over-rule the head. These emotions tend to drive panic decisions such as 'I need to get out of equities' or 'I want to be in cash' with serious consequences for your long-term wealth. Optimism combined with over-confidence can lead to poor decisions.

5. Do you see patterns in things?

The human mind tends to seek order in the world around it, and the search for patterns in investment data is an example. Acting on these so-called patterns seems to be a common human weakness.

Imagine the outcomes from two sequences of dice throws being 6,6,6,6,6,6, and 2,2,6,1,4,3. From a gut-feel perspective, the second sequence seems the one that is more likely to occur, although rationally we know that they both have the same chance of being rolled. If we rolled again for the first sequence, do you feel that there is a good chance of a 6? Some gamblers would; see how many double up on the roulette table the spin of the wheel after 'red 9' comes up, or track the patterns of results on different tables. Short-term random sequences are relatively common in investing but rarely warrant any attention. Some investors see patterns everywhere. Technical analysis, a practice that looks at charts of market movements, seeks to find meaning in them. This 'art' is sometimes referred to as 'reading the tea leaves' by some in the industry!

No: The ability not to get tempted into seeing patterns in random numbers is a bonus. Broker-inspired lines such as 'the trend is your friend' should be taken with a large handful of salt.

Yes: The danger is that you see signs everywhere, which if combined with overconfidence and optimism can result in damaging levels of investment activity and decision-making in your portfolio, ultimately leading to sub-optimal investment performance. An example would be the temptation to sell a fund you own because another fund has done better over the past couple of years, extrapolating what is in all likelihood a chance event, into a basis for judging future long-term outperformance.

6. Are you prone to being a hindsight expert?

It is tempting to try and make sense of events that have occurred and post-rationalise that there was some rhyme or reason to them. This behaviour may lead you to believe that events are more predictable than they actually are and may lead you to regret not taking appropriate action sooner. It is difficult to remember how you felt before a market event happened; after the event you may have conveniently forgotten your exuberance, for example for technology stocks in 1999!

Behavioural economist Robert Shiller undertook some research (1997) relating to the Japanese stock market crash in 1989. It showed that before the peak of the market, 14 per cent of people thought the market was overvalued. Afterwards, 32 per cent said they had thought the market to be overvalued at the time of the crash.

This trait frequently manifests itself in blaming advisors for missing what was, now in their minds, a perfectly predictable event: 'Why didn't you spot that technology stocks were overvalued? Anyone could have seen that.' This was probably a common comment to advisors in late 2000.

No: If you can accept that professionals' crystal balls are just as clouded as your own and that things always seem easier to make meaning of afterwards than at the time, then you will have considerably less angst in your life. Knowing that markets are not predictable in the short term reduces feelings of regret and blame and allows you to make decisions that are not clouded by these emotions.

Yes: The danger is that you blame your advisors or investment managers for decisions that they did or did not make. By all means talk through past events with your manager but don't blame them for events that you should have anticipated when establishing your portfolio in the first place. You may also fall into the trap that decisions are easier to make than they actually are.

7. Do you regret decisions that you make?

All the investment decisions that you make will have consequences for your wealth in the short term as well as the long term. However, some investors regret sensible long-term decisions when in the short term the markets seem to be working against them. Your ability to avoid regret in the short term in order to achieve your long-term purchasing power goals is critical.

No: If you can accept the consequences of decisions, you are in a good position to stay the course.

Yes: If you are prone to suffering regret over decisions in your life, then you are vulnerable to making decisions that can seriously jeopardise your wealth. If you establish a rationally structured portfolio and understand why it is structured as it is, then times when you may feel it was the wrong thing to do may arise. The classic case is investing part of your portfolio in bonds for downside protection and then regretting that you are not 100 per cent in equities when the market soars.

8. Do your losses hurt more than your gains?

You may feel a greater degree of pain from losses on your portfolios when markets fall, than the pleasure you feel when markets rise. Studies have shown that this ratio of pain-to-gain may be more than 2:1 for many investors (Kahneman et al, 1979).

No: You are lucky because you will be able to accept the overriding reality of investing that in order to achieve higher long-term investment returns, a greater tolerance for short-term market trauma will be required. You may feel uncomfortable and disappointed when markets fall but not to the degree that it makes you panic and sell out.

Yes: Unfortunately you are in a delicate position as you feel more pain when things go wrong than when things go right. That is fine. Feeling comfortable in your investing is important provided that is within sensible bounds. The danger for you is that when markets are rising you would like to participate in the returns on offer, but the pain you suffer when they sell-off frightens you away from these investments. You sell at the bottom and then become overly conservative in how you invest, focusing on avoiding further losses and sacrificing longer-term purchasing power potential.

Some investors have the unrealistic expectation that you can have the upside without the downside – sorry but that's not possible. Avoid any products or managers that purport to create this elusive asymmetry. The only way you can improve this trade-off is by structuring a highly diversified portfolio with several investment building blocks.

9. Do you like long shots and insurance?

On the surface this is less intuitive than the previous questions. In general people have a preference for gambles, i.e. low probabilities of high value outcomes, or insurance, i.e. greater certainty of outcomes with lower pay-offs. In other words people like gambling and insurance.

Some people are more than willing to pay more than £1 for a 1 per cent chance of winning £100, or more than £1 for raising a 99 per cent chance of maintaining £100 to 100 per cent certainty. Yet few are willing to pay £1 to raise the chance of maintaining £100 from 65 per cent to 66 per cent, even though it has the same utility as the other two options. Some products on the market prey on investors' desires to satisfy their irrational preference for long shots and insurance.

No: If you are able to understand and accept that investing is about trying to get the chances of a favourable outcome as high as you can in your favour then you are well on the way to becoming an astute investor.

Yes: Paying over the odds for products that incorporate gambling and insurance characteristics is poor investing. Favour investing in portfolios that have reasonable probabilities of survivable outcomes to you over gambles and insurance. Any products made up of the two should be avoided, e.g. structured notes, including equity-participation notes, where you invest your money for a set period, get a share of the market upside, or your money back, before inflation, if markets fall (except in the circumstances covered later in the book).

10. Do you have difficulty seeing beyond the short term?

Many investors find it difficult to see the long-term wood for the short-term trees. Their focus tends to be on the effects of recent market conditions on their wealth and this affects their ability to make good decisions for the long-term success in meeting their lifetime purchasing power needs.

The advent of online accounts and investment tracking software has made this a lot worse and too many investors now look at their investments too frequently, getting highly excited as the markets rise and desperately disappointed as they fall. On any day, the chance of seeing a loss on your equity investments is around 50:50 (Swedroe, 2002). Even once a year you have around a 30 per cent chance or more that you will see a loss. Given the ratio of pain to gain, the longer the period between peeks the better!

No: You are in a good position. You can control the pain that accompanies short-term losses because you can see beyond the short-term volatility, encouraging you to stick to your long-term plan.

Yes: The danger is that the losses you see regularly give you unnecessary

pain, blinding you to the gains you will make in the long-term. It may tempt you into changing your strategy, as the short-term pain seems too much to bear. The answer is not to look at your portfolio too often. Time smoothes out return volatility. If you look at your portfolio every day you will think you are riding a bucking bronco. Look at it yearly as a whole and you will be trotting along comfortably most of the time.

What the eye doesn't see . . .

11. Do you have trouble seeing the big picture?

Some investors tend to look at their investment portfolio, or for that matter other issues in their lives, from a big picture perspective, while others tend to focus on minutiae.

No: Looking at the big picture is a great asset as an investor. What you should be interested in is how your portfolio as a whole is progressing relative to the purchasing power targets you have set, not dissecting and feeling anxious about how each component has performed. The danger for holistic thinkers is that any rotten apples in the portfolio, perhaps a badly managed fund, may be jeopardising the portfolio goals as a whole. Just make sure that each component of your portfolio is doing the job you ask of it.

Yes: Looking at each separate component of a portfolio in isolation from the other pieces and the overall picture has the danger of making you focus on the wrong things. As an example, if your equity holdings do really well you may be tempted to sell some of your other investments, e.g. bonds that were not performing as well, and buy more equity. The problem is two-fold, timing markets is very difficult but, just as importantly, you have sold bonds that were part of the portfolio to protect you when equities suffer a severe reversal, which is almost inevitable at some point. Remember the big picture and keep your long-term goals in mind.

12. Do you prefer action to planning?

Time spent planning is a crucial step in successful investing: defining what your lifetime purchasing power goals are; working out what mix of portfolio building blocks has the greatest chance of attaining them; and pre-testing your emotions against this mix is critical to good investing and controlling your emotions.

No: If you enjoy the planning process and derive comfort from its thoroughness or if you merely acknowledge that it is a necessary evil, then that is a bonus. Whether you enjoy it or merely tolerate it, you are at the better end of the spectrum and are likely to end up with a workable and successful investment strategy.

Yes: Here lies danger. Whilst being action-orientated is not in itself a problem, action at the expense of planning is. For some of you, planning may seem mundane and boring compared with the excitement of the markets. However, counting the cost of a poorly thought out investment strategy is more painful. An action-orientation, combined with overconfidence and insufficient knowledge is a volatile cocktail. Simple, good investing, as you will see, requires relatively little action.

13. Are you more trusting than sceptical?

As you will see as this book moves along, a healthy dose of scepticism is a good thing.

No: Excellent. If you are a bit of a sceptic you are likely to make a good investor. Treat everything that you see or hear with an element of suspicion. If you ask yourself questions like: Where are the vested interests? Are the fees reasonable? Why is this supposedly such a good investment? Where's the catch? You will be rewarded in the long run. Starting from the premise that all advisors and much of the industry are working, at the margin, against your best interests, it sets up your defences for the conflicts of interest that you will encounter.

Yes: If you do not have much interest in or knowledge about investing, or are a merely a trusting soul, you may unfortunately believe that professionals must know what they are talking about, but worse than that, believe that they have a superior insight and understanding that allows them to outperform the market by stock-picking and timing markets. As you have seen, the evidence shows quite categorically that it is highly unlikely. Try to develop a healthy level of scepticism when making investment decisions. Remember three things:

■ There are no free lunches in investing, except perhaps for diversification.

■ If it looks too good to be true, it is too good to be true.

■ Everyone is trying to make his or her bonus from your money in one way or another.

5.4 Ms Rational versus Mr Irrational

As a summary of these behaviours that blur the edges between rational and irrational decision-making, let's take a look at caricatures of two investors: Ms Rational Investor and Mr Irrational Investor. I have made them female and male deliberately, because research shows that men have significantly worse investment track records than women – they are more overconfident and overly optimistic about their investing, which leads to higher levels of the ultimately irrational investment behaviour, over-trading.

Ms Rational Investor

Ms. Rational Investor may or may not understand the fundamentals of investing at this point, but she knows that she needs to. She may not be particularly interested in investing, but knows that whether she is or not, she has to face the fact that she must take it seriously as being integral to her financial well-being. Even if she decides to use professional advisors, she knows that she needs a good grasp of the basics of investing so she can evaluate the advice that she is given: in the end, she has to carry the responsibility for the investment decisions taken.

She is realistic about her abilities and that any overconfidence in her ability to make better decisions than others is delusional and likely to be detrimental to her long-term wealth. She uses her head rather than her heart to make decisions based on research and facts, not gut-feel and hearsay. She tries to remain stoical about the market's ups and downs and avoid getting sucked into the emotion accompanying these short-term situations, merely rationalising that that is how markets are. She avoids being influenced by any newspaper articles that start with the words 'Is now the time to be investing in . . .?'

When times get tough she remains calm and reviews where recent events fall in the range of expectations that she established when she first sat down with her advisor and carefully planned her investments.

She avoids being influenced by the wisdom of hindsight, knowing that in reality the evidence shows that virtually no-one can consistently guess the markets right, and as a consequence won't take out any short-term disappointment on herself or others.

In establishing her investment plan, she realises that she needs to seek investment options that provide a reasonably high chance of a satisfactory outcome. She understands the chances that the outcome may be unsatisfactory and this disappointing scenario's consequences for her. Taking long shots to try and reach her goals are resisted because this is gambling not investing, irrespective of how attractive these opportunities appear to be. Insuring the short-term downside may feel attractive but she knows that the premium paid, in terms of significantly reduced future purchasing power, is not a trade-off worth making long term.

She also understands that she may well feel more pain from short-term losses than short-term gains but fights hard to make sure that this asymmetrical short-term pay-off is balanced by the potential rewards of long-term wealth accumulation that comes with bearing the pain. She understands that you cannot have your cake and eat it and understands that anyone, or any product that aspires to do so, is not what it appears. If she needs greater comfort in short-term down markets, she accepts that she needs to be prepared to give up some of her long-term potential upside. To be overly influenced by short-term pain will be detrimental, long term, to her purchasing power.

She is wise enough to understand that as long as she has taken the time and planned her investment programme sensibly and put her plan into action sensibly, it is more important to focus on the total portfolio performance against her long-term goals, than on the individual components.

Ms Rational employs a healthy dose of scepticism whenever she meets with her private bankers, fund managers, or reads her unit trust investment reports. She reserves a large dose of scepticism for anyone who claims to be able to outperform the market consistently, or to provide upside returns while at the same time protecting her downside. She reviews, with care, all claims made in investment product marketing brochures and advertisements. She is also aware that most advisors, while being people of integrity, have vested interests in the advice they give in one form or another.

She avoids looking at her portfolio too frequently, comfortable that in the long run it has a good chance of delivering what is asked of it.

Mr Irrational Investor

He is a surprisingly common species, often spotted at parties bragging about the great investments he has made. He often knows less than he thinks he knows, and what he does know is often way off the mark in terms of simple, sensible investing.

Nevertheless, he is confident in his own abilities and believes that he and a few others out there can outperform all the other dozy suckers in the market. Not only does he feel he has a greater insight into individual companies, and valuations of markets, than most, but when he does use professionals, he is confident that he can pick those who will be future winners. He feels that he has control of the situation and understands the markets and has an insight that allows him to beat it. Good investments are down to his skill. Bad trades are due to bad luck. He has a few dog stocks in his portfolio that he doesn't want to sell because he will have to realise his losses on them as well as recognise his poor decision-making. They'll come back in any case as he chose them for a reason that is still valid in his mind.

He doesn't want to waste his time with some private banker or advisor care-fully planning what he should be doing but wants to get into the fray and start investing as soon as possible and tells them not to bother to ring him unless they have a good investment idea to talk to him about. However, he has confidence in his broker, trusting him implicitly, having been shown a couple of interesting 'deals' in the past.

When the market is bullish, he gets caught up in the excitement of the stampede, becoming over confident in where the market is going and his ability to outperform it through his own superior skills. He tends to end up taking bigger risks than he should.

However, when markets correct, he becomes overly pessimistic, sells his equities at the bottom, moves into bonds, bawls out his advisor and tells him that his blind grandmother could have seen a bear that size coming. He blames others for being incompetent and not protecting his assets from the downturn, in turn firing his broker. He doesn't regret the fact that last year he sold his conservative bonds, because they were only making 6 per cent a year in any case, because that would be apportioning blame to himself. But he'll crawl back once the bull returns.

This caricature is not too far away from the sad truth about how many people go about their investing.

Whilst these two examples may be extremes, they do make a point.

Recognising the degree to which you exhibit these emotional demons is a step towards getting them in control. While you may think Ms Rational Investor is a bit dull, it is better to be dull and successful than exciting and almost inevitably doomed to miss your investment goal. The choice, as they say, is yours. This book focuses on why being rational is the only rational choice that you have.

Interesting research to mull over

Take a look at the research below. It provides a good insight into the behaviour that many investors portray, to their great cost.

Investor behaviour destroys wealth

Research undertaken by Brad Barber and Terrence Odean (2000), which looked at over 60,000 household accounts of a discount brokerage firm in the USA, from February 1991 to December 1996, analysed the investment performance for equities held by these individuals. It revealed some interesting facts: average turnover, i.e. the percentage of the portfolio value bought and sold, was very high at 80 per cent a year and average net returns, after transaction costs, were 15.2 per cent compared with 17.1 per cent for the market, calculated on an annualised basis; most shockingly, the top 20 per cent of households with the highest turnover, of approximately 10 per cent per month, generated an annualised net return of only 10 per cent, being a full 7 per cent lower than the market.

The central message from this research is that trading is hazardous to your wealth, largely due to costs. Putting a monetary value on this is revealing. A $100,000 portfolio invested in an index (tracker) fund, assumed reasonably to return the benchmark less 0.5 per cent costs, or 16.6 per cent per year, would have grown to $250,000 during this period whereas the individuals with high turnover would have returned only $175,000. Being overconfident in their own perceived skills cost these people a staggering $75,000. A sobering thought.

Overconfidence destroys wealth

The same researchers also looked at 35,000 household accounts from a large brokerage firm from February 1991 to January 1997 (Barber and Odean, 2001). They found that, consistent with other research that shows that men tend to be more overconfident than women (although both are overconfident), men trade 45 per cent more than women. This is reflected in risk-adjusted returns 1.4 per cent a year lower than women. Looking at single women and men, single men trade 67 per cent more than women and generate annual risk-adjusted net returns 2.3 per cent less than single women. Given that by and large self-invested investors, i.e. those that buy and sell shares and other investments themselves through a brokerage account, underperform the markets, as we saw above, this is bad news for wealth accumulation for either sex.

5.5 Wise words to leave you with

Perhaps reflect a while on these wise words written by Charles D. Ellis in his excellent book *Winning the Loser's Game*.

'The hardest work in investing is not intellectual, it's emotional. Being rational in an emotional environment is not easy. The hardest work is not figuring out the optimal investment policy; it's sustaining a long-term focus at market highs or market lows and staying committed to a sound investment policy. Holding on to sound investment policy at market highs and market lows in notoriously hard and important work, particularly when Mr Market always tries to trick you into making changes.'

He shares more wisdom with us:

'Don't trust your emotions. When you feel euphoric you're probably in for a bruising. When you feel down, remember that it's darkest just before dawn and take no action. Activity in investing is almost always in surplus.'

5.6 Behavioural rules and tips

Try and be rational about your investing, from planning how you will invest to how you will respond when times get tough, as they will at some point. It's hard when markets are painful. But the costs of being irrational are far higher, as we have seen.

- Take time planning your investment strategy.
- Form an understanding of the chances you have of achieving the long-term outcome you want and the chances that you may not achieve it.
- Consider the ranges of returns that your portfolio will, in all likelihood, exhibit during the time you are investing, however unpalatable they may seem. Forewarned is forearmed.
- Put a plan in place, for when times get tough, that details how you should respond, based around: 'Don't panic, be brave, do nothing'!

- Stick to your long-term plan unless personal circumstances unexpectedly change significantly and you need to reassess your goals. Never change a plan because of what markets are doing today, or how a fund you don't own has done.

- Do not look at your portfolio too often; it will only make you feel overly euphoric or miserable. Think long term.

- When you do, look at your whole portfolio and judge how it is doing relative to your long-term purchasing power goals. Don't get over-anxious about short-term weak performance in a single element, or even your portfolio as a whole. That's the markets for you.

- Don't believe that you can outsmart the market – you are probably being overconfident, seeing patterns where none exist, being over-optimistic, or have an unrealistic hindsight view of events.

- Don't therefore try and own and individual stocks yourself through a brokerage account. There are far better ways of doing things.

- Avoid the temptation of gambles and insurance, however tempting they may be. These products play on your emotions and you often pay usurious costs that are hidden in the structure (unless you understand the Black & Scholes option pricing model – No? Then avoid these products).

- Maintain a healthy level of scepticism about all products and advice.

References

Barber, B. M. and Odean, T. (2000) Trading is hazardous to your wealth: the common stock investment performance of individuals, *The Journal of Finance*, vol. LV, no. 2 April, 773–806.

Barber, B. M. and Odean, T. (2002) Boys will be boys: Gender, overconfidence, and common stock investment, *Quarterly Journal of Economics*, vol. 116, no. 1, February, 261–292.

Bogle, J. C. (2003) 'The policy portfolio in an era of subdued returns', Bogle Financial Markets Research Center. Available from: http://www.vanguard.com

Buffett, W. (1998) *Chairman's letter to shareholders 1997*. Berkshire Hathaway Inc.

Buffett, W. (2001) *Chairman's letter to shareholders 2000*. Berkshire Hathaway Inc.

Graham, B. and Dodd, D. (1996) *Security analysis: the classic 1934 edition*. New York: McGraw Hill.

Kahneman, D. and Tversky, A. (1979) Prospect Theory: An analysis of decision under risk. *Econometrica* 47: 263–291.

Kahneman, D., Higgens, E. and Riepe, W. (1998) Aspects of investor psychology, *Journal of Portfolio Management*, vol. 24, no. 4, 52–65.

Shiller, R. (1997) *The Wall Street Journal*, June 13. As quoted on: http://www.investorhome.com/psych.htm. See also: http://www.econ.yale.edu/~shiller

Swedroe, L. (2002) *Frequent monitoring of your portfolio can be injurious to your financial health* [online]. Available from: http://www.indexfunds.com.

3

Building smarter portfolios

Now that you are a convert to the lose-the-fewest-points philosophy and you have your emotions in control, you can begin the process of defining your investment goals and building a portfolio that makes sense for you, providing you with a reasonable chance of success and survivability – about as much as you can ask for as an investor.

Chapter 6: Sorting out your goals

Here you have the opportunity to develop and narrow down your investing goals, whatever they may be. There are several tables that help you to work out what you need to be aiming for, what reasonably to expect from your portfolio and how much you need to contribute. Defining your goals is the first step to creating a suitable investment programme.

Chapter 7: Building a smart but simple portfolio

We will take a quick look how, in concept, you can put together a smart but simple portfolio made up of equities and bonds, the core building blocks of any portfolio.

Chapter 8: Equity and bond building blocks in brief

As a mix of bonds and equities forms the core of your portfolio and drives its characteristics, understanding what each brings to the table and how they work together is an important starting point.

Chapter 9: Getting your equity/bond mix right

By the end of this chapter you should feel confident that you can build a portfolio for yourself from a mix of equities and bonds that should give you a good chance of meeting your purchasing power goals as well getting a good feel for the potential troubles ahead, how severe they can be and the chances of them happening to you.

Chapter 10: Building a portfolio for all seasons

We will explore how you can enhance the characteristics of your portfolio by adding other building blocks, spreading your investment eggs between a number of different baskets and working out some simple rules for doing so.

Chapter 11: Fancy tools – getting technical

This is aimed at those of you who are interested in leading-edge portfolio construction techniques, some of which have been used in Chapters 9 and 10. These more technical approaches are discussed in simple terms; so don't be afraid to take a look. It is in your interests to understand their value and pitfalls, but I can empathise if you can't find the time or inclination to delve deeper!

6

Sorting out your goals

Let's spend a little time thinking about how to turn the question 'Where do I start?' into a definite plan of action.

A good friend of mine, who is a businesswoman in Melbourne, once announced to her long-suffering accountant that she had started investing her money seriously. Her much-relieved accountant asked her what she was investing in, only to get the simple response 'Me'. Unlike her, your challenge is to think ahead about your future purchasing power needs, rather than today's gratuitous consumption; while most of us understand that, we suffer a sort of fatal inertia, caused by the apparent complexity of the decisions (and maths) that we face.

Another friend of mine, in his early forties, recently that told me that he knows he needs to start thinking about what he should do about his pension, as his existing pension will only deliver around £10,000 a year. He knows he desperately needs to do something, but simply does not know where to start or who to ask. Familiar story? He is not alone by any means, and nor are you if you are struggling to get a handle on what you need to do to put things right, whether for your retirement or other investment goals you may have.

The answer is that you start right here; in the next few minutes you should have a pretty fair idea of what you should be doing.

6.1 Well thought-out goals underpin success

Understanding what you want from your investing is the critical starting point of any investment programme; being able clearly to articulate these goals will help you and any one else assisting you, to tackle the issues you face. One of the constants that I found in my discussions with clients over the years is that many of them have only vague notions about what they want to achieve with their money and relatively few have a precise set of articulated goals.

In many ways that's not really very surprising. We find it easy to think emotionally about our vision: 'I want to be comfortable in my retirement'; 'I want to be involved in more philanthropic works'; or 'I want to provide my children with financial security', but find it harder to articulate in much more detail what we really want our money to do for us such as 'I need a £1.2 million pool when I retire to generate an income equivalent to £50,000 in today's money (before tax) giving me a standard of living that is comfortable, without having to worry about running out of money before I die'.

Investment needs can be viewed as a hierarchy, with those at the bottom being essential to achieve because life will be difficult if you fail to meet them, e.g. not having any income in retirement, to those that are nice to achieve but perhaps less critical, such as lifestyle choices. This is similar to a behavioural scientist's hierarchy of human needs (Maslow, 1970), which I have bastardised in Figure 6.1.

Looking at your own goals in this way may help you to understand them a little better. Your focus may be on investment goals towards the top of the pyramid, if you are already financially secure, or your focus may be towards the bottom of the pyramid, as you strive to put in place some financial security for yourself and your family. Most institutional investors such as pension plans, endowments, foundations and corporate treasurers have basic financial survival goals.

At the lower levels of the hierarchy, attention to the nitty gritty detail of time, contributions, rates of return (and their associated uncertainty) and the size of your investment pot is more critical because the consequence of not being successful has serious repercussions. Those at higher levels have the luxury of being able to concentrate on higher-level objectives such as maintaining or increasing their purchasing power over the long run, and may need less detail in their planning.

I have not split investors down into the broad classifications that the industry uses of retail (up to £100,000 of investable assets), affluent (£100,000 to £1 million), high net worth (usually more than £1 million) and ultra-high-net-worth (£20 million upwards), to make a point. An 'affluent' individual with £200,000 of investments may have a good company pension to live on and may want to use this money to set up a small trust to benefit a pet cause in perpetuity – an example of financial altruism at the top of the pyramid. On the other hand, an individual with £3 million to invest critically needs these assets to generate income to live on and to avoid having to go back into the City everyday. This may be basic

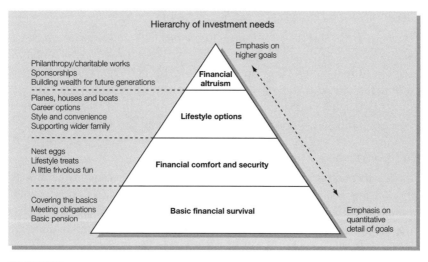

figure 6.1 **Different levels of needs**   *Source: Maslow (1970)*

financial survival. You will know where you stand. Let's take a quick look at some of the goals that investors have.

General goals for individuals

As you read through each of the generic goals below, think hard about those that are relevant to you.

Basic financial survival – retirement

Increasingly, people are having to plan and invest for their own retirement as traditional defined benefit (final salary) schemes, where your benefits are defined as a function of your time with the company and your final salary, become unavailable to employees. Many are rightly concerned with being able to generate an acceptable level of income for their retirement. Common goals may be to 'avoid being poor' or 'to be able to enjoy ourselves in our retirement' or to 'feel comfortable that we can live how we do now, for the rest of our lives'.

Today, with the ever-growing influence of defined contribution pension plans (where a set monthly contribution is made by an employer, into an employee's individual pension pot), you alone are responsible for investing to satisfy your basic financial survival. All of the investment responsibility and investment risk is on your shoulders, and getting your investing programme right, i.e. giving yourself the greatest chance of having the right level of purchasing power available at the right time, is critical.

Basic financial survival – school/university fee

'I want to be able to give my children the best education I can,' is a common goal for some parents, which is often achieved by building reserves to meet school and university fees, through regular savings plans as the children grow up. Fortunately, many schools provide indications of future expected fees; the downside is that these seem to be growing faster than inflation. How important this is to you, only you will know.

Nest eggs

'I want to put something aside for a rainy day', 'We want to be able to afford a few small luxuries in our retirement', or 'It's good knowing that there is a little extra' are all familiar investment visions. These types of goals often apply to investors who have sufficient sources of income to take care of their basic financial survival and represent funds to provide an additional layer of security.

Lifestyle options

'I want to be free to pursue the things that I want to do', 'I want to be able to have some fun with my wider family', are examples of higher-level goals. No one is at risk of being hungry or not being able to afford their heating bills, but these goals are as important to those fortunate enough to be in this position as any other investor's goals, even if they are not, in an absolute sense, as critical.

Philanthropic works

Fortunately for society, there are many investors who use their wealth for philanthropic purposes. 'I would like to set up a foundation to provide annual scholarships ...' and 'We would like to provide a trust to maintain ...' are philanthropic objectives, for investors who feel that their other financial needs have been taken care of and they would like to put their wealth to good use within society or their local community.

6.2 Five steps in defining your goals

Sitting down and thinking hard about what you want your wealth to achieve may feel like a daunting and tiresome proposition. But a little time spent thinking about and planning what you want to achieve is time well spent. This task is made easier by dividing it into five manageable steps.

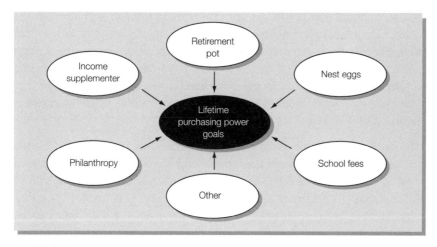

figure 6.2 Identifying each of your purchasing power goals

Step 1: Divide your plan into appropriate pools

The first easy step is to divide up your money into different goals. These can usually be defined by the function that they will serve: retirement funds; school fees; future gifts; house purchase, etc., and Figure 6.2 provides some examples of some common pools of investment funds. Identifying them allows you to set clear and relevant objectives for each pool. Lumping all your money together and managing it as one pool is possible, but most investors tend to segregate their wealth into different pools – a form of mental accounting – even though, at the end of the day it is an aggregated pool of money that is meeting a series of lifetime purchasing power needs.

Step 2: State your vision for each pool

Express the ultimate outcome that you want to achieve and which would make you content, within the bounds of realism. Usually your vision is relatively easy to state and understand. Examples include: 'I want to lead a comfortable life throughout my retirement'. 'I want to establish a charity that provides money for malaria research'. 'I want my children to be financially secure when I am no longer around'.

Step 3: Define your investment horizon for each pool

Your investment horizon is the amount of time that your money can remain invested for and largely defines the mix of portfolio building blocks that you should use. The longer your investment horizon is, the greater the chance that your investments will act like their generalisations, rather than their exceptions. Longer-term investors can afford to have more of their money invested in building blocks that have the potential to generate higher returns, but will suffer periods when returns can be painful. The link between your investment horizon and your portfolio of investments is explored in depth in Chapter 9.

The horizon should be as long as possible to allow you to maximise the use of your money through time and compounding. Build a small pot of cash to cover contingencies or arrange overdraft facilities to allow you to get through temporary liquidity needs, say six months' salary. Mismatching your investment horizon with your portfolio mix can be costly.

Choosing a portfolio that is too conservative

Your portfolio mix should match your investment horizon. If you choose too conservative a portfolio for a long-term horizon you will generate lower returns. Compounding lower returns over time cuts your future purchasing power and may require you to scale back your goals. This is illustrated in Figure 6.3.

Choosing a portfolio that is too aggressive

On the other hand, if a portfolio is too aggressive for your investment horizon, purchasing power may be at risk just at the time you need it. If

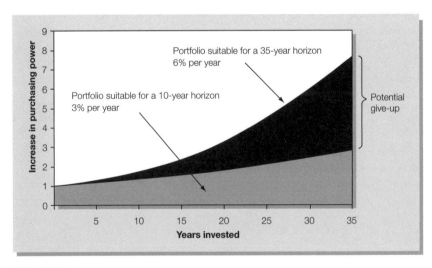

figure 6.3 **Your opportunity cost is high**

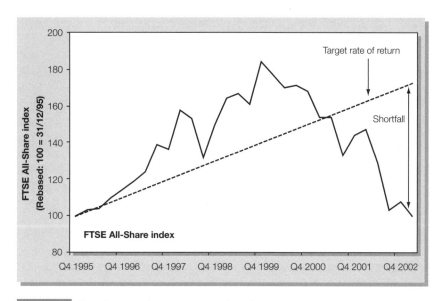

figure 6.4   **Too long and you may not be able to meet your commitments**

Source: Thomson Datastream

markets fall and do not recover before you need the cash, you will have a shortfall between what you hoped for and what you end up with.

A sobering example of this occurred at the end of the 1990s. Some investors, with only a handful of years to go in the accumulation phase, were tempted into holding too great an exposure to equities, lured by high equity returns that they had just experienced. Markets fell by 40 per cent and still remained well below the high five years later. The wealth to fund their retirement dreams was irreparably damaged; for some, their retirements have been delayed or their plans scaled back. This is illustrated in Figure 6.4.

Remember that the accumulation phase reaches a point at which your accumulation ends and your distribution phase begins, e.g. the start of your child going to school or the day you retire and need to begin drawing a pension from your pool of assets. You need to determine how long each phase is likely to be. This may be from three years to beyond your mortal lifespan; anything less than three years and you are probably better off putting your money in an interest-bearing bank account or money market fund.

Getting it right and matching a sensible portfolio to it is key to successful investing.

Step 4: Consider the consequences of failure

Each of your goals will have consequences for you if they are not met and some of these goals might be more important to you than others. Being able to afford to send your child to the university of his or her choice or not having to worry about how you will pay the bills in your retirement may be critical; however, passing on assets to future generations may not be a life-and-death consequence. Only you can decide. You need to work out what represents a survivable outcome and what does not. There are three stages to working this out: the first is to define what the worst case would be for you; the second is to understand how likely it is to occur; and the third is to understand how you would respond if it did occur.

An example may help. Imagine that you are planning a party in your garden in the summer and will invite one hundred friends. The worst-case scenario is that it pours with rain and it is a complete washout. We all know that that is a possibility, but that does not help you to decide whether to go ahead or not. This alone is insufficient to base a decision on. However, if I tell you that the chances of a torrential downpour are less than 5 per cent you would probably go ahead. If on the other hand I tell you there is a 50 per cent chance of rain, that might result in a different decision. If you are consequence-orientated, the thought of mud in the house and disgruntled friends is too great. If you are possibility-orientated, the opportunity of catching up and having a few drinks with your friends will be worth it, despite the mud. The outcome of rain and mud is the same, yet your response to it may well differ from someone else's. Only you will know which you are.

You need to understand the equivalent as it relates to each of your investment goals: what would happen if your portfolio were ultimately only £500,000 instead of £1 million when you retire? What are the chances of this outcome happening? Can you live with this outcome? Answer these questions and you will be well on the way to setting the parameters for a successful investing programme. Figure 6.5 illustrates the mental process you need to go through for each pool of money.

For the moment, try and define for yourself what you think the worst case would be for each of your pools of money. Decide what is an acceptable probability that you can live with that it happens, e.g. 5 per cent chance, 20 per cent chance, etc., and designate yourself either possibility- or consequence-orientated for each.

We will look at worst-case scenarios and the chances of success or failure for different portfolio structures in Chapter 9, depending on your investment

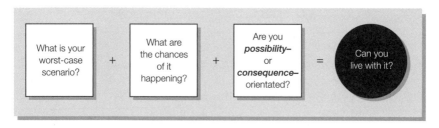

figure 6.5 **Evaluating the consequences of investing**

table 6.1   **How bad does it get?**

Pool	Examples of possible worst-case outcomes
Pension	■ Ending up with less than half of your current salary ■ Running out of money before you die ■ It's a bonus – you have other income to fall back on
School fees	■ Having to pay more than 30 per cent of the fees due to a shortfall ■ The kids have to go elsewhere
Nest egg	■ Without this nest egg, life will be spartan ■ Pity, but you can get by without it
Lifestyle	■ You really don't want to have to go back into the City ■ You need this for your sanity
Philanthropy	■ This is the culmination of your life's work. It's critical ■ Disappointing, but life goes on

horizon. This will allow you to work out which portfolio structure makes most sense for you. Table 6.1 sets out some examples of possible worst-case situations.

Step 5: Explain your goals in financial terms

At some point you need to translate your vision in Step 2 into hard numbers.

Defining higher-level financial goals

If you are describing higher-level goals that are over and above basic financial survival goals, translating them into financial terms is a little easier because your can afford your objectives to be a little looser. Table 6.2

table 6.2	Common financial goals – filling in the gaps	
Criteria	Requirement	Financial terms used
Returns	Absolute (nominal or real)	I expect to make [ ]% a year
	Relative to cash	I want to beat cash by [ ]% a year
	Relative to something else	I want to beat [ ] by [ ]% a year
Inflation	Increase purchasing power	I want to beat inflation by [ ]% a year on average
	Maintain purchasing power	I want to at least maintain my purchasing power
Assets	Amount (nominal or real)	I want my assets to grow to £[ ] over [ ] years
	Doubling (nominal or real)	I want to double my money in [ ] years
Income	Withdraw income as %	I want to withdraw [ ]% of the value of the portfolio a year
	Withdraw income £ amount	I want to take an income in today's money of £[ ]
	Withdraw income and capital	I want to take £[ ] from my portfolio over [ ] years
Chances	Good chance	I want to be pretty sure I will achieve my goal
	Reasonable chance	I want a fair chance of being successful
	Gamble	I will try and shoot the lights out on this
Constraints	Annual losses	I can accept losses of [ ]% in any 1 year
	Over [ ] years	I can accept losses of [ ]% in any [ ] year period
	Over economic cycle	I expect real gains over an economic cycle
Attitude	Possibility-oriented	I am looking for upside and can live with the downside
	Consequence-oriented	I need to make sure that I succeed

provides an example of some of the goals that investors often state when they set up their investment portfolios. Few, though, ever have much of a feel for how likely they are to succeed – something that we will try and put right.

Defining Basic Financial Survival goals

If, on the other hand, your investment goals are of the basic financial survival variety, such as planning your retirement income, it becomes critical that you define what it is you are hoping to achieve in tight financial terms, as the consequences of not meeting them will affect your life significantly.

6.3 The nitty-gritty of basic financial survival goals

You need to work out what the nitty gritty numbers that underlie your emotional investment goals are, however boring that may sound. This is not difficult if you think about it logically.

At this point, some people throw their arms up in horror. Don't panic! With a few simple calculations you can begin to get a rough idea of what you should be aiming for. Most of the maths is done and the results are set out in the tables that follow. These provide estimates to help you to understand the task in hand and some of the challenges that you face. Don't switch off at this point, however tempted you are!

Essentially, investing is about growing a pool of money (which may start at zero), over time, through the returns that your asset mix delivers and additions that you make to the pool, in order to allow you to do something at the end of the accumulation phase. This may be either to meet a capital commitment, or to provide an income over time, such as a retirement plan. Figure 6.6 illustrates this process.

For many, investing for retirement is the main investing challenge that they face and it may be for you too. Therefore this section is structured to help you explore how you can define your goals in financial terms where

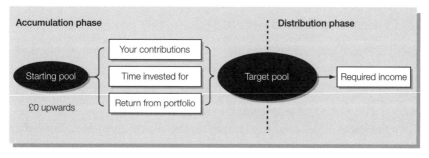

figure 6.6   **The process and goals of an investment programme are simple**

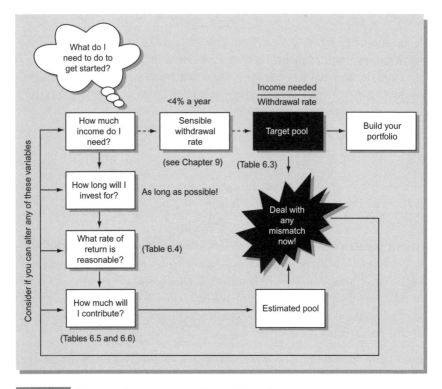

figure 6.7   **The road map to your financial goals**

you are looking eventually to take an income from your portfolio (the *distribution phase*) and will make regular contributions into the pool up to this point (the *accumulation phase*). You will be able to see the effect that changing time, contributions, the returns from your portfolio and the level of income you withdraw, will have on the overall programme.

What do you need to do to start?

Getting started is straightforward, and simply looks at Figure 6.6 in a different order. Take a minute to study Figure 6.7 above.

One of the biggest problems in saving for retirement is that while people may have a picture of a comfortable retirement, they have no real idea just how big their target pool needs to be to deliver the level of income they would wish for. In addition, they have little idea whether the contributions they or their employer are making into their pension plan (if they have one) and the way it is invested is going to deliver what they need. A mismatch often exists between dream and reality. You may be surprised just how much you need to accumulate and how much you will need to save regularly to get there – but get there you will, with a little planning and a sensible portfolio. You need to answer the following questions for yourself.

Question 1: How much income do I need?

The goal of investing for retirement is to be pretty sure that you will be able to pay yourself an acceptable level of income that keeps pace with inflation throughout your retirement, so the first thing is to decide how much income you will require. Thinking in terms of the income you require in terms of today's money is the easiest way to look at things: 'I need 75 per cent of my salary today to live comfortably'.

This is a good way to think because it allows you to talk about things in today's money terms and know what your income will buy you. It's hard to conceive how comfortable your retirement will be unless you factor in the effects of inflation. Will an income of £80,000 a year in tomorrow's devalued money provide a comfortable retirement? Not if a loaf of bread costs £15 and a pint of beer £35! To allow yourself the ability to talk about things you want in the future, in today's money terms, you must always use real, i.e. post-inflation, returns in any calculations you make. Using real returns on the asset side of your personal balance sheet allows you to ignore inflation on the liability side. Throughout the rest of this book, we will use real returns.

Sit down with a piece of paper and decide what level of income you need. Remember to allow for any state or other pensions or sources of income that you will have. Use the level of income you decide for the remainder of this section. I leave it to you to work out how much this represents!

Question 2: How large does my target pool need to be?

A significant challenge is that we do not know how long we will live and therefore cannot be certain how quickly we can spend the capital. Obviously, if you spend your capital over time, your target pool size does not need to be as large as if you wish preserve the purchasing power of your capital pool. You have three options on retirement:

■ Maintain the purchasing power of your portfolio and your income. This implies that you withdraw an income that is equal to or less than the real return generated by your portfolio. Given that we are living

table 6.3 How large does your target pool need to be?

Withdrawal rate p.a. Income required

	£10,000	£20,000	£30,000	£40,000	£50,000	£60,000	£70,000	£80,000
2%	£500,000	£1,000,000	£1,500,000	£2,000,000	£2,500,000	£3,000,000	£3,500,000	£4,000,000
3%	£333,333	£666,667	£1,000,000	£1,333,333	£1,666,667	£2,000,000	£2,333,333	£2,666,667
4%	£250,000	£500,000	£750,000	£1,000,000	£1,250,000	£1,500,000	£1,750,000	£2,000,000
5%	£200,000	£400,000	£600,000	£8000,000	£1,000,000	£1,200,000	£1,400,000	£1,600,000
6%	£166,667	£333,333	£500,000	£666,667	£833,333	£1,000,000	£1,166,667	£1,333,333

= You have a serious danger of running out of money (see Chapter 9)

longer, perhaps into our nineties, this is a sensible approach, particularly if it represents the bulk of your retirement income. Although as the US comedian Henny Youngman once said:

'I went to the bank today and I have all the money I need . . . if I die tomorrow.'

▪ Pay yourself an income that includes capital, using up the capital over a designated period of time. This is an option suitable for some. However, trying to predict when exactly you might run out of money is not easy with unpredictable markets and longevity.

▪ Use some or all of the accumulated pool to buy an income from an insurance company in the form of an annuity. Basically, you hand over your money in return for an income for the remainder of your life. They now hold the risk of you outliving the standard mortality tables and you take the risk that you die sooner and your estate loses monies that would have existed by controlling these assets yourself.

As a general rule of thumb, you should withdraw 4 per cent or less from your portfolio (well balanced between equities and bonds), if you want to avoid the possibility you will run out of money before you die, as this represents the level of real returns that such a mix of investments would hope (but is not certain) to achieve.

The level of income required divided by the withdrawal rate defines how much money needs to be in your target pool at the end of your accumulation period. Table 6.3 provides an indication of the size of pool you require at different rates of withdrawal, to generate your required annual, pre-tax income. You can see that in real terms these pool sizes can be frighteningly large (and appear even bigger in before-inflation terms) and just how valuable non-contributory final salary schemes really are. We will explore the chances of you running out of money for different withdrawal rates and portfolio mixes in Chapter 9.

Don't be discouraged by the magnitude of the task. As you will see from later tables, the combined effect of compounding of moderate returns over time and regular drip feeding of contributions into your pot have the ability to create substantial wealth.

Question 3: How long will I invest for?

At first glance that appears an easy question to answer, perhaps picking your 65th birthday, the normal 'retirement' age in the UK, as the end of your accumulation phase (unless of course the Chancellor decides we all need to work longer). In reality, as organisations narrow rapidly near the top, and loyalty to long serving employees fails, you should perhaps consider that being in gainful, full employment at 60, let alone 67, is no longer going to be the norm. Perhaps you should consider having more in your pot at an earlier stage (say 55 perhaps), which means investing higher, regular contributions, to provide security and flexibility in your later working years; working if you choose, or when you can.

Question 4: What portfolio returns are reasonable to use?

This is probably the most used, abused and misunderstood area of investing. Overly optimistic estimates of return will always come back to haunt you, as they did the endowment mortgage sales industry. As you will see, the 'reasonable' annualised rates of return used throughout this book for equities and bonds are 5 per cent and 2 per cent in real terms, which are relatively conservative. In Chapters 15 and 16 you can see where these come from. Remember back to *Shocker 7* at the start of the book: Most advice is wrong more than half of the time. Over the time frame that you will be investing, it is unlikely that the return for equities and bonds will be 5 per cent and 2 per cent. You may be lucky and get higher returns or unlucky and get lower returns; even over long periods of time, returns can vary significantly from their averages. Understanding your chances of achieving an acceptable rate of return from your portfolio is therefore critical.

You face a trade-off between choosing a higher rate of return, with less chance of success but with lower contributions, or a lower rate that you have a good chance of achieving but with higher contributions. If your goals are critical to you, err on the side of caution. Too many investors ask too much of their portfolios – markets don't deliver just because you hope they will! If your expectations are unrealistic, given long-term and recent history, they will probably catch up with you later.

As you embark on your investing programme, there are many possible investment outcomes that your portfolio may deliver, depending on what happens to the markets. The problem is that you do not know what your investment life will look like until it has happened. Fortunately, these days, with the help of multiple life simulations of portfolios, we can at least get a sense of what the chances are that we will achieve a certain level of return – a very useful piece of information. (The process used is called Monte Carlo simulation, which you can read more about in Chapter 11.)

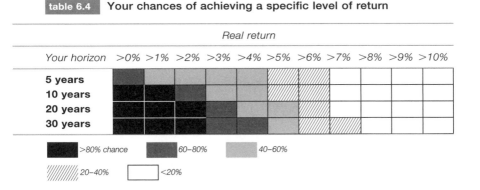

table 6.4   **Your chances of achieving a specific level of return**

					Real return						
Your horizon	>0%	>1%	>2%	>3%	>4%	>5%	>6%	>7%	>8%	>9%	>10%
5 years											
10 years											
20 years											
30 years											

■ >80% chance   ■ 60–80%   ▨ 40–60%   ▥ 20–40%   □ <20%

Table 6.4 shows the chances of achieving a specific rate of real return, or better, over different investment horizons. It was created by looking at the most appropriate portfolio structure for a given investment horizon (as defined in Chapter 9) and seeing what chance a portfolio has of meeting or bettering different levels of annualised return.

As an example, over thirty years, you have a chance of 40–60 per cent of achieving an annualised return of 5 per cent or better, but a pretty good chance, 60–80 per cent or more, of generating a real return of 4 per cent. You can look at what the consequences are if you change the rate of return that you use on both target pool size and contribution level, using other tables in this chapter. Used sensibly, you should be able to arrive at reasonably detailed financial objectives for your investing programme, which, if you are consequence-orientated, will err towards more cautious return expectations, higher contributions and the longest investment horizon you can stretch to.

Question 5: What contributions will I need to make?

At this point, you know what income you need, have worked out what target pool size you are aiming for with a given withdrawal rate, and have chosen a rate of return that has a reasonable chance of being achieved over the time that you will be investing for. You now need to work out how much you should contribute every month.

As you saw in Figure 6.6, the pot of money you end up with is a function of the regular contributions you make, the time over which you make them and the real return that your portfolio generates. Many would-be investors become too focused on the rate of return that their portfolio will achieve,

table 6.5	Approximate monthly contributions to build £1,000,000							

	Real rate of return							
Years	1%	2%	3%	4%	5%	6%	7%	8%
10	£8,000	£7,600	£7,300	£6,900	£6,600	£6,300	£6,000	£5,800
20	£3,800	£3,400	£3,100	£2,800	£2,500	£2,300	£2,000	£1,800
30	£2,400	£2,100	£1,800	£1,500	£1,300	£1,100	£900	£800

even though you cannot control this with any certainty – the best you can do is to choose a rate that gives you a reasonable chance of success, but with no guarantees. On the other hand, time (in some cases) and the contributions you make may well be variable and can play a significant role in increasing the chances of a successful outcome. As they are in your control, they are all the more valuable.

There are two approaches tackling the question of contributions.

Approach 1: Contributions to build £1,000,000

This first approach calculates the monthly contributions that you would need to make to accumulate £1,000,000 of purchasing power, depending on your investment horizon and the real rates of return you expect from your portfolio. You can scale the contributions up or down depending on your target pool size. For example, to accumulate £1 million at 4 per cent over thirty years you would have to contribute approximately £1,500 a month. To build £300,000, then multiply £1,500 by £300,000/£1,000,000 or 30 per cent, to give £450 a month. Take a look back at Table 6.4 before you choose a rate in Figure 6.5 above.

Approach 2: Target pool size based on set monthly contributions

The second approach estimates how large the target pool will be depending on the level of monthly contributions that you make at different rates of expected real returns and the investment period (Table 6.6). Again, see what the effect is on your potential pool if returns are worse than you expect. Remember to take into account any tax relief on the contributions you make. Running a few 'what if?' scenarios using these tables will be time well spent.

table 6.6	How large will your target pool be?

Real return				*Monthly contribution*			
2%	*£100*	*£200*	*£400*	*£600*	*£800*	*£1,000*	*£1,500*	*£2,000*
10 years	£15,000	£25,000	£55,000	£80,000	£105,000	£130,000	£195,000	£265,000
20 years	£30,000	£60,000	£115,000	£175,000	£235,000	£290,000	£435,000	£585,000
30 years	£50,000	£95,000	£195,000	£290,000	£390,000	£485,000	£730,000	£975,000

3%	*£100*	*£200*	*£400*	*£600*	*£800*	*£1,000*	*£1,500*	*£2,000*
10 years	£15,000	£30,000	£55,000	£85,000	£110,000	£140,000	£205,000	£275,000
20 years	£30,000	£65,000	£130,000	£195,000	£260,000	£320,000	£485,000	£645,000
30 years	£55,000	£115,000	£230,000	£345,000	£455,000	£570,000	£855,000	£1,140,000

4%	*£100*	*£200*	*£400*	*£600*	*£800*	*£1,000*	*£1,500*	*£2,000*
10 years	£15,000	£30,000	£60,000	£85,000	£115,000	£145,000	£215,000	£290,000
20 years	£35,000	£70,000	£145,000	£215,000	£285,000	£355,000	£535,000	£715,000
30 years	£65,000	£135,000	£270,000	£405,000	£540,000	£675,000	£1,010,000	£1,345,000

5%	*£100*	*£200*	*£400*	*£600*	*£800*	*£1,000*	*£1,500*	*£2,000*
10 years	£15,000	£30,000	£60,000	£90,000	£120,000	£150,000	£225,000	£300,000
20 years	£40,000	£80,000	£160,000	£240,000	£315,000	£395,000	£595,000	£795,000
30 years	£80,000	£160,000	£320,000	£480,000	£640,000	£795,000	£1,195,000	£1,595,000

6%	*£100*	*£200*	*£400*	*£600*	*£800*	*£1,000*	*£1,500*	*£2,000*
10 years	£15,000	£30,000	£65,000	£95,000	£125,000	£160,000	£235,000	£315,000
20 years	£45,000	£90,000	£175,000	£265,000	£355,000	£440,000	£660,000	£880,000
30 years	£95,000	£190,000	£380,000	£570,000	£760,000	£950,000	£1,425,000	£1,900,000

7%	*£100*	*£200*	*£400*	*£600*	*£800*	*£1,000*	*£1,500*	*£2,000*
10 years	£15,000	£35,000	£65,000	£100,000	£135,000	£165,000	£250,000	£330,000
20 years	£50,000	£100,000	£195,000	£295,000	£395,000	£490,000	£740,000	£985,000
39 years	£115,000	£225,000	£455,000	£680,000	£905,000	£1,135,000	£1,700,000	£2,265,000

Increasing your chances of success

At the end of the day, there will always be some uncertainty. However, you can control most of the elements involved: you can choose a rate of return that has a high chance of being achieved; pay in higher contributions to compensate for this lower rate of return; and if necessary either scale back your goals or extend the investment period. Perhaps these are unpalatable actions, but all are preferable to a long retirement spent scrimping and saving to meet basic needs. I leave it up to you at this point to decide.

table 6.7	The effect of time and return on lump sum investments						

Growth of £1				Expected real return			
Years	1%	2%	3%	4%	5%	6%	7%	8%
10	£1.10	£1.20	£1.30	£1.50	£1.60	£1.80	£2.00	£2.20
20	£1.20	£1.50	£1.80	£2.20	£2.70	£3.20	£3.90	£4.70
30	£1.30	£1.80	£2.40	£3.20	£4.30	£5.70	£7.60	£10.10

Lump-sum investing

Your investment programme may consist of making a lump-sum invest-ment, perhaps due to monies acquired through the sale of a business, an inheritance, work related bonuses, or the sale of a property. In this case, the end value of an investment pool is based on three things: the amount you invest as a lump sum, the time it is invested for, and the real rate of return from the mix of portfolio building blocks used. This would also apply to any capital you already have in your investment pool, and to which you will make additional regular contributions.

You can see the effect of time and return on the purchasing power of £1 in Table 6.7. You can multiply any lump sum investment that you plan to make by this number. Choose your investment horizon and the real rate of return that gives a suitable chance of success.

A caveat to using the numbers

Always bear in mind that using these outputs only provide rough figures and cannot fully describe the uncertainty of the markets that you face. You can never be certain of the returns in advance, although by choosing a rate of return that has a good chance of being achieved over your investment horizon using Table 6.4 is a start. You can hope that your investments achieve such returns and, if they do, then these numbers will give you an indication of what to expect.

Even if you receive your expected return, this will in all likelihood be made up of negative as well as positive periods and the interim value of your port-folio will be out of line with the straight-line projections. This means that you need to think carefully about how you monitor your portfolio and judge how it is doing against your long-term goals (Chapter 12). The actual value of your portfolio will be different from this in tomorrow's debased money: don't worry, so too will the income you withdraw from it later. Just remember that if you use real return numbers, as you have, this does not matter.

Remember, too, that any contributions that you make need, in real life, to be scaled up to reflect the nominal amount you need to invest. You can use an inflation index to do this simply. Finally, remember that investing will cost you. Build in investing costs into your expected returns. If you use index funds, then 0.5 per cent a year in costs is a reasonably conservative deduction.

The danger of using simplistic models like the ones above is that they can lull you into a false sense of security. Be smart and think about some of their limitations. At this point you at least have a reasonable chance of finding the right ballpark for your financial targets.

6.4 A working example

Imagine a professional couple, both in their mid-thirties, with a gross annual combined income of £100,000. They have a daughter, who is three years old. They have two main investment goals: the first is to be able to retire on a similar standard of living to that they have today; the second is to buy a property for their daughter for her twenty-first birthday. With this gift, they won't feel so bad about spending the rest of their capital.

The retirement pool (basic financial survival)

The couple want to make sure that they have £70,000 of purchasing power available in total when they retire. Part of this income will come from company pension plans, which they estimate will bring in £40,000 (in real terms) a year. The remaining £30,000 needs to come from an investment programme. The current balance of their savings is £50,000 from a recent inheritance. If they fail to generate at least £15,000 additional income a year then this will severely hamper some of their plans for travelling in their retirement, which they would be pretty upset about. They have 30 years to accumulate the assets and intend to live well into their nineties.

The flat purchase (nest egg)

While this goal is a nice altruistic gesture, they are not that fussed if the amount that they end up with is less than the price of a one-bedroom flat in a reasonable area, which they estimate to be about £150,000 in real

table 6.8	Work out your five-step plan	
Step	Pot 1	Pot 2
Step 1: Investment pools	Retirement income	Property purchase
Step 2: Vision	Comfortable retirement	Foot-up on the property ladder at 21 for daughter
Step 3: Horizon	30 years to retirement at 65 Live until at least 90	18 years
Step 4: Consequences	Critical. Need at least half the income target (£15,000)	Non-critical. Something is better than nothing
Step 5: Goals in financial terms	Nitty-gritty calculations required. Need £30,000 income	Nitty-gritty calculations not essential but useful

terms. After all, a small mortgage never hurt anyone and might instil some financial discipline in their daughter. They currently have nothing put aside. They want to try and keep the contributions into this pool at a reasonably low level, given the investment they are going to have to make to generate the retirement income they need. As a consequence, they may ask a bit more from the investment portfolio they choose, i.e. more aggressive with a higher expected return, because failing to meet their target is not so important. Something above the level of their contributions, after inflation, is better than nothing.

Five steps to building the plan

They scribble down the five steps that this book suggests they should take to unravel their goals. They come up with Table 6.8.

As you can see, retirement income is their main concern and they need to be pretty sure that they will be able to generate at least half of what they are hoping for.

The nitty gritty of the plan

The calculations they need to make are based on the step-by-step approach of Figure 6.8.

To generate an income of £30,000 a year without eroding their pool of capital in retirement, they need a target pool of £750,000, if they are com-

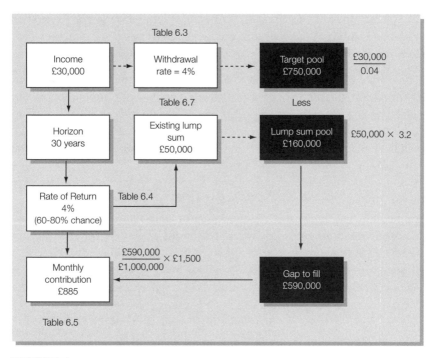

figure 6.8 Determining financial goals is easy

fortable with an annual withdrawal rate of 4 per cent. This target pool figure is obtained from Table 6.3. From Table 6.4, you can see that there appears to be a 'good chance' of 60–80 per cent that a real rate of return can be achieved of 4 per cent over the period they expect to be retired (thirty years or more), which should allow them to protect the purchasing power of their capital and the income derived from it.

The £50,000 in savings they have will grow and cover some of the capital they require. In the thirty years over which they will be accumulating assets, there is a 'good chance' that 4 per cent real returns will be achieved (Table 6.4). Let's assume they feel comfortable with this. Using this rate of return over their investment horizon, we can see that £1 compounds up to £3.20 (Table 6.7). So, we can multiply the £50,000 lump sum they have by 3.2 to give £160,000, making the gap to be filled by their regular savings plan to be a mere £590,000.

Next we can calculate the level of monthly contributions needed to fill a hole of £590,000. From Table 6.5 the monthly contribution over thirty years to build £1 million using the 4 per cent rate of return is about £1,500. But they only need £590,000. So, the monthly contribution required is

£1,500 multiplied by £590,000/£1,000,000 which is around £885 a month. Remember this is in today's terms and would need to be scaled up each year to take account of inflation.

The couple could have decided to be conservative and choose a 3 per cent withdrawal rate and 3 per cent real return during the accumulation phase, which would increase the monthly contributions they need to make to £1,600 to achieve their target income of £30,000 until they die, with greater certainty. These are the kind of trade-offs that you face and need to decide for yourself.

Calculations for the property purchase

In the same manner, but using a 6 per cent rate of return gives them a 'reasonable' chance of getting to where they want to go over the next twenty years or so, they would need to invest £350 per month (from Table 6.5: £150,000/£1,000,000 × £2,300). Don't get hung up with the fact that it is eighteen years and not twenty or that £345 has been rounded to £350. The actual return on the portfolio will not be exactly 6 per cent. If you are lucky or unlucky, it may be nowhere near 6 per cent! To be more certain of the outcome, they could save more, but they don't want to.

6.5 Useful calculations

In Figure 6.9, if you are interested, you will find the formulae to calculate basic estimates for your own investment plan. You probably need to use a spreadsheet, as the calculations are laborious using a calculator. Always bear in mind the limitations of such calculations. They do, however, provide you with a useful tool to look at the consequences of different courses of action, allowing you to make decisions aligned more closely with your goals.

$$\textit{Final value} = \frac{\text{annual contributions} \times [(1 + \text{rate of return})^{\text{Number of years}} - 1]}{\text{Rate of return}}$$

$$\textit{Annual contributions} = \frac{(\text{final value} \times \text{rate of return})}{[(1 + \text{rate of return})^{\text{Number of years}} - 1]}$$

$$\textit{Pool size} = \frac{\text{required income}}{\text{withdrawal rate}}$$

Where ^ = to the power of

figure 6.9 Formulae for your own calculations

6.6 Summary: investment goals

■ Have a clear idea of what you want to achieve from your investing and express it clearly.

■ Spend some time thinking about your goals using the simple five-step process.

■ Use the tables to calculate your target pool size and contribution levels given your investment horizon and expected portfolio return.

■ It is important to bear in mind that the actual return that your portfolio delivers is unlikely to be that chosen as your expected return. This is the great dilemma all investors face. Use Table 6.4 to get a feel for the chances that a specific rate of return can be achieved over the investment period you choose.

■ Failing to understand and use this type of data creates a large risk that you will be disappointed with the outcome of your investments.

■ More analysis on what type of portfolio mix has a good chance of delivering the returns you need and what some of the worst-case extremes that you may face is covered in Chapter 9.

■ You can change any or all of the following four things to increase your chances of success: scale down your goals; reduce the rate of expected return you use; increase the contributions you make; extend the time you invest for. The right combination for you, only you will know. But at least you now have the tools to work out what the implications are.

References

Maslow, A. (1970) A theory of motivation. In: *Motivation and personality*, 1st ed. Upper Saddle River, NJ: Pearson Education.

7

Building a smart but simple portfolio

At last you can begin to start thinking about building a portfolio that will provide a good chance of meeting your investment goals by generating the returns that you need, but still allowing you to sleep well at night when markets get tough.

7.1 Choices, choices

There is an ever-widening choice of investment building blocks, from the more familiar cash, bonds, equities, and property, to the less familiar and esoteric, such as commodities, hedge funds, gold, art, wine and cars. You have to decide in a rational way which to discard and which to use, and

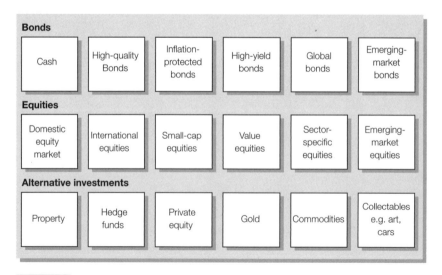

figure 7.1 The choice can feel bewildering

how much of each you should include. Pick up the money section of your Sunday paper and see how many 'opportunities' are on offer each week. Traditionally, these are categorised by the industry as equity, bond and alternative investments, which is helpful up to a point (Figure 7.1).

You need to develop a mental framework that will help you to decide:

■ what each building block brings to the table;

■ whether you want to use them; and

■ if you do, how much you should use in your mix.

In fact, with some common sense, a basic understanding of a few simple concepts, drawn together with some simple rules, you can put together a sensible portfolio with these building blocks.

7.2 Two steps to building a portfolio

The process of building this sensible portfolio can be reduced to two main steps. This chapter looks at the first step and considers the two central building blocks that you will use – equities and bonds. Chapter 10 addresses the issue of moving beyond a two building block portfolio as the second step.

Step 1: Pick your spot on the risk/return spectrum

The first step is to decide what characteristics your portfolio has to deliver – the balance between returns and sleeping easy. In more industry-like language, you are trying to identify where you fall on the risk/return spectrum, where risk is defined at the volatility of returns (the bumpiness of your investment journey). Understanding your portfolio in terms of how bumpy a ride to expect, how deep the falls can be and how long they generally persist, will be crucial to picking the right spot on the spectrum.

Step 2: Adding to the equity/bond mix

The second step searches for ways to refine your portfolio's characteristics. This is an optional step, but one worth considering. Each building block brings useful characteristics. Some help to smooth the ride further and protect your portfolio from certain risks, while others tend to add extra returns; few manage to do both to any great extent. A skilful mix of blocks can help to improve the trade-off between the return you achieve and the risks you need to take to get there. In other words, you want to try and improve the bang (of return) for your buck (of risk).

Why use equities and bonds?

At its simplest, these building blocks have certain properties that complement each other. Equities have an economic rationale for and history of delivering mid-digit real returns (after inflation) and are considered the engines of portfolio returns, but with considerable and sometimes extreme swings in returns – at times leaving investors with large holes in their wealth. High-quality domestic bonds on the other hand, tend to have far smoother return patterns at a cost of lower returns, which come in the low single digits, after inflation. Both are broad, deep, markets in which it is easy to invest, either directly or through funds. Mixing them in different proportions creates a good range of portfolios. Chapter 8 explores their characteristics further.

However, for many investors, bonds and equities are as far as it goes. You can gain much of what you need from these two building blocks, without the increased complexity of owning other types. Let's stick to such a simple portfolio for now.

7.3 Understanding return and risk

A good starting point is to remember that return and risk go hand in hand. For higher returns you need to take higher risks, it's as simple as that (well almost). Generally, risk is regarded as the volatility of returns, but may include other risks, such as liquidity, political, or bankruptcy risk. For taking on this risk, you should, theoretically, have a potential for higher returns. If not, you would be putting your money into investments where you are exposing yourself to unrewarded risks.

We can measure historic risk and return characteristics of different building blocks, and make guesstimates of what they are likely to be looking forward to and come up with a view of where different building blocks fall on the risk/return spectrum. Figure 7.2 shows where each box sits, approximately, on the spectrum and the zigzag chart shows the bumpiness of the road at each point along it.

What does this tell you? First, you can see that a relationship does appear to exist; second, it may make you begin to see that although you may want to achieve higher returns, there are consequences to doing so (sleepless nights); and third, the equity-like universe of building blocks are the real drivers of returns, but they come with a very bumpy ride. Don't worry about what each of these blocks represents at this point, just look at where high-quality domestic bonds and domestic equities fall.

7.4 Step 1: Picking a spot on the risk/return spectrum

In general, most investors are looking to maximise the level of return they can achieve from their portfolio, for a survivable level of bumpiness in the value of wealth, over the time they will be investing for. They accept this as the price they pay to give themselves a good chance of meeting their goals. In reality, this statement describes a continuum from those merely seeking purchasing power preservation, with as smooth a path as possible, to those in pursuit of aggressive wealth accumulation, prepared to live with the roller-coaster ride that comes with it. From Figure 7.2 again, you can see that the expected real return for equities is around 5 per cent and for High Quality Domestic Bonds 2 per cent, but the ride for equities is about twice as bumpy as that for bonds.

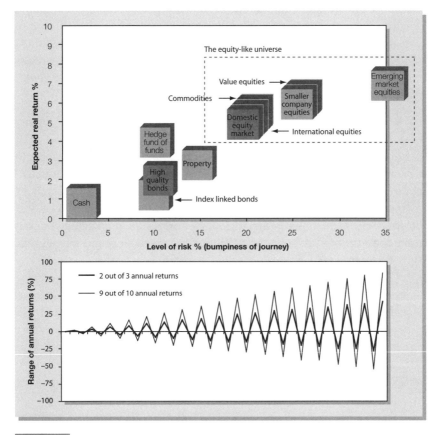

figure 7.2 Return and risk are inextricably linked

Finding your way to the right place

Perhaps think about the problem in this way: as an investor, you want to achieve as high a return as you can, but you know that returns come with a bumpy investment ride. Your ability to survive extremely poor periods of equity markets is a function of how long you will be able to invest for, the financial damage from falls in your wealth and your emotional stomach for coping with a big reduction in wealth, even if you have time on your side. Time is a great smoother of returns as the good times generally negate the bad, in the longer term.

Let's imagine an extreme case. You are very wealthy individual and intend to pass on your wealth for the benefit of future generations. You have no real need for the money in your lifetime and you have the emotional stomach to survive the severe and sometimes prolonged equity market crashes that occur. You have a choice between bonds and equities, or a mix of the two. It's quite a simple choice – owning 100 per cent in equities would make sense. Any addition of bonds to your portfolio would result in you giving up the returns you want, and would provide you with downside protection you neither want nor need. Buying bonds would be like buying insurance to cover something that you don't value, or can afford to repurchase.

In real life, few investors have an infinite investment time horizon, many have financial implications associated with big falls in the value of their wealth, such as the retiree living off their portfolio (even if they expect to live another thirty years) and, as is evident, many can't live with stomach-churning losses. As you will see in Chapter 15, some markets have disappeared altogether, and many have suffered severe crashes: the UK was down 70 per cent in real terms in 1972–74 and some markets have taken more than thirty years to recover. The sobering words of Lord Keynes may ring loudly in your ears:

'Markets can remain irrational longer than you can remain solvent.'

So where does that leave you? In general, investors with a long-term investment horizon should have a bias for domestic equities (and the wider equity universe) and their return-driving properties or at least use this as their conceptual starting point. I am not suggesting that you have to own a high allocation of equity type investments; after all, I don't know what your investment horizon is, what effect falls in wealth will have on your situation, or whether you can emotionally stomach them; simply, you may find it helpful to think of this as your starting point from which you make conscious decisions to move yourself down the risk spectrum to a place where you feel most comfortable, and what the addition of bonds in this case (or other building blocks for that matter) have on the characteristics of your portfolio.

Generically, two things are likely to make you move down the risk spectrum: the first is that you may not have a particularly long time frame to invest for and exposing yourself to potentially severe and perhaps long-lived falls in the value of your wealth is not advisable, as you may not recover from them in time to meet your objectives; the second is that you simply can't live with bumpiness of the journey, either from an emotional or a financial perspective. With a shortening horizon, investors wisely move further out of equities. With very short time frames (less than 3 years) you should move out of equities entirely and probably into cash.

Buying protection for a smoother ride

There are two ways in which you can protect yourself from the downside of equities. The first is to substitute a portion of your conceptual starting allocation in equities for a building block(s) – bonds in this case – that is capable of *dampening* the pattern of returns by virtue of the fact that bonds have a substantially smoother return pattern than equities, in absolute terms. Market extremes are generally less severe than those of equities, at least in the short term.

The second level of protection comes from the fact that the return patterns of bonds and equities, while generally somewhat in line with each other, are not perfectly matched. This helps to smooth the pattern of returns further and is known as *diversification*. In the case of bonds this effect is beneficial but not overly substantial, most of the time. At times of equity market crisis, however, investors have a propensity to flee riskier assets and move into high-quality domestic bonds issued either by the government or financially strong companies.

It's buying insurance

You could think of this process as like buying insurance: you want protection from equity market trauma and you can get it by buying some cover (owning bonds). Imagine you buy cover for half your portfolio so you have an equal mix of bonds and equities: as bonds have a level of return bumpiness half that of equities, you would expect, with a bit of basic maths, this mix to have a level of return bumpiness that is only three-quarters that of equities. This is the *dampener* effect and the premium you pay is the returns you lose by owning bonds instead of equities. In this policy, however, you find in the small print that you get an extra bit of cover (i.e. additional smoothing of the bumpiness of returns) for free – yes free. This is the *diversification* effect caused by the fact that bond and equity returns do not move exactly in step, creating a smoothing of the pattern of returns. Diversification, the only 'free lunch' in investing, is covered in Chapter 10.

Choosing your spot

Deciding where you fall on the risk spectrum, defined in a two-building block portfolio by the mix you choose between equities and bond cover, is the critical decision. Imagine that you can slide the circle in Figure 7.3 from equities to bonds; as you do, the returns that you could potentially make will fall, but in return you gain some protection from equity market downturns.

As you slide the circle towards bonds, it would be useful to know a few things about the characteristics of each mix. These would include:

■ The expected level of return.

■ The chances of achieving this level of return (remember Table 6.4) or perhaps understanding what level of return you have an 80 per cent chance or so of achieving.

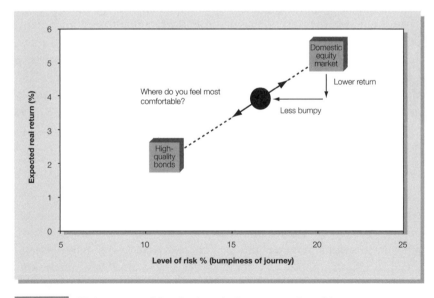

figure 7.3 Giving up equities for bonds for a smoother ride

■ What the chances might be of losing purchasing power over your investment horizon and interim time periods.

■ How this type of portfolio would have fared in the big equity market crashes of 1972–1974 and 2000–2002.

■ What the worst returns experienced were over different investment holding periods, e.g. the worst year, and the worst five, ten, twenty and thirty years.

Chapter 9 provides the opportunity to slide this scale up and down the risk spectrum, seeing for yourself the consequences of doing so is in these terms. Working out where you feel most comfortable is an iterative process and you will have a number of insightful and innovative tools to assist you.

8

Equity and bond building blocks in brief

So far, we have avoided talking about the way in which markets behave and the characteristics of different building blocks, except for brief illustrative examples. This has been deliberate because many investors have a fascination for the short-term workings of the market, which tends to blind them to some of the more important issues. At this point, though, you do need to begin to form a picture of the general characteristics that bonds and equities display.

If you are interested beyond this point, you can refer to Chapters 15 and 16, where you can get a deeper insight into how they work.

8.1 Equities in brief

Let's briefly explore the general characteristics of equities. In this case, what we are talking about is a broad exposure to the UK market as a whole (or whatever your domestic market is).

A definition of equities

A company wishing to raise money to invest in its business can do so by selling part of its ownership to others. The ownership of a company is divided up into shares, which are either sold privately or through a public exchange, where anyone can buy them. Buying shares, otherwise known as equities or stocks, therefore gives you part ownership in a real business that sells its products or services in its chosen markets, develops products and, hopefully, services its customers well.

The ultimate objective of the managers and workers should be to increase the value of the enterprise over time, by increasing its earnings, through a well thought out and executed strategy, good product development and distribution, and integrity in dealing with all of its stakeholders, although in reality this is not always the case. As a part-owner in a business, you also have certain rights and responsibilities to vote and influence company policy at shareholder meetings and so do fund managers who manage money on an investor's behalf. As reward for the capital you have invested in the business, you can expect to receive regular dividends that are paid in cash and hopefully an increase in the value of the enterprise, which is reflected in an increase in the share price.

Simplistically, if you own a broadly diversified equity portfolio, say through an index tracker fund, you effectively own part of public UK plc, or whatever economy your fund tracks. Capitalist economies can be expected to grow in real terms over time, as companies drive relentlessly to make money for the owners and other stakeholders in the business. This may come about, for example, through increased efficiency, the development of products, and the exploitation of new customer segments. In an inflationary environment, a company can raise its prices and its real assets should maintain their value, so you would expect equities to have a built-in hedge against inflation in the long term and create wealth in real terms.

It is useful to remind yourself from time to time that you own a stake in the real world and real companies, not a mythical market that appears to be able to generate unreal returns, consistently throughout the years, well above long-term rates of growth. When markets lose touch with this reality, gains or losses result for speculative rather than economic reasons. When the business environment is tough and sentiment is weak, large capital losses can and may occur, and vice versa. Continual changes in the underlying fortunes of a company combined with market sentiment about it and the general economic outlook, leads to volatility of returns and consequently a bumpy investment journey.

The return engines of investment

The next few of pages look at the historic returns of UK equities in a number of ways and draw conclusions that can guide your thinking. First, consider the annual returns that have been experienced from 1900 to 2004, the longest reliable data available, which are used throughout the book.

Figure 8.1 provides an insight into just how volatile the annual returns of equities were in the last century. You can see that the extremes are wide. In some years, the market has performed exceptionally well and in others it has fallen dramatically. In fact, you can expect to experience negative

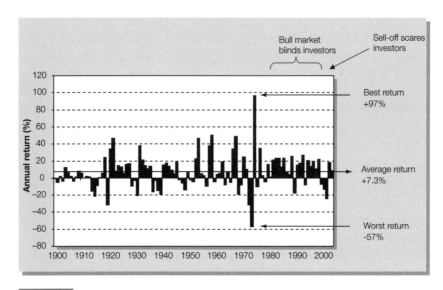

figure 8.1   **UK equity real returns (1900 to 2004)**

Source: DMS Global Data (Ibbotson) © 2006 E Dimson, P Marsh and M Staunton

returns in about one in three years. Just bear Figure 8.1 in mind the next time you decide to compound up returns in a straight line. The 1980s and 1990s bull market made many investors naive to this fact.

As a good investor, you should always be trying to understand what the chances are that you will be successful in your investing. Knowing that you have about a one in three chance of losing money in any single year is a useful piece of information for an investor with a one-year horizon, but little use to you. To estimate the range or returns within which two out of three of all annual returns usually fall, or even nineteen out of twenty annual returns to fall, would be a useful next step. By reworking these returns we can see what this has been historically, which may provide a useful proxy for the future. It's a start anyway.

Figure 8.2 shows the number of times that different annual returns have occurred during the 105-year period plotted. With a little bit of statistics, which you don't have to worry about, we can then work out these ranges.

So far, we know that the average return is around 7 per cent (this is actually the *arithmetic average* where we take all the annual numbers and divide by the number of years). The best return has been +97 per cent and the worst return –57 per cent in any one year. We can also calculate that two out of every three returns were approximately between +27 per cent and –13 per cent and nineteen out of twenty were between 47 per cent and –33 per

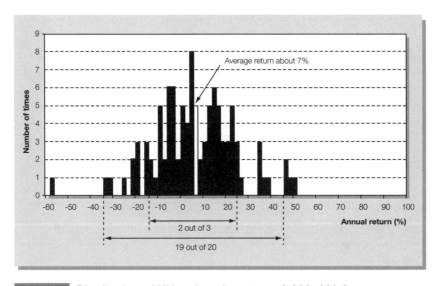

figure 8.2   **Distribution of UK real equity returns (1900–2004)**
Source: DMS Global Data (Ibbotson) © 2006 E Dimson, P Marsh and M Staunton

cent. We are slowly building a picture of the characteristics of equities. Note too the outliers that lie well above and below the ranges. On the downside, it is these extremes that bite investors hard.

As an aside, in statistical terms this range either side of the mean is referred to as the *annualised standard deviation of returns* and is the industries measure of *risk*, which results in the notion that equities are risky just because the potential range of annual returns is wider than for some other building blocks. This measure is of little use to a long-term investor because the real risk you face is not meeting your purchasing power goals. Cash is low risk in this industry sense, but high risk to an investor building or even just protecting purchasing power, over the longer term.

Looking a little closer at the returns since 1900, we can calculate what annualised returns have been generated by equities over different windows of time. An *annualised return* reflects interest-on-interest when you compound numbers up over time; this is known as the *geometric average*. Looking at the period as a whole, the past fifty years, and the decades that make up this period, you can see in Figure 8.3 that returns have varied considerably relative to the long-run average. The 1980s and 1990s were an exceptional period and making future return assumptions based on this period would greatly overstate the returns that a portfolio is likely to deliver. You could get lucky, but don't bank on it.

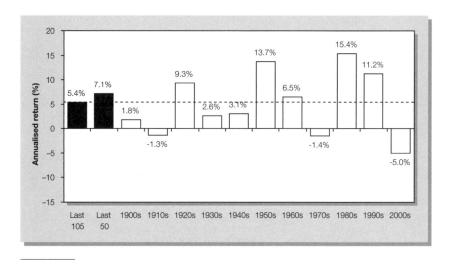

figure 8.3 Annualised real returns of UK equities (1900–2004)

Source: DMS Global Data (Ibbotson) © 2006 E Dimson, P Marsh and M Staunton

This raises two interesting questions. First, what are returns going to look like over the period you will be investing? Second, what effect does time have on the range of returns that you might experience? Manipulating the data again, we can look at the range of returns that investors with different investment horizons would have experienced in the past century. This is done by looking at, say, a ten-year window from 1900 to 1909 and calculating the annualised return for the decade, then moving to the next window and so on. Figure 8.4 illustrates this for ten and thirty-year windows, known as *holding periods*.

There have been occasions when ten-year returns have been very strong, but also occasions when returns have been negative. Remember that an annualised return of –5 per cent a year every year for ten years substantially erodes your capital. You can begin to see from this diagram why a 5 per cent real return is a reasonable target for a longer-term investor.

As an investor, it is helpful to examine the range of returns exhibited by different portfolio structures over your time frame: you will get a chance to do so in the next chapter. Figure 8.5 covers the range of returns that have been experienced in the period 1900–2004 over different holding periods. The striking point is the way in which, over time, the range of annualised return outcomes narrows dramatically, and even the worst case returns have, over any period above twenty-five years, always yielded positive real returns. In other words, long-term investors should probably weight their portfolios to

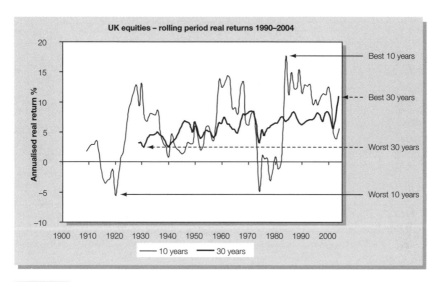

figure 8.4 **Equity returns can be negative over ten years or more**

Source: DMS Global Data (Ibbotson) © 2006 E Dimson, P Marsh and M Staunton

higher levels of equities as they have the timeframe to recover from the shorter-term bumpiness that they exhibit. The caveat is that some markets have experienced worse outcomes than this, which is explored in Chapter 15. Always bear in mind that the Japanese equity market still languished at only a quarter of its 1989 peak after 15 years. We can rework Figure 8.5 to illustrate the effect on £100 of purchasing power for different time periods,

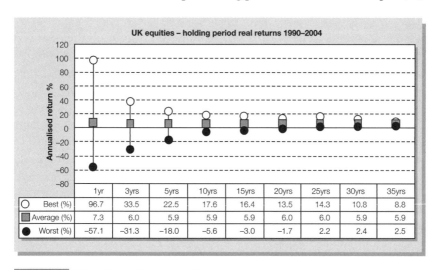

	1yr	3yrs	5yrs	10yrs	15yrs	20yrs	25yrs	30yrs	35yrs
○ Best (%)	96.7	33.5	22.5	17.6	16.4	13.5	14.3	10.8	8.8
■ Average (%)	7.3	6.0	5.9	5.9	5.9	6.0	6.0	5.9	5.9
● Worst (%)	−57.1	−31.3	−18.0	−5.6	−3.0	−1.7	2.2	2.4	2.5

figure 8.5 **Time helps to narrow the range of returns**

Source: DMS Global Data (Ibbotson) © 2006 E Dimson, P Marsh and M Staunton

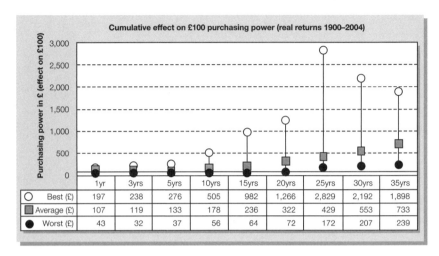

Cumulative effect on £100 purchasing power (real returns 1900–2004)

	1yr	3yrs	5yrs	10yrs	15yrs	20yrs	25yrs	30yrs	35yrs
Best (£)	197	238	276	505	982	1,266	2,829	2,192	1,898
Average (£)	107	119	133	178	236	322	429	553	733
Worst (£)	43	32	37	56	64	72	172	207	239

figure 8.6 **Cumulative effects increase over time**

Source: DMS Global Data (Ibbotson) © 2006 E Dimson, P Marsh and M Staunton

taking time and compounding into account, to produce Figure 8.6. Even in the worst-case thirty-five-year period, purchasing power more than doubled. Note that small differences in average returns make big differences in final purchasing power terms over long periods. If you look at twenty-five-year holding periods, in the worst case you would have not quite doubled your money and in the best case you would have improved your purchasing power by more than twenty times (this was the period leading up to the top of the bull market in 1999/2000).

Investing is not a game of certainties; you have to weigh up the odds you face and decide what balance of upside to downside you can live with. To balance the odds, you have to have a feel for the chances of one outcome occurring over another. To that end, let's take our analysis of equity returns and risk to another level. Figure 8.7 illustrates the chances that you have of building or losing wealth by investing in equities over different time frames. For the calculations I have used my own reasonable estimates of expected returns for equities, which are very similar to the historic long-run characteristics used above. These are 5 per cent annualised real returns and a standard deviation of 20 per cent for those who are interested. The process used to create this illustration is known as a Monte Carlo simulation. You can read more about this useful multiple-life probability-orientated tool in Chapter 11.

You can see by reading from the vertical scale in Figure 8.7 that in any one year there is a pretty high chance (45 per cent or so) of losing money. This

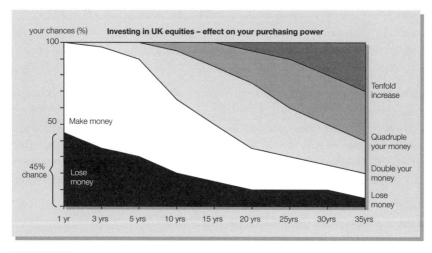

figure 8.7   Chances of outcomes in equity investing

is a little higher than experienced in the past, but the message is the same. Investors with a long-term horizon of, say, thirty-five years, dramatically reduce the chances of losing purchasing power. The chances of losing money over this period are 5 per cent. While this has not been experienced in the UK, other markets have seen periods of thirty-five years where purchasing power has been eroded. I think it is fair to say that you would be unlucky to suffer negative returns over thirty-five years, but it is possible. Investors who made twenty times their money in the twenty-five-year period up to 1999 were in the lucky minority. Anyone hoping to emulate this has a less than a one in ten chance of doing so. Reading from the vertical scale, where each notch represents a 10 per cent chance, you can see that you have about a 60 per cent chance that you will quadruple your money or better and a one-in-four chance that you could multiply it ten times or more over thirty-five years.

Don't get too caught up in the precise probabilities – this analysis is meant to provide a sense of magnitude and type of outcome, not exact probabilities. The top and bottom 5 per cent or so of outcomes are extremes of good or bad years. While we may expect markets to revert eventually to their long-term average, a process known as mean reversion, thirty-five years is not that long and who knows what extremes may exist in the future. You and I may get unlucky and have really stinking markets for the next thirty years. We cannot know for sure, but at least the probabilities are in our favour, which is as much as we can ask. As Laurence Siegel of the Ford Foundation so encouragingly once said:

'Risk is not short-term volatility, for the long-term investor can afford to ignore that. Rather, because there is no predestined rate of return, only an expected one that may not be realised, the risk is that, in the long-run, stock returns will be terrible.'

The upside of long-term equity investing for most investors outweighs the slim possibility that returns will be negative over substantially longer periods than have been experienced in the past. With information analysed and presented in this way, you are now able to make that call on whether or not to hold that party in your garden we addressed earlier. You always knew it could rain but now you know what the chances are of it happening.

Equities – summary of characteristics

From this brief analysis you can draw some useful conclusions, which include:

- It seems fair to call equities the drivers of wealth creation, generating over the long term, above-inflation returns of around 5 per cent annualised.

- In the shorter term, returns fluctuated historically within wide ranges from plus 100 per cent to minus 60 per cent or so for annual returns.

- Equities generate negative annual returns 30 per cent to 40 per cent of the time.

- Two out of three annual returns historically fell within the approximate range of 25 per cent to –13 per cent.

- Nineteen out of twenty annual returns historically fell within the range of 47 per cent to –33 per cent.

- Over longer periods (twenty-five years or more) even the worst cases have generated positive purchasing power growth in the past, for UK equities.

- Don't bank on it – there is a chance that we could be unlucky in the next thirty years.

- Equity investors have a significant chance of losing money up until about fifteen to twenty years, somewhere in the region of a 20 per cent chance. At thirty-five years, the chances are small but they do exist. This should be balanced against the significant opportunity to increase purchasing power.

8.2 Bonds in brief

Let's now explore the characteristics of our other basic building block – bonds. Here, we are talking about high quality bonds where the company or government you lend your money to is unlikely to go bust.

A straightforward definition

Another way in which a company (or government) can raise money is by borrowing it. A company may borrow from its creditors, from its directors, from its bank by way of loans or an overdraft, or from the investing community.

Bonds are IOUs issued by companies and governments to investors. In return for lending them money, a bond pays you a fixed rate of interest (*coupon*) and promises that the principal amount you lent them will be returned at a set date, its *maturity date*. Bonds are for this reason known as *fixed income* investments. When a bond is issued, the interest it pays should compensate you, broadly speaking, to cover the anticipated inflation eroding your capital, the risk that you might not get your money back and the time that your money is tied up for. As you can see, this is a very different animal from equities. Your return comes largely from the income you receive. If inflation rises unexpectedly, you will not be adequately compensated by the interest payments. Unanticipated inflation is the largest risk for an investor with a diversified portfolio of high-quality domestic bonds.

There is a public market for most government and corporate issued bonds, which allows investors to buy and sell them. However, because bonds pay fixed levels of interest in an environment where interest rates are constantly changing as investors' perceptions of risk change, the new rates demanded by investors are reflected through changes in the price of the bonds, creating capital gains and losses. As interest rates go up, often in response to the perceived threat of rising inflation, bond prices go down and vice versa.

The sensitivity of a bond's price to changes in the interest rate depends in a large part on how long it is until you get paid back your money. The longer to go, the more the price will fluctuate. It's a bit more complicated than that but at this point it is irrelevant, as for a long-term investor the effect is not significant. For more on this subject refer to Chapter 16.

Bonds generally provide more stable returns than equities

Just as we did with equities, let's look at the history of real bond returns from 1900–2004, to try and get a feel for their general characteristics. It is worth noting that looking at nominal (pre-inflation) returns overestimates the stability and positive return generation characteristics of bonds and you should always seek to look at real returns.

Figure 8.8 shows that the extreme annual returns are significantly narrower than for equities, but the average return of 2.3 per cent is significantly lower (compared with 7 per cent). Many investors have recently become blinded to the risk of bond investing, as returns have been largely positive since the 1980s and especially during the stock market crash of 2000–2002, when they generated positive returns. Negative real bond returns do occur, with surprising frequency.

Again, we can work out the ranges within which two out of three and nineteen out of twenty returns fell during this period, giving you an idea of what the future may hold. From Figure 8.9, these ranges are approximately +16 per cent to −12 per cent and +30 per cent to −26 per cent respectively, narrower than those for equities.

Looking at this data in another way, Figure 8.10 shows that while the annualised 105-year return may be 1.3 per cent, returns for shorter periods can vary quite significantly. In estimating what the future holds, we need to be careful to place our expectations in the context of history.

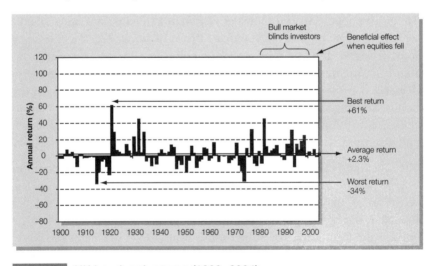

figure 8.8 **UK bond real returns (1900–2004)**

Source: DMS Global Data (Ibbotson) © 2006 E Dimson, P Marsh and M Staunton

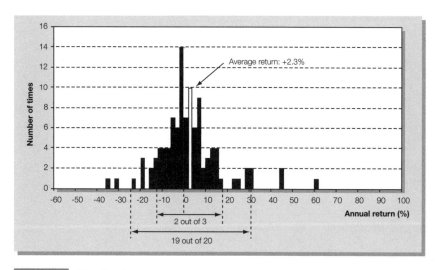

figure 8.9 **Distribution of UK bond real returns (1900–2004)**

Source: DMS Global Data (Ibbotson) © 2006 E Dimson, P Marsh and M Staunton

Clearly, returns have varied considerably, rising well above the long-run average and well below it too. The 1980s, 1990s and 2000s (so far), have been a major bull market for bonds and have perhaps lulled some investors into believing that bonds are safe havens generating strong returns and are a long-term alternative to equities; in fact, the past thirty years have been the best on record. A quick look at the data would indicate that this is a naive claim. If again, we look at holding period returns of ten years and

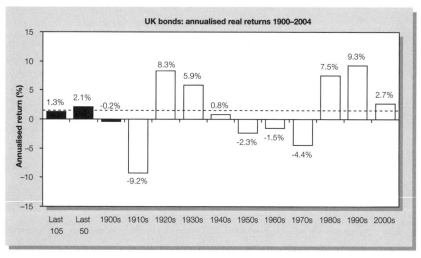

figure 8.10 **Bonds returns are not as smooth as you may believe**

Source: DMS Global Data (Ibbotson) © 2006 E Dimson, P Marsh and M Staunton

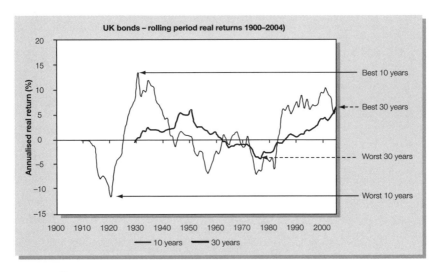

figure 8.11   At times, bonds have fared very poorly

Source: DMS Global Data (Ibbotson) © 2006 E Dimson, P Marsh and M Staunton

thirty years, we see a very different picture from equities, as Figure 8.11 illustrates.

For both of these holding periods, returns have been substantially negative in some periods. Figure 8.12 plots the ranges of annualised returns for different holding periods, as was done for equities.

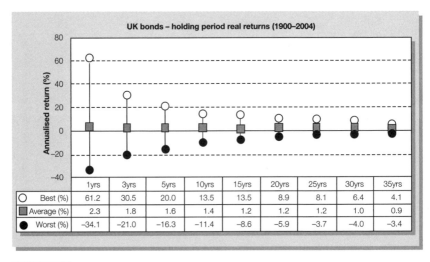

figure 8.12   Ranges narrow but long-term worst case is still poor

Source: DMS Global Data (Ibbotson) © 2006 E Dimson, P Marsh and M Staunton

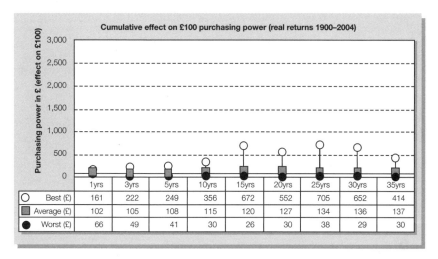

Cumulative effect on £100 purchasing power (real returns 1900–2004)								
	1yrs	3yrs	5yrs	10yrs	15yrs	20yrs	25yrs	30yrs	35yrs
○ Best (£)	161	222	249	356	672	552	705	652	414
■ Average (£)	102	105	108	115	120	127	134	136	137
● Worst (£)	66	49	41	30	26	30	38	29	30

figure 8.13 **The growth of purchasing power is limited over time**

Source: DMS Global Data (Ibbotson) © 2006 E Dimson, P Marsh and M Staunton

Two points of comparison with equities stand out: first, bonds have less severe short-term falls; second, the worst-case returns over all holding periods up to and including thirty-five years have experienced erosion of investors' purchasing power. You may conclude that bonds may provide short-term protection from equity market trauma but will have a significant cost for longer-term investors. Translating this into its effect on £100 shows the effects of time and compounding. The vertical scale in Figure 8.13 used is the same as that used for equities to provide a visual comparison. Over thirty-five years, the best case for equities was to increase your purchasing power twentyfold, whereas for bonds the best case was only a fourfold increase. In an inflationary environment, long-term ownership can be punishing.

The main points to note are that in the short term, bonds tend to have smaller extreme downturns, but over even significant periods, they can, on occasion, significantly erode investor purchasing power dramatically. You can also see that there have been periods of fifteen to twenty-five years or so when some investors received strong returns. Again, this is a little bit like knowing that the sun could come out for your garden party and temperatures soar or it could be rainy and cold. What you want to know is what the likelihood of it raining actually is.

So, again, what are the chances that different outcomes will occur? The results are illustrated in Figure 8.14. You may have heard somewhere that bonds are safer than equities. If you are looking at the volatility of

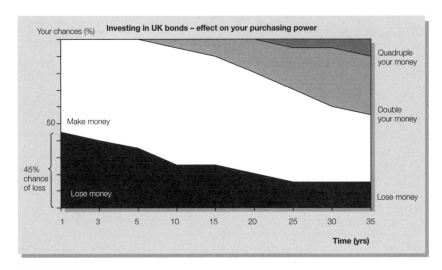

figure 8.14 Chances of outcomes in bond investing

short-term returns, this is true; looking at longer time periods, bonds are not that safe and have nowhere near the ability that equities have to maintain or increase your wealth in real terms. You can see from Figure 8.14 that there is a significant chance that bonds may erode purchasing power in any year. As the holding period increases to thirty years the chances of losses decrease, but less sharply than for equities. Your long-term upside is also dramatically curtailed relative to equities. Compare and study Figures 8.7 and 8.14 carefully because they are invaluable tools.

You can hope that inflation will be under better control in the years ahead that you will be investing for. If so, then real downside extremes may be less severe, but don't bank on it.

Bonds – summary of characteristics

From this analysis of the long-term return data for bonds, a number of conclusions can be drawn:

■ Bonds returns come largely from income in the longer term.

■ In the short term, returns may also include capital gains or losses that result from price changes to reflect the compensation that investors are demanding for the risk they are assuming.

■ Short-term returns have fallen in narrower ranges than equities have with the highest annual return being around 60 per cent and the lowest being around −35 per cent over the past 105 years.

▪ Perhaps a little surprisingly, bonds have generated negative real returns in just under half the years. However, the past twenty-five-year bull market in bonds, as governments have managed to curb inflation reasonably well, have given some investors a false impression of bonds being strong and steady generators of returns.

▪ Going forwards, with bond yields at an all-time low, will such consistent and spectacular returns be seen again? Probably not.

▪ The real risk to bonds is that of an unanticipated rise in inflation, and the price falls that accompany this, as investors demand higher yields.

▪ Over the long term, bonds have done a poor job at growing investors' purchasing power compared with equities.

▪ Investors should look to use bonds to smooth their investment journey, but be aware that owning too high a level of protection could, and is probably likely to, curtail their ability to increase their purchasing power over their investing lifetime. Finding the right balance is important.

8.3 Why use high-quality domestic bonds as market trauma protection?

Investors' requirements for yield can be broken down into two main components – the real yield (after inflation) they require and an expectation level for future inflation. As you saw above, changes in yields on bonds affect bond prices – when yields fall, prices rise and vice versa.

At its simplest, the effects on both these components provide the underlying basis for why you can use high-quality domestic bonds as market trauma protection. First, during short-term periods of financial crisis, large numbers of investors flock towards safe havens of quality and liquidity to place their funds, driving real yields down and prices up. Where safer than the highly liquid bonds issued by governments of strong economies? Generally, in the US investors' funds flow to US treasuries and in the UK to gilts. The increased demand pushes prices up.

Also, at times when future inflationary pressures appear to ease, the second component of yield, the required compensation for expected inflation falls and bond prices rise. At times of financial stress and falling equity markets, inflation expectations may well fall as people worry about the effect on the strength of the economy.

This occurs too at times of deflation (when consumer prices fall), which may occur from time to time and holders of high-quality domestic bonds receive a double boost. First, in periods of deflation, yields demanded by holders of bonds fall and bond prices rise and, second, at maturity you will receive the nominal value of your initial investment, which now buys more goods than it did when you invested. Given that during periods of deflation many firms find themselves in financial trouble, money will likely flow into the safest bonds, such as treasuries and gilts.

Owning bonds that have a few years to go before they mature helps to magnify these beneficial effects in the short term as their movements in price are more sensitive and greater than those just about to mature (i.e. pay you back your capital). More on that in Chapter 16.

Some notable investors believe that owning anything other than the highest-quality, long-term government bonds in your base currency and without any bells and whistles attached and only to the minimum point where you receive the level of short-term market trauma protection you want, is the only rational way to invest in bonds. Perhaps they are right. Logically, taking credit risk, i.e. getting a higher yield because the company is less financially secure, through owning lower-quality or even high-yield (junk) bonds does not make sense, as the environment when you need protection most is probably when these companies are themselves under most pressure. Look at Figure 8.15.

This scenario is the period of time covering the fall of Long Term Capital Management, a hedge fund full of Nobel Prize winners, leading traders and professionals who got it badly wrong. The ensuing fall-out could have created a severe financial crisis had not a small group of leading banks stepped in with a $3 billion rescue package, at a few days' notice, to stabilise markets. While this happened in the USA, the fall-out was global. Investors flocked to high-quality domestic bonds, whereas low-quality (high-yield) bonds suffered.

An example of the value of owning bonds is more recent. Following the great equity bull run of the 1980s and 1990s, the market began to revert towards its long-run mean returns, as overstretched valuations of companies were not supported by economic reality. In early 2000, the equity market began to fall and did so for three straight years. Bonds held up well as the inflation outlook remained benign, global economies strug-

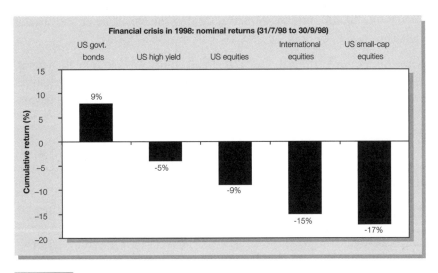

figure 8.15 **Flight to quality in times of financial crisis**
Source: US Bonds and US Large and Small Cap Equities (Ibbotson), International Equities – (MSCI), US High Yield – Lehman High Yield Long – B (Source: Thomson Datastream)

gled on the verge of recession, and in some case, deflation, and many investors flooded out of equities into safe havens. Bond yields fell in most major economies resulting in strong capital gains. Ironically, as a smarter investor, you need active, market timing and philosophy-free investors to

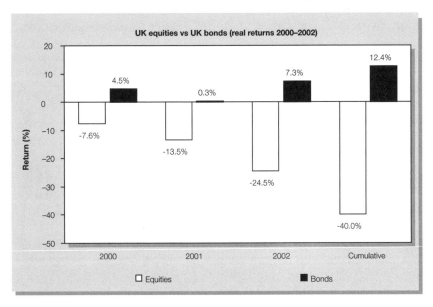

figure 8.16 **Bonds have provided good insurance against recent trauma**
Source: DMS Global Data (Ibbotson) © 2006 E Dimson, P Marsh and M Staunton

switch into bonds at these times to maximise the beneficial effects of your defensive bond position! Figure 8.16 illustrates this clearly.

However, bonds are not the panacea to all equity market falls. In general, they do help, but by and large they fall less than equities, rather than by returning positive real returns like they have done recently. Positive returns are the exception rather than the rule, as you will see below.

8.4 By and large bonds help dampen market trauma

The degree to which the returns of equities and bonds move together, i.e. how highly *correlated* they are, is worth looking at. The lower the correlation between the returns of each, the greater the smoothing effect of returns will be together. Generally, the return patterns of bonds and equities are related. Over the past 105, fifty and twenty years (to 2003) the correlations between bonds and equities have been 0.55, 0.49 and 0.45 respectively, where a correlation of 1 means they move identically in the same direction and –1 where they move in the opposite direction. This lowish level of correlation should have a beneficial diversification effect on the bumpiness of returns in a portfolio.

Hopefully, a picture is emerging of how you might use bonds and equities. From Figure 8.17, you can see that when equity markets fall, often bond

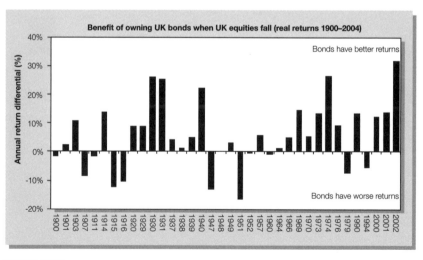

figure 8.17 **Bonds may fall but not generally as much as equities**

Source: DMS Global Data (Ibbotson) © 2006 E Dimson, P Marsh and M Staunton

markets have performed less badly, providing a positive contribution in relative terms, if not always in absolute terms. As you saw above, on occasion, such as 2000–2002, bond markets have risen as equity markets have fallen but this is not always the case, otherwise the correlation between the two would be negative, which it is not.

As a general rule, there appears to be a beneficial effect from holding high-quality domestic bonds in a portfolio to protect against short-term market trauma, but it's not an infallible solution. The key to protecting your wealth is by being diversified in bonds and other suitable building blocks, as you will see in Chapter 10.

8.5 Summary: rationale for owning some bonds

- Bonds tend to have less severe market falls than equities (although bond holders of Imperial Russian bonds when the Bolsheviks took power in 1917 might beg to differ).

- Bond and equity returns do not move in exact synchronisation, providing the opportunity to smooth returns and increase the certainty of outcomes.

- By and large, but not always, bonds tend to do less badly than equities when equity markets turn bad.

- Investors seek out quality bonds in a flight to safety and liquidity when markets are in turmoil.

- Sometimes, bonds return positive real returns when equity markets crash, but don't bank on it.

References

Siegel, L. (1997) Are stocks risky? two lessons, *Journal of Portfolio Management*, Spring, 29–34.

9

Getting your equity/bond mix right

You should now have a fair idea of your goals and a basic understanding of the characteristics of equities and bonds, so the time has come to focus attention on building a portfolio. The mix you choose is the primary decision you make as an investor as it almost entirely defines the returns that your portfolio will generate, as you saw in Chapter 4.

9.1 Focus on your end goal, not bumps in the road

In deciding what mix to choose, try to focus on the chances that you have of achieving a successful final outcome and then on the effects of periods of market trauma along the way. Being overly influenced by short-term events is like choosing where you want to go on a cycling holiday by looking at the bumpiness of the terrain, not by the scenery at your destination. If you are looking for a smooth ride you will always end up in the Netherlands, but if you choose by the scenery at your destination you will end up in the Alps. That said, if you are going to fall off on the first steep corner, you have chosen the wrong route.

As Figure 9.1 illustrates, the focus should be on giving yourself the highest chance of achieving a survivable purchasing power outcome, rather than avoiding short-term market wobbles. Only you will know the true consequences of what the latter mean to you.

The only advice I can give is to try your best to see the long-term benefits of your mix, over the period you will be investing for. Any decision to dampen the bumpiness of your ride should be made in the knowledge that you might well be significantly affecting your lifestyle in the future.

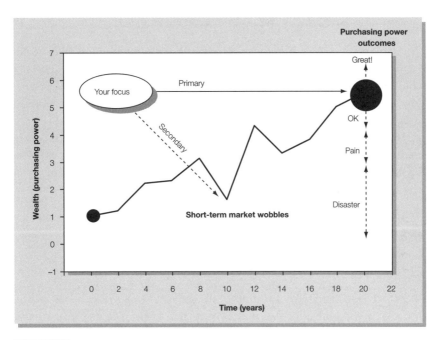

figure 9.1 Focus primarily on outcomes not interim market wobbles

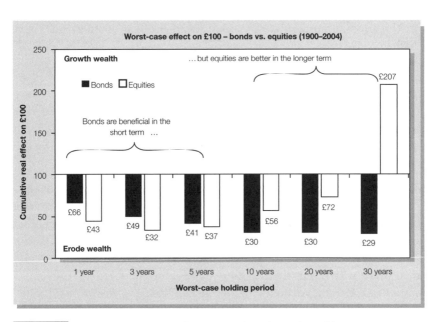

figure 9.2 Worst-case trade-off between bonds and equities

Source: DMS Global Data (Ibbotson) © 2006 E Dimson, P Marsh and M Staunton

The trade-off between equities and bonds

The trade-off you face is between protecting your downside in the shorter term by adding bonds against the long-term return that you potentially could have achieved by owning more equities; equities seem to do a better job than bonds of protecting your wealth in worst-case longer-term outcomes – well they have done over the past century or so, as you can see in Figure 9.2. If you can't live with the short-term consequences of equity market crashes then you need more bonds in your portfolio at the expense of the long-term upside. If you can survive these periods reasonably well then don't buy unwanted insurance by putting too much in bonds.

At the end of the day, investing always carries a risk that you will not be successful; a fact of life that we all need to contend with.

9.2 Rules of thumb to decide your mix

Many advisors use rules of thumb to decide what mix makes sense. While broadly useful, the problem is that they fail to provide any real understanding of what you are letting yourself in for. Invariably you have no feel for what your chances of success (or failure) are long term and little clue as to the magnitude and longevity of any market trauma that you might experience on the way and whether you would be able to stomach it. Below are three common rules that get you to a similar mix of equities and bonds.

Rule 1: a common-sense lifetime approach

The grid in Figure 9.3 is widely used in the industry to provide broad, common-sense parameters for establishing the mix between your core structural building blocks, although different practitioners use different mixes. It is only a generic guide and you need to reflect on your own circumstances and tolerances.

As you can see, investors starting out in the accumulation phase of their investing, with perhaps a thirty-year time-scale, should have a mix of building blocks that heavily favours equities. Conversely, an older investor who may be spending the fruits of his or her accumulation years may want to reduce their equity holdings to a more moderate 50 per cent or so, commensurate with their shorter time frame and the need to generate a sustainable income, without eroding the purchasing power of their capital. This is a reasonable starting point. You could do worse than to follow such these guidelines if you are saving for retirement and intend to take an income for your portfolio once you retire.

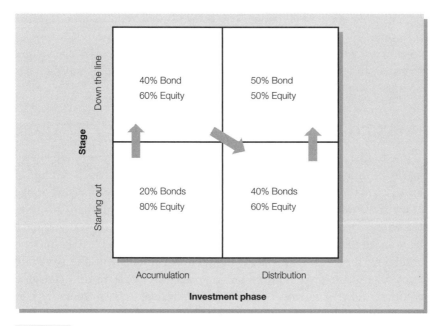

figure 9.3   Lifetime rules of thumb

Rule 2: 100 less your age = your equity allocation

This links the investment horizon to your age. For example, if you are thirty years old, you should have 70 per cent of your mix dedicated to equities and 30 per cent to bonds; fifty years old and this should be 50:50 and so on. A simple approach, but again it does not prepare you for the consequences of your decision.

Rule 3: your investment horizon times 4 per cent

Take your investment horizon and multiply by four; this is an approximate percentage of equities that you should hold in a portfolio. I have also seen this as 10 per cent a year but that seems far too bullish, suggesting a 50 per cent allocation for an investor with a five-year investment horizon. Using 4 per cent per year would suggest a 20 per cent allocation to equities for someone with five years to invest. You reach 100 per cent in equities at 25 years. Most long-term investors could probably benefit from at least a small exposure to bonds.

Again, this implies that the longer you have to invest, the less equity you need to give up to bonds, as you hopefully have time to recover from periods of equity market trauma. This rule of thumb reduces your exposure to equities as the end of your accumulation phase draws near; it is a useful approach if you intend to buy an annuity with your money for your retirement or if you need cash for any other reason at the end of your accumulation phase.

9.3 Making an informed choice

While these rules of thumb are useful, understanding why they are appropriate is important. One mistake that investors make is failing to understand the consequences of owning the portfolio they do. Lying awake at night worrying about your investments is either the sign that you are in the wrong type of portfolio, or that you don't understand what you have let yourself in for. Understanding and resolving the trade-off that you face and being able to live with the consequences is fundamental to surviving your investment programme intact and keeping those wealth-damaging emotions at bay. Remember – your fortitude will be tested at some stage in your investing.

As an example, many young investors in the 1990s looking to accumulate assets would rightly have had a high proportion of their assets in equities using any of the rules of thumb above. Many would only have experienced the strong bull market in equities, where the market nearly always went up, and when it didn't, it rebounded quickly to new highs. Yet between 2000 and 2002 they would have lost 30 per cent to 40 per cent of their purchasing power. The stress of losing money no doubt drove some to act emotionally and embark on the 'buy-high, sell-low' wealth-destroying strategy you read about earlier. Yet if they had understood at the outset that this was a possibility, resolved to hang on in and invest their regular contributions in now significantly cheaper assets (remember Warren Buffet's hamburgers in Chapter 5), then they would still be able to reap the long-term upside of their courage and their chosen mix.

Choosing a mix that is right for you

A powerful way of arriving at your portfolio mix uses an iterative process that allows you to compare the characteristics of different portfolios from all equities to all bonds. Table 9.1 is a simple tool that allows you to do so, providing you with a feel for the likelihood of success or failure and the really rotten times that investors have had to endure in the past and may well have to do so again. In fact, this table is one of the most important in the book (along with Table 6.4). Study it and try and work out how you feel about the trade-offs.

You should start by choosing the column that most closely matches your investment horizon and your outlook, which we explored when you were establishing your goals. It defines a generically appropriate mix of equities and bonds that can at least be a starting point in the process. By and large, the longer you have to invest, the greater your bias to equities should potentially be. Run down this column through each of the different headings to get a feel for the characteristics of this mix. Decide whether it provides you with the upside you are looking for and whether you could live with it when times get tough. If not, then choose another mix and see whether this gives you a better trade-off.

At the end of the day, your personal circumstances in terms of your job, business, debt levels, family responsibilities, etc, will influence your choice. Only you can decide what is right for you.

What do you see?

On the upside, you can see that by owning a higher level of equities, you have the chance of generating higher levels of returns. Remembering that using average returns leaves you with a high chance (50 per cent) that you will not achieve your goals, Table 9.1 provides an estimate of the minimum level of return that you have a fairly high chance of achieving (80 per cent likelihood) to help you out. Remember that you need to factor in the cost of owning investments and that keeping costs to a minimum is important. The more important it is to meet your goals, the more prudent you should be with the return you expect.

On the downside, while a possibility exists with all portfolios that you could lose money, you can see that the longer you have to invest, the lower the chances are that you will, as building blocks begin to act more like their generalisations than their exceptions. With twenty or more years to invest, you can see that the chances of losing money drop to manageable levels for most people. Owning a balance between bonds and equities reduces the chances of losing money. Owning some bonds can help to mitigate the effects of equity market crashes, although rarely as beneficially as in the early 2000s. Bonds tend to have a beneficial effect in lessening shorter-term market extremes, but in the long run, equities seem to do a better job of preserving wealth. Only you can decide the balance that makes sense for you.

table 9.1 **Use an iterative approach to determine your mix**

Your investment horizon and possible portfolio mixes

| 30-year horizon   Possibility ◄————————————► Consequence |
| 20-year horizon   ◄——————► |
| 10-year horizon   ◄————————► |
| 5-year horizon   ◄——————————► |

Equity/bond mix starting point

Equity allocation %	100%	80%	60%	40%	20%	0%
Bond allocation %	0%	20%	40%	60%	80%	100%

Return expectations

Historic returns 1900–2004*:	5.4%	4.8%	4.1%	3.2%	2.3%	1.3%
Reasonable estimates:	5.0%	4.4%	3.8%	3.2%	2.6%	2.0%
80% chance over 10 years of:	>0%	>1%	>1%	>1%	>0%	*
80% chance over 20 years of:	>2%	>2%	>2%	>2%	>1%	>0%
80% chance over 30 years of:	>2%	>2%	>2%	>2%	>1%	>0%
Years to double your money:	14	16	19	23	28	36

* <80% chance of a positive return

Your chances of losing money

Over 5 years	30%	25%	25%	25%	30%	35%
Over 10 years	20%	15%	15%	15%	20%	25%
Over 20 years	10%	5%	5%	5%	10%	20%
Over 30 years	10%	5%	3%	3%	5%	15%

Equity market crashes (effect on £100)*

Market crash: 2000–2002	£60	£69	£79	£89	£100	£112
Market crash: 1972–1974	£29	£34	£39	£45	£51	£57

Shorter-term worst case*

1 year Annualised return	−57%	−52%	−47%	−41%	−36%	−34%
Effect on £100	£43	£48	£53	£59	£64	£66
3 years Annualised return	−31%	−29%	−26%	−24%	−22%	−21%
Effect on £100	£32	£36	£40	£44	£47	£49
5 years Annualised return	−18%	−16%	−15%	−13%	−13%	−16%
Effect on £100	£37	£41	£46	£50	£49	£41

Longer-term worst case*

10 years Annualised return	−6%	−7%	−8%	−9%	−10%	−11%
Effect on £100	£56	£50	£45	£40	£35	£30
20 years Annualised return	−2%	−2%	−3%	−4%	−5%	−6%
Effect on £100	£72	£61	£52	£43	£36	£30
30 years Annualised return	2%	2%	1%	−1%	−2%	−4%
Effect on £100	£207	£182	£128	£87	£54	£29

◄———— Compare ————►

Source: *DMS Global Data (Ibbotson) © 2006 E Dimson, P Marsh and M Staunton

The 105 years of data used covers some significant market extremes including periods of very high inflation. Perhaps in the future inflation will be better controlled, but don't bank on it. Getting a feel for what the worst-case outcome has been over your investment horizon and in between, is extremely useful. In our summer garden party analogy, this is like knowing there could be a severe thunderstorm in the middle of summer. Knowing that this is a possibility and deciding whether you can live with even the possibility is important.

Nominal versus real worst-case returns

For those of you who feel that the Bank of England has inflation in control I have included worst-case nominal (before inflation) returns (Table 9.2). Personally, I am not as confident as some that inflation will not rear its ugly head again over the period I will be investing for and I believe that it is prudent to factor in such a scenario. Remember that even low levels of inflation hurt over long periods of time. Owning bonds protects you quite well from short-term equity market trauma in nominal terms. Over thirty years bonds deliver positive nominal growth in your assets, growing £100 to £140 in a worst-case scenario – a seemingly reasonable downside.

table 9.2	Worst-case nominal returns (1900–2004)						
Your equity/bond mix							
Equity allocation %		100%	80%	60%	40%	20%	0%
Bond allocation %		0%	20%	40%	60%	80%	100%
Downside – worst case							
1 Year	Annualised return	−49%	−43%	−36%	−30%	−24%	−19%
	Effect on £100	£51	£57	£64	£70	£76	£81
3 Years	Annualised return	−23%	−20%	−17%	−15%	−13%	−11%
	Effect on £100	£46	£51	£57	£62	£67	£71
5 Years	Annualised return	−9%	−7%	−5%	−4%	−1%	−6%
	Effect on £100	£62	£69	£76	£83	£88	£74
10 Years	Annualised return	2%	1%	0%	−1%	0%	−2%
	Effect on £100	£117	£110	£102	£95	£95	£78
20 Years	Annualised return	4%	3%	2%	1%	1%	−1%
	Effect on £100	£219	£187	£159	£133	£111	£91
30 Years	Annualised return	4%	4%	4%	3%	3%	1%
	Effect on £100	£345	£318	£287	£254	£208	£140

Source: DMS Global Data (Ibbotson) © 2006 E Dimson, P Marsh and M Staunton

However, this is a money illusion, which is illustrated by comparing this with the worst-case thirty years for bonds in real terms, where £100 was turned into £29 (Table 9.1).

Looking deeper at your investment horizon

Let's look at the choices you face based on your own specific investment horizon. In the next few pages, you will find some additional analysis that focuses on investment horizons of thirty years, twenty years and ten years. Choose the horizon that suits your circumstances best. You may also want to consider the challenges that different investment horizons present. You are unlikely to see this sort of analysis elsewhere.

9.4 A thirty-year investment horizon

This section applies if your investment horizon is thirty years or more.

Your generic dilemma

You have a long-term investment horizon and the powers of compounding and time are both working in your favour. The dilemma is that you will inevitably need to weather some significant market trauma events. You need to decide if you can handle them or whether you need to buy some market trauma protection and give up some return of the wealth you could potentially create from equities. Some equity markets have taken thirty years to recover purchasing power back to pre-fall levels (see Chapter 15). Review the information below carefully, and try to resolve the trade-offs between your long-term goals and the risks of poor equity market returns in the interim. Refer back to Table 9.1 when necessary.

Understanding your chances of success

You can get a feel for the chances you have of growing a lump sum investment. Remember that if the chances of success are too low for you, then you will either need to make higher contributions to your portfolio or scale back your expectations. You can ask your portfolio to perform the impossible but you will have a high chance of being disappointed!

In Figure 9.4 below, you can see that you have a 90 per cent chance of making money with all equities and a 10 per cent chance of losing money (each notch on the vertical scale representing a 10 per cent chance). You

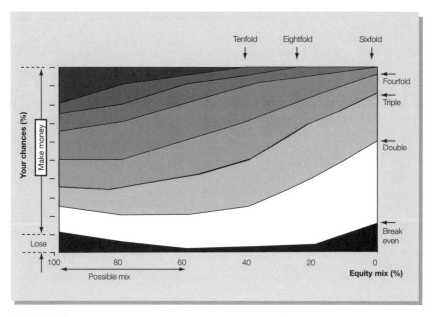

figure 9.4   **Your mix should be biased towards equities (30-year span)**

have a 75 per cent chance of doubling your money or better, which equates approximately to an annualised rate of return of 2 per cent an annum over thirty years. On the other hand, with 100 per cent in bonds (0 per cent equity), you can see that the chance of achieving doubling your money is around 50 per cent and the chance of losing money is 10 per cent or so. The upside with all bonds is significantly more limited than that for all equities. Study this diagram carefully as it tells you a lot about the choices you face.

Your chances of achieving a specific rate of return

You may be making regular contributions to a portfolio and as such will be more interested in the chances of achieving a specific rate of return, than the multiples of growth that a lump sum might achieve. Table 9.3 illustrates the chances of achieving specific annualised rates of returns for each port- folio mix over your investment horizon of 30 years. For example, you have a 70 per cent chance of achieving 3 per cent or better if you hold 100 per cent in equities.

You may wish to note that the numbers for an 80/20 mix (a reasonable portfolio choice) provide the thirty-year line in Table 6.4.

table 9.3	Chances of achieving specific real annualised returns over 30 years

	Equity/bond mix (%)					
Return	100/0	80/20	60/40	40/60	20/80	0/100
>10%	5%	1%	0%	0%	0%	0%
>9%	10%	5%	2%	0%	0%	0%
>8%	20%	10%	5%	1%	0%	0%
>7%	30%	20%	10%	5%	1%	0%
>6%	40%	30%	25%	10%	5%	1%
>5%	50%	45%	35%	25%	10%	5%
>4%	60%	60%	55%	45%	25%	10%
>3%	70%	75%	75%	65%	45%	25%
>2%	80%	85%	85%	80%	70%	50%
>1%	85%	90%	95%	90%	85%	70%
>0%	90%	95%	97%	97%	95%	85%
<0%	10%	5%	3%	3%	5%	15%

= Greater than 80% chance of achieving

Choosing a reasonable mix

You could argue that a reasonable portfolio would be 80 per cent in equities and 20 per cent in bonds. With this mix you have a very high chance of generating 2 per cent (around 80 per cent chance), a reasonable chance of generating returns of 3–5 per cent and a 50 per cent or so chance of generating 5 per cent or better. A slim possibility exists, of around 5 per cent, that in your investing lifetime equity returns will be terrible and some of your purchasing power will be eroded. That's unfortunately the nature of the game.

Conclusions for a thirty-year horizon

■ The mantra 'equities for the long run' has both logic and history on its side.

■ A bias towards equities will give you a good chance to grow your purchasing power. But all rules have exceptions.

■ You should probably own some high-quality domestic bonds to dampen short-term periods of equity market trauma and look to find other ways of diversifying your equity exposure, without giving up too large a portion of their returns, perhaps by using additional building blocks (Chapter 10).

■ If you are, for example, investing for your pension and cannot get
your hands on the money before you retire, you should seriously
consider riding out shorter-term storms for the long-term gains that
you have a good chance of accumulating.

■ Remember though that in such a case, your investment horizon may
be decreasing and you will need to change your allocation over time.
See 'lifecycle' investing later in this chapter.

■ A suggested mix is 80 per cent in equities and 20 per cent in bonds.
Less if you are consequence-orientated and really can't stomach severe
equity market trauma either psychologically or financially; more if you
are possibility-orientated and can live with the downside.

9.5   A twenty-year horizon

This section applies to you if your investment horizon is around twenty
years.

Your generic dilemma

You have a reasonably long investment horizon and are likely to be able to
weather most short-term market downturns. Owning some bonds may help
to reduce the severity of short-term falls in your wealth, but owning too

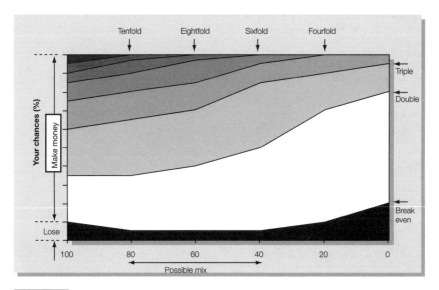

figure 9.5   **Your mix should be biased towards equities (20-year span)**

much can be costly in the long run. While most markets falls are recovered within this time frame, some are not. If this happened, could you survive it? If you can, bias your portfolio towards equities, if not own more bonds and other return-smoothing building blocks.

Understanding your chances of success

A twenty-year horizon allows you have a significant equity bias, balanced to some extent by some bonds (Figure 9.5).

The chances of achieving a specific rate of return

While Figure 9.5 gives the outcomes of a lump sum investment, you may be making regular contributions to a portfolio and will be interested in the chances of achieving a specific annualised return. Table 9.4 provides a feel for the chances of achieving certain returns for each portfolio mix over your twenty-year investment horizon.

The chances of achieving a 4 per cent return are relatively constant at around 50 per cent to 60 per cent likelihood, with between 80 per cent and 40 per cent of your portfolio in equities. Fortunately too, your chances of

table 9.4   Chances of achieving specific real annualised returns over 20 years

| | Equity/bond mix (%) | | | | | |
Return	100/0	80/20	60/40	40/60	20/80	0/100
>10%	10%	5%	1%	0%	0%	0%
>9%	15%	10%	5%	1%	0%	0%
>8%	20%	15%	10%	5%	1%	0%
>7%	30%	25%	15%	10%	2%	1%
>6%	35%	30%	25%	15%	5%	2%
>5%	50%	45%	40%	25%	15%	10%
>4%	60%	60%	55%	45%	30%	20%
>3%	70%	70%	70%	60%	45%	25%
>2%	80%	80%	80%	80%	70%	50%
>1%	85%	90%	90%	90%	80%	65%
>0%	90%	95%	95%	95%	90%	80%
<0%	10%	5%	5%	5%	10%	20%

= Greater than 80% chance of achieving

suffering a loss to your purchasing power is low at around 5 per cent with a well-balanced portfolio.

Choosing a reasonable portfolio mix

As you can see, somewhere in the region of 60 per cent in equities is not unreasonable and provides you with only a small risk that you will lose money, although this has happened in some twenty-year periods in the UK and certainly elsewhere. A well-balanced portfolio will serve most investors well.

Conclusions for a twenty-year investor

- Twenty years is a reasonable time period for the return-generating and inflation-protecting properties of equities to come to the fore. However, prolonged market trauma is a risk.

- The greatest challenge is being able to survive the periods of down markets that could significantly erode your purchasing power.

- If the consequences of this interim trauma are too great for you, then you should own a higher level of bonds. Be prepared to trade off a potentially higher level of future spending power for a smoother ride.

- Suggested mix: around 60 per cent in equities. However, you need to make sure that you can emotionally and financially weather periods of market stress and the associated bumpiness of your ride.

9.6   A ten-year horizon

This section applies to you if your investment horizon is around ten years.

Your generic dilemma

You have a reasonable time period to invest, but you are getting into the territory where an overexposure to equities could leave you in a significant hole if the market crashes and fails to recover, despite the fact that in the past equity markets have frequently recovered in ten years. An even balance between bonds and equities makes sense. The risk of bonds ownership is predominantly that of significant and unexpected increases in inflation and you could look to mitigate this risk by owning index-linked bonds that provide protection from inflation – more on that in Chapter 10.

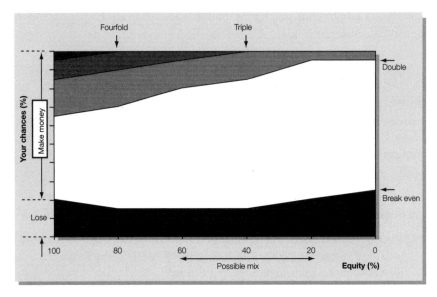

figure 9.6   **A well-balanced mix helps to reduce the chance of losses (over 10 years)**

Understanding the chances of success

As you can see from Figure 9.6, the risk of losing money has increased significantly compared with a thirty-year or twenty-year horizon, across all mixes. The nature of your portfolio should be one of balance and realism, as ten years doesn't give your portfolio that much time to benefit from the effects of compounding or to reflect the general characteristics of bonds and equities. Your chances of doubling your assets or better are not that great – you may get lucky and have strong returns, but don't bank on it. If you want a larger pool of assets then put more aside in your investment programme.

The chances of achieving a specific rate of return

Figure 9.6 illustrates the outcomes for a lump sum investment, but you may be making regular contributions to a portfolio and will be interested in the chances of achieving a specific annualised rate of return. Table 9.5 provides a feel for the chances of achieving certain returns for each portfolio mix over a ten-year investment horizon.

The chances of achieving a 3 per cent return are relatively constant at around 50 per cent to 60 per cent likelihood with between 60 per cent and

table 9.5	Chances of achieving specific real annualised returns over 10 years

	Equity bond mix (%)					
Return	100/0	80/20	60/40	40/60	20/80	0/100
>10%	20%	15%	5%	3%	1%	0%
>9%	25%	20%	10%	5%	2%	1%
>8%	30%	25%	15%	10%	5%	2%
>7%	35%	30%	25%	15%	10%	5%
>6%	45%	40%	35%	25%	15%	10%
>5%	50%	45%	45%	35%	20%	15%
>4%	55%	55%	50%	45%	35%	25%
>3%	60%	65%	65%	55%	50%	35%
>2%	70%	70%	70%	70%	60%	50%
>1%	75%	80%	80%	80%	75%	60%
>0%	80%	85%	85%	85%	80%	75%
<0%	20%	15%	15%	15%	20%	25%

▓ = Greater than 80% chance of achieving

20 per cent of your portfolio in equities, although you have a meaningful chance that you could suffer a loss to your purchasing power. The chances of a loss can be reduced with a well-balanced mix between bonds and equities. Again, you may wish to consider using index-linked bonds to protect against rises in inflation.

Choosing a reasonable portfolio mix

A reasonable mix of investments would be somewhere around 40 per cent to 60 per cent in equities and the rest in bonds; 40 per cent would be consistent with the third rule of thumb, provided at the start of the chapter.

Conclusions for a ten-year investor

■ Your dilemma is that over a relatively short period in investing terms, there are quite a few periods when markets have fallen and failed to recover.

■ With ten years to invest, you can still afford to retain a reasonable equity exposure.

■ Don't expect too much from your investments. You will need a real return of 7 per cent to double your money over this period, which is well above the long-run average real return of a 40/60 equity/bond portfolio.

■ In a raging bull market you might get lucky, but don't bank on one. In fact, you only have about a one in ten chance of doubling your money or better. In this context, the 1980s and 1990s were exceptional periods.

■ Suggested mix: around 40 per cent in equities. Up to 60 per cent if you are prepared to trade off the chances of higher returns for a higher level of short-term volatility and the small chance that you might suffer a prolonged market downturn and recovery period.

9.7 A five-year horizon

The short investment horizon limits your choices and you should err on the side of caution, unless you can financially and emotionally accept a gamble that has a high chance of not coming off. You should be focused more on saving wealth than increasing wealth.

■ However tempting it is to own higher levels of equities, hoping to get lucky during your five years is a gamble, not an investment strategy. Only play this game if you can afford to get it wrong.

■ Your worst case could be severe, but 80 per cent to 100 per cent in bonds will help to limit short-term losses, particularly if inflation is stable and stays within anticipated ranges.

■ If you are very concerned about inflation, you have the option of purchasing index-linked gilts and holding them to maturity in five years' time. These bonds guarantee a low real return of 1 per cent to 2 per cent a year and your original purchasing power is returned to you at maturity.

■ Suggested target: 20 per cent in equities and 80 per cent in bonds – possibly index-linked. If you are comfortable that inflation is in control you will probably do marginally better by being in normal bonds. That's a trade-off you need to consider. Overall, be sensible and conservative and don't expect too much other than protecting your money and the contributions you make from inflation.

■ For some, investing in a structured product that provides a guarantee of return of your nominal capital (remember that 3 per cent inflation a year eats into your spending power pretty quickly) and gives you some participation in any upwards movement in equities, could be an option. This may appeal, for example, to someone approaching retirement, who wants to limit their downside but perhaps provide a boost to returns. Over a five-year period, you have a two in three chance that equities will be positive. You choose.

9.8 A 'lifecycle' approach to investing

If you are in the accumulation phase of an investment programme, your investment horizon may be constantly decreasing towards a fixed date in the future when you need cash, such as the day the kids go to university and need funding, or the day you retire and need cash to buy an annuity. As a consequence, your mix needs to change over time in order to maximise the returns that you can achieve while minimising the risk that you will be left at this landmark point with less funds than you require. The more critical these funds are to you, the more certain you need to be about their existence when you need them. As your investment horizon decreases, so, as a general rule, should your bias towards equities.

Figure 9.7 takes the suggested portfolios for each investment time horizons provided previously, illustrating the changing mix of assets in your portfolio. Your mix should reflect your shortening horizon and tolerance for short-term market volatility, such as the period 2000–2002. This figure includes index-linked bonds as part of the bond allocation. Owning these

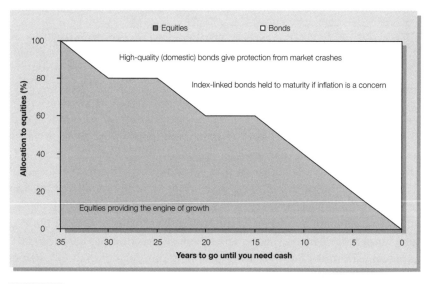

figure 9.7   The mix should change as your horizon shortens

inflation-linked bonds to maturity is the only sure way to protect your money's purchasing power. If the funds are critical then you may want to consider this strategy. You may be able to effect this *lifecycle* transition by redirecting new contributions into bonds, rather than selling equities. This makes particular sense if this money is taxable (i.e. outside a pension plan or ISA). You only need to ask one of the many people approaching retirement who had too much money in the equity markets in 2000 with five years or less to go, how painful not thinking this through properly can be.

The rate of return is hard to compute

When you established the financial goals for your portfolio, you choose a rate of return that had a fair chance of occurring (Table 6.4). This chance was based on investing over the whole horizon in the suggested mix of assets. However, in the case here, where you need the cash at the end of your investment horizon, and your mix changes significantly over time, your rate of return is likely to be lower in later years. In addition, the level of your assets benefiting from the longer time period and higher rate of return is lower, as this is at the start of your programme.

Computing your investment horizon rate of return is complex and this issue is best resolved by lowering your overall expected rate of return, and contributing more to your portfolio during the investment programme. Remember the rule of thumb: save 20 per cent of your gross income throughout your life for an acceptable retirement.

9.9 Drawing an income from your portfolio

As your investing moves from the accumulation phase to the distribution phase, the questions that concern you move from being those related to pool size, contribution levels and your chances of getting there, to questions relating to the income you need, and the rate of withdrawal that allows you to sustain this level of purchasing power over time. A classic example is a portfolio that provides income in retirement. The scenario is different from the one above, in that you do not need cash at the end of the accumulation phase, but you may decide to modify your portfolio so that it has a sensible balance between bonds and equities with a good chance of generating solid real returns over the remainder of your life and providing a stable income. For many investors it is critical to be able to take an income from the portfolio without risking running out of money before they die. The three main linked questions that you need to answer in this case are:

■ How much income should I withdraw?

■ What are the chances of running out of money before I die at this level of withdrawal?

■ What mix of investments is best suited to delivering this?

Rule of thumb

Understanding what chance you have of eroding all your capital and running out of money before you die is critical in deciding how much income you can take from your portfolio. An industry rule of thumb is that you should withdraw 4 per cent at most from a portfolio balanced between 40 per cent and 60 per cent in equities, with the rest in bonds. The logic behind this is that if equities return around 5 per cent real returns on average and bonds around 2 per cent then your real portfolio's rate of return is approximately 4 per cent. If your portfolio returned 4 per cent in real terms, every year without fail, you could be confident that this strategy would work, but you know that real life is not like that.

What strategy will be successful?

Again, we can use a multiple-life, Monte Carlo simulation to try and get a handle on this. This time, costs of 0.5 per cent have been deducted, being about the cheapest cost of replicating the markets in the UK. This simulation assumes that you are going to live for at least 30 years, which is not unreasonable, and that you don't intend to take the risk of spending your capital. This is a fair and prudent assumption to make for many investors.

Take a look at Figure 9.8 below. The percentage figure on the right shows the annual rate of withdrawal as a percentage of the value of the portfolio. To read the chart, choose a withdrawal rate line, say 4 per cent per year. For example, with no equities, i.e. 100 per cent bonds, you can see on the left-hand vertical axis that the chance of having enough money is only 50 per cent, whereas with 100 per cent equities it is 75 per cent. Both of these may be unacceptable to you and a lower rate of income withdrawal may be required to increase the chances of success. If you look at a 3 per cent withdrawal rate, there is a 95 per cent chance of having enough money with 40 per cent to 60 per cent in equities. You may infer from Figure 9.8 that the 4 per cent rule of thumb may be a little aggressive for some.

If you wish to maintain the purchasing power of your portfolio over time and thus have an inflation-protected income then a withdrawal rate of 3–4

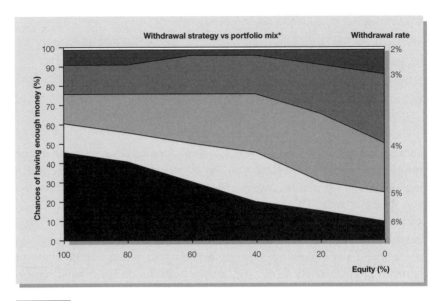

figure 9.8 **Withdrawal rates and portfolio mix are both important**

per cent, maximum, probably makes more sense. In real life, if you seem to be suffering continued losses on your portfolio, you can always see if there is room for tightening the purse strings and reining in your spending. Build this into the equation when you are establishing your goals.

If you intend to use your capital up over a number of years, you can withdraw at a higher rate from your portfolio. You will need to be careful though as a couple of bad years can dent the size of a portfolio and you may risk running out of money too soon. You can find the details of a simple calculator to test out your assumptions, in the Bibliography.

9.10 Finally, wise words from a respected investor

By minimising your allocation to high-quality domestic bonds, you reduce the premiums you pay and leave room to diversify further, as succinctly put by David Swensen of the Yale Endowment:

'Sensible investors focus on the superior diversifying characteristics of long-term government bonds, holding only the amount necessary to protect portfolios against financial trauma. If portfolios include the minimum allocation necessary to provide insurance against catastrophe, investors free up assets to

diversify into alternative asset classes, achieving volatility reduction without sacrificing return.'

You may find that owning these two core building blocks in your portfolio will be sufficient to allow you to plan a suitable long-term and manageable investment portfolio. This is the main decision that you must make and, hopefully, by now you will have a pretty fair idea of what it means for you. On the other hand, you may wish to make use of other building blocks to diversify short-term market trauma further and/or add additional returns to your portfolio. If so, read on.

9.11 Summary: getting the mix right

■ This is the primary decision that you face as an investor because it determines the upside and downside characteristics of your portfolio. The asset allocation (mix) drives the bulk of the returns that a portfolio will make. Time spent thinking about this and deciding how you resolve the trade-offs is time well spent.

■ Try and focus on the chances of achieving a successful outcome, before worrying about the bumpiness of the road that takes you there.

■ Your investment horizon helps to define a generic mix between equities and bonds that at least puts you in the right ballpark. Simple rules of thumb can help.

■ Start the iterative process of deciding what mix makes most sense for you by seeing what chances you have of growing your purchasing power, or achieving a certain level of return and what the risk is of losing money over this investment horizon with each mix.

■ Carefully review the historic ranges of return over the past one hundred years or so to give yourself a feel for what to expect if times get rough.

■ Take a close look at the worst-case scenarios over different periods. Over longer time frames, equities have provided better returns than bonds, but over shorter periods, their returns can be significantly worse than for bonds.

■ Therefore, own bonds to mitigate this shorter-term equity market trauma, but remember that the premiums that you pay will be high for the cover you receive. Understand and accept the trade-offs that you make.

■ If your investing programme is counting down to a finite point in time when you need cash, you should change your mix accordingly.

■ Withdraw a maximum income of 4 per cent from a well-balanced portfolio to give yourself a good chance of not running out of money during your retirement.

References

Swenson, D. F. (2000) *Pioneering portfolio management*. New York: The Free Press.

10

A portfolio for all seasons

In Chapters 7 to 9, we focused on building a sensible and eminently workable portfolio for you using just two building blocks – domestic equities and high-quality domestic bonds. For many investors, that is sufficient; it is easy to implement, monitor and manage over time. There is a real effectiveness in such simplicity.

The opportunity does exist, however, for you to refine your chosen equity/bond mix further, creating a portfolio that has a good chance of seeing you through the wide variety of circumstances that could well occur over your investment lifetime. This is Step 2 we referred to in Chapter 7.

You only need to look back at the past thirty years or so to register just what might be thrown at you and your portfolio. We've had oil crises, war, terrorism, rampant inflation, low inflation, two equity market crashes, irrational exuberance in the dotcom world and the housing market, and the recent spectre of deflation, to name a few. It doesn't seem unreasonable to think that it makes sense to cover a few of these bases. You have the opportunity to build a portfolio for all seasons. As ever, in investing there are no right or wrong answers, just those that probably give you a better chance of surviving with your investment programme intact. It is worth bearing in mind the words of John Bogle:

'Asset allocation [your mix of building blocks] is not a panacea. It is a reasoned – if imperfect – approach to the inevitable uncertainty of the financial markets.'

And as William Bernstein succinctly agrees:

'Since the future cannot be predicted, it is impossible to specify in advance what the best asset allocation will be. Rather, our job is to find an allocation that will do reasonably well under a wide range of circumstances.'

10.1 Creating a diverse portfolio

If you look up the meaning of the word 'diversify' in the Oxford English
Dictionary, you will see that it means to: *'Introduce variety into, redeem from
uniformity or monotony'*. Many people intuitively and rightly feel that they
should diversify their investments, spreading their investment eggs around
a number of baskets. Recent history illustrates why this makes sense and
provides an example when those who had invested in a wide array of
investment building blocks benefited significantly, as you can see in Figure
10.1. On the other hand, many of the big pension plans and insurance
companies failed to do so and held surprisingly high levels of equities that
were out of line with their liabilities, which is surprising given the level of
their responsibility and their access to professional advice. An investor who
spread his or her eggs around with, say, equal levels of equities, bonds, real
estate and commodities would have gained over 10 per cent during this
period when equities were down by almost 40 per cent; now that is a good
result at such a difficult time. I am not saying that this is the mix for you,
or that you will be so lucky every time, but it provides an example of how
spreading your investment eggs around can be beneficial, on occasion.

The effects of owning a diverse portfolio are not always, or even usually, so
beneficial and indeed a day may come when all building blocks crash
together – it is possible, as in Figure 10.2. It is also widely observed that

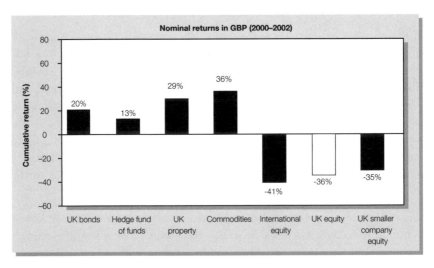

figure 10.1 **Great results happen sometimes**

Source: UK Equities and Bonds – DMS Global Data (Ibbotson) © Copyright E Dimson, P Marsh and M Staunton, UK
Small Companies – HGSC Index: International Equity – MSCI World ex-UK: Commodities – Dow Jones AIG Commodities
Index: UK Property – IPD All Property Index: Hedge Fund of Funds – CISDM Hedge fund of fund median

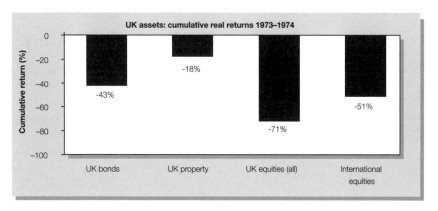

figure 10.2 **Spreading your eggs around helps but is not always perfect**

Source: UK equities and Bonds – DMS Global Data (Ibbotson) © Copyright E Dimson, P Marsh and M Staunton; UK
Property – IPD All property Index: International Equities – MSCI World ex-UK

some building blocks that don't seem that related in normal circumstances end up being highly related in the return patterns they deliver during times of shocking markets.

The challenge is to put together a mix of building blocks that covers a number of different bases that does not blow your Level 1 mix of equities and bonds out of the water. You will need some skilful substitution of these blocks by those you introduce. As you will see below, there are two approaches: one is to use some simple rules and common sense that take into account the expected returns, bumpiness of the ride, and the interrelationship of the block being added with equities and bonds. The other approach is to throw all the building blocks into a software-based mixing tool that spits out a combination of blocks that you can choose from (or pay someone to do this for you). This approach is covered in Chapter 11.

Covering the bases

Keeping in mind that your goal is to build a portfolio for all seasons, let's take a quick look at some of the circumstances and risks that exist and pick out which building blocks appear to have the ability to mitigate them.

Investing is a very personal business and I cannot tell you which you should include; for example, if you are particularly worried by inflation, it would make sense to allocate a significant proportion of your portfolio to building blocks that seem to do a good job protecting you from it – index-linked bonds, property, equities and commodities – as you can see below.

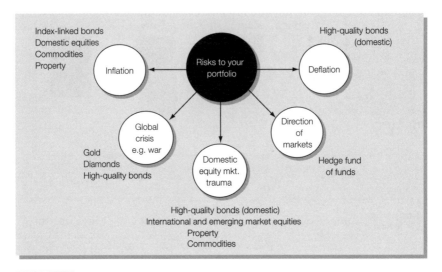

figure 10.3 **Covering the bases**

In your equity/bond mix, you have a return driver in domestic equities, which gives protection in the longer term by delivering around 5 per cent after inflation, but with a bumpy and at times viciously bumpy ride. Adding high-quality domestic bonds, which have an inherently less bumpy ride than equities, dampens this ride. Let's take a look at these risks in a little more detail (Figure 10.3).

Inflation eats away at your wealth

As you know, inflation is the scourge of long-term investors and adding protection against it should be on your radar screen. The high-quality domestic bonds you own are susceptible to periods of unanticipated inflation as the coupons become insufficient to compensate investors for the higher level of inflation and bond prices fall to compete with newly issued bonds that reflect the latest level of inflation.

The risk of deflation

Deflation, i.e. when prices fall rather than rise, is a rare but punitive risk that all investors face. Companies' performance and thus share prices tend to suffer as consumers delay making purchases, anticipating further price falls. An example of deflation has been seen in Japan over the past decade. The residual value of corporate assets also falls, including the value of property. As mentioned above, high-quality domestic bonds do a good job in protecting against deflation.

Domestic equity market trauma

Owning equities can give you a vicious kick at times when the markets decide that the price it is prepared to pay for future earning is too high. The combination of economic and speculative pressures can result in some very sharp and painful episodes such as 2000–2002 and 1972–1974 where markets fell by 40 per cent and 70 per cent respectively. Added protection can come from a number of different building blocks – a combination of them may be worth considering.

Times of global crisis

Market trauma caused by a global event, such as the prospect of a widespread war or another Cuban missile crisis is always a possibility. In the past, money has frequently flowed into safe assets such as government bonds and hard assets, such as gold and diamonds, when this spectre looms.

Direction of market returns

This last category of risk is a bit more esoteric, and certainly more controversial. A portfolio that is made up of a number of building blocks, will, despite its diverse nature, reflect the aggregate market movements that it consists of. If at times of market crisis they all fall as one, then your portfolio could suffer losses, as investors found out in the crash of 1974. How do you protect yourself from this happening?

We will explore in a moment how each of the building blocks can help. First, let's take a deeper look at the concept of diversification.

10.2 A free lunch from Harry Markovitz

When you come to add additional building blocks to your portfolio, and thus give up part of the allocation that you have made to equities and bonds, the challenge is doing so in a way that provides coverage of the bases that are important to you without destroying your initial return expectations and your ability to tolerate the bumpiness of the road ahead. Hopefully, you can improve the trade-off between return and the bumpiness of the ride with a bit of thought.

While each building block has, individually, an expected level of return and a certain level of bumpiness of its returns, when you add them into a portfolio, the portfolio behaves differently from a pro-rata sum of its characteristics, improving the relationship between return and risk (i.e. bumpiness – or volatility – of returns). This is due to the interrelationships that exist between the return patterns of different building blocks. Putting a portfolio together with two building blocks as you did to create your core mix is relatively easy because you are only dealing with one interrelationship, that between equities and bonds. With two blocks you have one interrelationship between their return patterns, with five you have ten and with ten blocks you have forty-five. So, working with ten building blocks gets complicated when you are looking for the 'best mix'. As you add a block, you change these interrelationships and the effect on risk and return of the portfolio.

This phenomenon of being able to increase the return of a portfolio without increasing its bumpiness, or keeping the same level of return and decreasing the bumpiness, was first explored by Harry Markovitz in the 1950s (Markovitz, 1952). Its underlying concept – Modern Portfolio Theory – still lies at the centre of much investment industry thinking. He demonstrated how investors are able to reduce the bumpiness of the ride by selecting investments whose return patterns do not move perfectly in step with one another. Simply put, you can smooth portfolio returns by owning blocks that are zigging, while other blocks you own are zagging, without giving up return. The more they zig and zag without relationship to each other the better. This is in known as *'diversification'*.

Put another way, Markovitz demonstrated that you could add a higher risk building block to a lower risk building block, and up to a point, you could

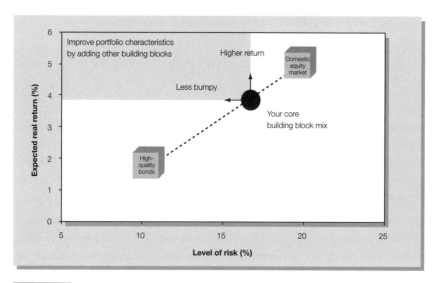

figure 10.4 **Taking advantage of the free lunch on offer**

increase returns without adding any more risk (Figure 10.4). That's the remarkable property of well constructed portfolios, so building one that takes advantage, wherever possible, of this quality makes sense – it is the only free lunch in investing and represents the free cover provided in the small print in our insurance policy analogy in Chapter 7.

Markovitz wrote a quadratic equation that works out the risk and return for a portfolio made up from a number of building blocks, using the return and risk dimensions for each block and the degree to which each block's pattern of returns are related to every other block. He won a Nobel Prize for his efforts. His equation allowed other smart people to develop software that could work out the best (or most *efficient* – in industry speak) portfolio, in terms of risk and return, for every level of risk, using an iterative process to calculate many portfolios until the most 'efficient' was found for each point.

For those of you who are interested, Chapter 11 provides an insight into the pros and cons of using these tools. It is, though, important to realise that this mathematics forms the basis for most asset allocation models on investment websites, or are provided by your investment manager or private banker. Understanding them allows you to challenge their outputs. Just because the pie chart of investments looks pretty, it does not mean that the outcome for you will be.

> **Correlation – The zig and zag of two building blocks' returns**
> If you compare the pattern of returns between two building blocks, you can get a measure of the degree to which they are similar. This statistical measure of this similarity (or otherwise) of returns between two blocks is known as its *correlation coefficient*. This ranges from 1 where two building blocks have returns that move identically together; and is known as *perfect correlation*. When building blocks have a correlation of –1, they are said to be *inversely correlated* and their returns move in the opposite direction with the same magnitude. Pairs of building blocks whose returns bear no relationship to on another are said to be uncorrelated with a correlation coefficient of 0.

In the real world, a free snack is probably a better description

In an ideal world, you would look for building blocks whose pattern of returns bear no relationship to other blocks in your portfolio (in this case they are said to be uncorrelated). If, for example, you could find a building

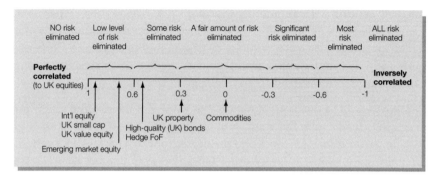

figure 10.5 **In the real world we have to make do**

block where this were true in relation to equities, which generated the same levels of return and risk, you could reduce the level of bumpiness in the level of your wealth over a quarter, by combining them in equal parts. Find four such blocks and you would halve the bumpiness of your ride – and all this without giving up any return at all. Don't spend too much time looking though because you aren't going for find more than one, or at most two. That comes down to the fact that these building blocks need to be uncorrelated with each other to achieve this effect and four blocks require all six interrelationships (possible pairs of blocks) to be unrelated. In reality though, very few building blocks have returns entirely unrelated to those of equities.

Figure 10.5 shows the effect that different correlations have in smoothing the bumpiness of the ride of a domestic equity portfolio, from a diversification perspective. Of course, some building blocks have lower levels of risk that add further dampening of returns and some have higher levels of risk that add further risk to the portfolio, overpowering the diversification benefit at some point.

You can see that other equity building blocks provide little diversification benefit, and most other blocks only provide limited diversification benefits. A common mistake is to believe that they provide significant levels of assistance. Thinking that you will significantly diversify your equity exposure simply by adding some international equities is likely to leave you disappointed at times of market trauma. All in all, it's hard to find building blocks that provide significant levels of diversification, but you should try and make the best of what there is to play with.

10.3 A practical framework for adding building blocks

Unless you are particularly bright, and have a couple of weeks to spare testing multiple portfolios combinations using Markovitz's quadratic equation in your head, we need to come up with a straightforward way of adding building blocks. We are going to do that in a few simple steps; first we will narrow the menu; second we will categorise them into the roles that they play to help you determine how to use them; and then we will create some simple rules for using them in your portfolio so the bumpiness of the ride and your return expectations will at the very least remain the same as when you started out, but hopefully will be improved. You will also find some portfolio structures to consider that provide possible portfolios for all seasons.

Narrow your choices

First, the choice of building blocks is wide; no doubt at some time or another, you will have read articles or heard some commentator expounding the virtues of investing in China, Japan, hedge funds, emerging markets, property, fine wines, vintage cars, gold, forestry plantations, venture capital trusts and so on. You need a way of deciding what each block brings to the party, which you should add to your portfolio and in what quantity. We will develop a simple framework for doing so in the next few pages. As part of this simple process, let's start by creating a short list of building blocks you should consider. We already have domestic equities and high-quality domestic bonds which we will call our Level 1 assets.

The next building blocks to consider are based on these criteria: their data set is reasonable, so you have an indication of what their characteristics are; the role they could play in your portfolio is reasonably distinct; and success lies in capturing these characteristics easily through accessible and cheap investment vehicles. Let's call these Level 2 building blocks. The exception is hedge fund of funds, which we will explore in Chapter 17.

Other building blocks we will call Level 3 building blocks and these should be left to the most sophisticated and interested readers. Issues exist that make them less attractive to the individual investor: for some, their characteristics are either unproven or not particularly useful to your portfolio; others, such as private equity have access, liquidity and manager selection issues that inhibit their usefulness to the individual investor (Figure 10.6).

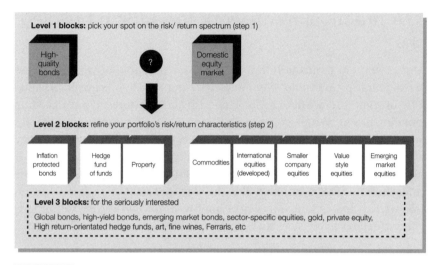

Level 1 blocks: pick your spot on the risk/ return spectrum (step 1)

High-quality bonds

?

Domestic equity market

Level 2 blocks: refine your portfolio's risk/return characteristics (step 2)

Inflation protected bonds | Hedge fund of funds | Property | Commodities | International equities (developed) | Smaller company equities | Value style equities | Emerging market equities

Level 3 blocks: for the seriously interested

Global bonds, high-yield bonds, emerging market bonds, sector-specific equities, gold, private equity, High return-orientated hedge funds, art, fine wines, Ferraris, etc

figure 10.6 Building blocks categorised by decision-making level

The menu of opportunity in Level 2 is ample for most investors. Some may question this selection, but that is their prerogative. These choices can be easily defended and make sense for the individual investor. You may decide that you want to consider one or more Level 3 building blocks; fine, that's your call, but I would just recommend that you do it after you are totally happy with your Level 2 decisions. That leaves you with a workable armoury to improve your portfolio with. A well-spread portfolio can be achieved by using a limited number of building blocks. It's really a question of applying the 80/20 rule: 80 per cent of the benefit for 20 per cent of the effort. Don't overcomplicate things unless you love the intellectual challenge.

Decide what roles each building block plays

With the choices narrowed down, you can more or less forget about anything else that is thrown up at you by the media, managers, or on a whim, takes your fancy. To complete our framework for thinking about how you can get the most out of these building blocks, it would be useful if we could somehow categorise these blocks by the role they can play. Earlier in this chapter, we identified a few of the risks that you may well face over the life of your investment programme and how different building blocks can help to mitigate them to some degree.

We can refine this further and look at building blocks in terms of the return characteristics they bring to a portfolio, the pattern of return bumpiness

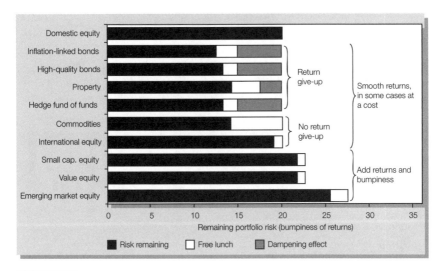

figure 10.7 **The primary role is either one of smoothing returns or adding returns**

(volatility) they have on their own, and the degree to which they provide a free lunch when added to a portfolio. Take a close look at Figure 10.7. Here, half a domestic equity portfolio has been substituted with each building block in turn to see what effect it has. For example, the line marked 'inflation-linked bonds' is half domestic equities and half inflation-linked bonds. It shows the degree to which the bumpiness of returns is affected either because the building block being added has a lower (or higher) level of return bumpiness in the first place, or because the pattern of returns is out of step with equities to some degree, and you get a free snack (i.e. a diversification benefit).

It is unlikely that you will be substituting half of your equity allocation with a single building block, but it does at least provide an indication of the roles and the degree to which the bumpiness of your portfolio's returns will be affected.

Some blocks (bonds, index-linked bonds, hedge funds, property), because their returns are less volatile than equity returns in the first place, provide a dampening effect on portfolio returns, but at a cost of lower returns; they also provide additional reduction in the bumpiness of portfolio returns through their diversifying properties, which vary from block to block. Other building blocks provide diversification benefits without return give-up (commodities and international equities). The primary role of all these blocks is to smooth portfolio returns. On the other hand, some equity-like building blocks (small cap, value and emerging market equities) primarily

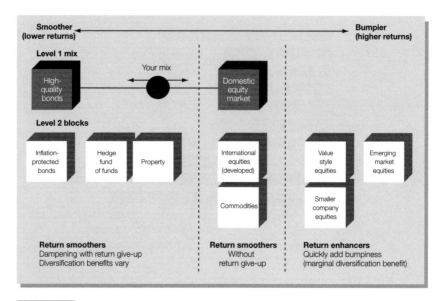

figure 10.8 **Categorising by role is useful**

provide the potential to increase portfolio returns, whilst generally providing marginal diversification benefits.

If we divide our Level 2 building blocks up by these two primary roles, which we will call *return smoothers* and *return enhancers* respectively you end up with the categorisation in Figure 10.8.

This gives you a solid framework to apply when considering which blocks to use (Level 1, 2, or 3) and why you should use them. It is a very useful framework to have in your head, for filtering out the noise and making sense of what you are hearing. The next time you read an article about investing in something, e.g. oil, you should ask yourself the following questions: what level of building block decision is it (usually Level 3!), what role will it play in my portfolio (do you have any indication of its level of return, return bumpiness or the degree to which its returns are in sync with equities)? You should know pretty quickly if you should look further or discard it as irrelevant.

10.4 A paragraph on each

It may be helpful at this point to summarise the characteristics of each of the additional Level 2 building blocks. You have already had a brief look at Level 1 bonds and equities. You can take a deeper look at each of these in

table 10.1 Reasonable estimates of additional building blocks in the future

Role	Building block	Level	Expected real return	Correlation to equity	Risk
Return smoothers	UK inflation-linked bonds	2	1%	0.3	10%
	UK high-quality bonds	1	2%	0.5	10%
	UK property	2	3%	0.3	15%
	Hedge fund of funds	2	4%	0.5	10%
	Commodities	2	5%	0.0	20%
	International equity	2	5%	0.8	20%
	Domestic (UK) equity	1	5%	1	20%
Return enhancers	UK small cap. equity	2	6%	0.85	25%
	UK value equity	2	6%	0.85	25%
	Emerging market equity	2	7%	0.7	35%

Diversification benefit ▮ Weak   ▮ Fair
(i.e. free lunch potential)   Limited ☐ Strong

Chapters 15–18, which covers all of the Levels 1 and 2 building blocks. The more you know about each the better – unless you are convinced as to why you should include them and what the downsides are, you will in all likelihood be fickle in your perception of them when things go badly and risk the age-old, wealth-destroying strategy of buying high and selling low, as you run for cover. If you are not convinced by a building block's attributes, don't include it.

In Table 10.1 you can compare the different level of return each is expected to deliver, judge how much return give-up or enhancement they will contribute and see how their pattern of returns is in step with equities. You can see that risk and return go hand-in-hand.

Return smoothers (with some return give-up)

This first category are the smoothers of returns that provide protection for your wealth, in part by having less a bumpy pattern of returns in the first place, thereby dampening the ride. You do get some of your lunch paid for, as their return patterns do not match those of equities, as you saw in Figure 10.7.

Inflation-protected bonds

These bonds are issued predominantly by governments and can protect your principal and income from the effects of inflation, if you hold them until they mature. You'll basically get your spending power back, plus around 1 per cent to 2 per cent a year depending on market conditions. These are the basic spending power protection blocks. Unexciting, but they get the job done, particularly if you are worried about unanticipated rises in inflation, a scenario in which regular bonds perform particularly poorly as prices fall. If inflation is in line with expectations then you will do marginally better by being in high-quality domestic bonds.

Property

Bricks and mortar have an inherent medium- to long-term hedge against inflation, because replacement values rise with inflation. Speculative distortions, however, where supply and demand for space is out of kilter, can result in shorter-term periods when property falls in value. By and large, it is a good protector of wealth over time, delivering a combination of income and capital gains, below that of equities but above that of bonds.

Hedge fund of funds

Hedge funds, as you might have read, claim to be able to deliver returns that provide protection from detrimental market movements because the returns they generate come from exceptional skills, not the direction of markets. By implication, exceptional skills are likely to be rare, so careful manager selection is necessary. Theoretically, hedge fund of funds could provide a strong diversification benefit, but don't take it for granted. This is an area of some controversy, as you can see in Chapter 17. This is the 'wild card' Level 2 building block.

Return smoothers (providing a free lunch)

These building blocks have more or less comparable return expectations to domestic equities, but again, their pattern of returns are out of sync with them so they provide the opportunity for, but not always the guarantee of, a free lunch – reduced risk without giving up return.

Commodities

These are the raw materials on which global economies feed, increasingly those of huge producers such as China. Commodities encompass the likes of oil, gas, coffee, wheat, livestock, metals and timber. From an inflation-protection point of view, commodities provide protection over the medium to long term. Commodity futures (see Chapter 17) have returned solid mid digit real (after inflation) returns, comparable to equities, when looked at as a diversified basket. They are one of the few building blocks where returns patterns are unrelated to those of equities and bonds, but correlated to inflation, providing significant level of return smoothing without return give-up and protecting against inflation. Well worth considering in moderation.

International equities

Investing in a range of developed equity markets such as those in North America, the European Union, Japan and Australasia, provides the potential to deliver comparable returns, given similar levels of risk, long-term rates of economic growth and reasonably comparable levels of governance, law, political stability and capitalist economics (please excuse the sweeping generalisations). These markets, though, may well have economic cycles and pressures out of sync with those in your domestic market. This provides the scope for some return smoothing, although some evidence does exist (1987, 1998 and 2000–2002) that at times of severe market turmoil, global equity returns all seem to head south. Remember, though, that non-domestic equities come with currency exposure that adds another dimension to the equation. For the long-term investor, it is probably best just to ignore it, hoping that it will equalise out in the long run. Again, moderation is the key.

Return enhancers

These building blocks predominantly add additional returns relative to domestic equities in compensation for a bumpier ride and in some cases other additional risks. Their ability to provide a contribution to your lunch bill is limited, and adding them to your portfolio will quickly add additional bumpiness. They are useful counter balances to the return give-up that adding return smoothers, that dampen as well as diversify risk, will incur.

Smaller company equities

'Small cap' equities cover the smaller companies in the economy. They tend to exhibit a higher level of return bumpiness than the wider market and may arguably deliver a return premium that cannot simply be explained away purely by the increased bumpiness of returns. The increased risk provides an opportunity to enhance returns when included as part of the equity portion of your portfolio. The debate rages about what this premium is, and even if it exists. Read Chapter 18 to find out more. Moderation, moderation, moderation!

Value equities

The term 'value equities' may seem esoteric, but what it refers to are companies that appear to be trading at a discount to their real value and to be out of favour with the markets (at the other end of the spectrum are 'growth stocks' that tend to be companies with strong momentum in either earnings or share price). Value stocks are more risky and investors demand a premium for assuming these risks, referred to by the industry as the 'value premium'. Academics have shown this premium to exist in most major markets, although over some, often prolonged, periods of time it can be negative. Again, like smaller company stocks, the debate rages as to what this premium is for, and whether it is worth taking the risk to try and capture, or even if it exists in reality. Again read about this debate in Chapter 18 and make up your own mind.

Emerging market equities

Investing in equity markets, this time those of economies developing from an agricultural base to industrial and service based economies, e.g. China, much of Asia, Brazil and Eastern Europe, offers two benefits. The first is the prospect that these economies may be out of sync with your domestic market, which you can see from Table 10.1 earlier is limited but better than international equities. Second, investors expect higher returns for investing in companies in these economies as a reward for the additional risks, which are considerable: political instability; a lack of open and free markets; insufficient legal protection; and poor corporate governance, to name a few. Long-term economic growth rates are higher and if they are reflected in higher corporate earnings then this also supports the case for strong emerging market returns, too. On their own, they represent a wild roller-coaster ride, but may have a valuable part to play in a portfolio when employed in moderation. The evidence to date is that the theory lags behind reality. One day perhaps?

10.5 Simple rules for constructing a portfolio

Remember, there are no definitive answers, just those that have a better chance of surviving the uncertainty that lies ahead. A portfolio made up of a diverse array of building blocks, put together with logic and a basic understanding of returns, the bumpiness of the ride and the effect that adding blocks together has, is as much as you can do. If you feel uncomfortable with a building block, don't use it.

One piece of advice, though, is be prepared for the psychological downside of a owning a diverse portfolio in order to smooth your portfolio's return. If equities do well and the rest of your portfolio by its very nature lags behind, you may be tempted to change your mix. The more diverse a portfolio is, the greater this influence. As David Swensen states on owning a diverse portfolio:

'Years go by without reward other than the knowledge that the portfolio embodies the desired risk–reward characteristics.'

Stick with your mix – it should pay in the long run. At least you know you have the right protection in place.

Refining your Level 1 mix

Your starting point is your Level 1 mix of domestic equities and high-quality domestic bonds. This mix was arrived at by adding bonds to your conceptual equity bias, to a level that provides sufficient comfort to sleep at night; you tested this to ensure it was the right one for you in Chapter 9. Whatever you do in creating a diverse portfolio should protect you from a range of market environments but not move you materially away from this point.

If we were using fancy *optimisation* software, we could throw in all the blocks, set a level of risk that suits us, and see what it spits out. However, we would take the results with a pinch of salt, because they are often unusual-looking mixes unless you constrain the boundaries for each block, in which case you might question how much value you are getting out of the process! Badly run software is worse than no software at all.

Our approach has to be based on simplicity, common sense and some straightforward calculations. Start by thinking of the parts of your Level 1 mix separately and how you can mitigate the risks that you are exposed to in each one further.

Looking at your high-quality domestic bonds

The big risk in your high-quality domestic bonds allocation is that inflation unexpectedly rears its ugly head and they deliver substantial real losses. The key here is 'unexpectedly' because expected levels of inflation should be reflected in a bond's coupon (interest rate) at the time it is issued. If this is a worry, you could replace some or all of your Level 1 bonds with index-linked bonds. There may be other ways to reduce the risk of bond investments, but these are generally with Level 3 assets where the pay-off is marginal and things get complicated quickly.

Looking at your domestic equity allocation

Equities is where most of your focus should be because this is where much of your portfolio's remaining risk is, particularly if you are a longer-term investor and have a strong equity bias. You have already smoothed the potential bumpiness in the level of your wealth over time by owning bonds, from both the dampening and diversification effects illustrated in Figure 10.7 earlier. You also own a building block that provides protection in turbulent times. However, you are still exposed to the vagaries of the domestic equity market and spreading the investment eggs around further makes good sense.

Ideally, you would want to put these eggs into building blocks that are uncorrelated with, and have comparable return levels with, equities. Commodities should be considered because they have the potential to deliver strong equity-like returns with a similarly bumpy ride, but have unrelated patterns of returns with equities. International equities too have similar levels of risk and return, but only provide a marginal diversification benefit. Throw them in the pot too. Property and hedge funds both have return patterns that while not unrelated to those of equities do provide reasonable diversification potential; however, they are lower-risk assets delivering lower returns, which will cost you in the long run. Add them to the list but be aware that your portfolio returns will need boosting somehow. Return enhancers can play this role, but you need to be aware that they will add to the bumpiness of your portfolio's returns, not reduce it, as you saw earlier (Figure 10.7).

How much should you own and what should you give up?

You now need to answer two questions: how much of each building block should you own?; and where will this allocation come from? Remember, in this common-sense approach, we are trying to make sure that we do not destroy the original Level 1 mix's return-generation capabilities, or the level of wealth fluctuation that you can live with. To get to the answers, try following the following guidelines.

■ **Make material allocations**: When you add an additional building block, anything less than 5 per cent is not worth the effort.

■ **But make allocations in moderation**: Don't risk overpowering the main characteristics of your Level 1 mix by getting carried away with adding other building blocks.

■ **Level 2 assets**: Don't risk your Level 1 equity/bond mix by investing more than 20 per cent in any Level 2 building block, with the exception of index-linked bonds, which could replace your entire Level 1 bond allocation, if you are very worried about inflation.

▪ **Level 3 assets**: Put a maximum of 5 per cent on any Level 3 building block, with an overall maximum of 15 per cent in the portfolio.

▪ **Level 1 bond allocations**: Take other bond market allocations (e.g. index-linked), and hedge fund of fund allocations from this allocation, because their risk levels are comparable. Take half of any allocation to property from here too. That's because the risk and the return of property lie between those of bonds and equities.

▪ **Level 1 equity allocation:** Take international equity and commodities from this allocation as they have comparable return and risk properties to domestic equities. Take the other half of any property allocations from here.

▪ Be careful adding return enhancers such as small-cap, value and emerging market equities because they add volatility quickly – perhaps set a limit of 5 per cent each, unless you have an aggressive outlook. These should just be tilts on your portfolio, i.e. small bets that you will capture the premiums due to you over your investment horizon.

▪ **Combined totals**: Generally, don't allocate more than a half of your broad Level 1 allocation to domestic equities to other Level 2 building blocks unless you really are striving for returns, or for that matter more than half of your high-quality bond allocation, unless you are really comfortable with their beneficial effects.

Use common sense; there are no definitive rules here!

10.6 Possible portfolios

By taking the Level 1 allocations associated with thirty-, twenty- and ten-year investment horizons from Chapter 9, for investors in the *accumulation phase* of investing and applying the above guidelines, we come up with the portfolio structures illustrated in Table 10.2.

If you are in, or perhaps planning for, the *distribution phase* of investing, you need to be careful that you do not run out of money. If you look back to Figure 9.8, you can see that it makes sense to withdraw 3–4 per cent of your portfolio a year at most, and be invested in 40–60 per cent equities, with the rest in bonds, if you plan to be long-term retired!

Look carefully at the difference in risk and return between the Level 1 portfolios and those that include additional building blocks in Table 10.2. What is striking is that the Level 1 mix between bonds and equities is what drives the return and risk profile of a portfolio, and while adding additional

table 10.2 Common sense allocations

Accumulation phase

Your investment horizon Orientation	30-Years Possibility	30-Years Consequence	20-Years	10-Years
Distribution phase				
Orientation	Avoid	Possibility	◄──────►	Consequence
Level 1 portfolio mix				
Level 1 UK equities	*100%*	*80%*	*60%*	*40%*
Level 1 UK bonds	*0%*	*20%*	*40%*	*60%*
Expected return	5.0%	4.4%	3.8%	3.2%
Risk	20%	17%	14%	12%
Return per unit of risk	**0.25**	**0.26**	**0.27**	**0.27**
Portfolio for all seasons				
Level 1 UK bonds	*0%*	*5%*	*15%*	*30%*
Index-linked gilts	0%	5%	15%	20%
Property	0%	10%	10%	10%
Hedge fund of funds	0%	5%	5%	5%
Commodities	10%	10%	10%	5%
International equities	10%	10%	5%	5%
Level 1 UK equities	*50%*	*40%*	*25%*	*25%*
Small cap equities	10%	5%	5%	0%
Value equities	10%	5%	5%	0%
Emerging market equities	10%	5%	5%	0%
Total	100%	100%	100%	100%
Expected return	5.4%	4.6%	4.0%	3.1%
Risk	19%	14%	12%	10%
Return per unit of risk	**0.28**	**0.33**	**0.33**	**0.31**

building blocks can improve this profile, their inclusion is a refining, rather than a structural change. For example, substituting half of your allocation to Level 1 UK equities with other building blocks in the left-most columns improves the return from 5 per cent to 5.4 per cent and reduces risk by 1 percentage point; a small yet worthwhile improvement. You have to weigh up the difference in terms of the trade-off between the added administrative effort of including additional blocks with the benefits they deliver.

These are not optimised portfolio in the mathematical sense, i.e. having used Markovitz's quadratic equation to arrive at the best mix, but diverse structures with reasonable underlying assumptions, sensible construction logic with both protection and upside potential across a range of different market environments – your portfolio for all seasons.

It is worth remembering that, statistically, the bounds between one portfolio and another often overlap; in fact, portfolios have to be quite different before they are statistically different, given the inherent errors in estimating the parameters of each building block. So, a percentage point or five in your allocation probably has little long-term practical significance.

You can see that the *efficiency* of the portfolio, defined as the 'return per unit of risk', has been improved by an increase in return without adding, and in most cases actually reducing, risk. Index-linked bonds can be substituted for high-quality domestic bonds, depending on your personal perspective. The thirty-year 'possibility'-orientated portfolio is quite aggressive and seeks to maximise returns, relying on equities to deliver their long-term expected returns. For most, a more diverse structure probably makes sense.

Looking at the ten-year investment horizon, the logic for not including emerging, value and small-cap equities is that this horizon represents a short time frame and if you value the consequences of your decision more highly than the possibilities, then you are taking a big risk that the small-cap and value premiums will not be collected and that highly volatile emerging markets may suffer a very severe sell-off and not recover. Stick to a broad domestic-equity allocation to provide returns and diversify some of the risk by investing in international equities, and other potentially favourable return smoothers.

10.7 Summary of the portfolio construction process

▩ In a consistent and predictable world, you would have a strong bias towards equities, because they are the engines of real wealth creation, based on the industriousness of those competing in the economy they represent. However, equities can exhibit short and sometimes prolonged periods of vicious erosion of your purchasing power.

▩ As such, you need to temper this with other building blocks that can help you to smooth out, the ride of our investment journey, and increase the certainty of outcome. Adding high-quality domestic bonds (Level 1) is your first step.

■ Step 2 of the process is adding Level 2 (and 3) blocks to provide the potential to improve the characteristics of your portfolio at the margin, although, as ever, there are no guarantees.

■ Many building blocks that can smooth returns materially, by dampening, tend also to have a cost in the long term because they tend to generate lower returns than equities on account of their lower risk. So, you trade a less bumpy ride and greater outcome certainty for a lower eventual outcome. Buy enough cover to live with, but don't pay excessive premiums for cover that you do not need.

■ Some building blocks do a better job than others providing a free lunch, measured by their correlation to each other. To keep things simple, focus on the correlation of each block you add to equities.

■ On the other hand, some building blocks appear to have the capacity to deliver equity-plus returns, although these tend not to provide much of a free lunch and quickly add to the bumpiness of portfolio returns. By adding them to a portfolio, you can raise the overall return. This should be done in moderation.

■ Unfortunately, very few blocks exist that can deliver both equity-like returns while smoothing the investment journey significantly. Building blocks that apparently promise both characteristics are highly attractive, hence the simplistic appeal of hedge funds at the moment.

■ Balancing these trade-offs helps to improve the quality of the investment portfolio, by providing a better chance of achieving a specific required rate of return with the smoothest ride possible.

■ For many investors, the Level 1 decision between bonds and equities gets them as close as they need to be. Remember that a sensible balance of Level 1 blocks is better than a badly thought out mix that includes Level 2 and 3 building blocks.

■ Add additional blocks to your portfolio using the simple guidelines provided to build a portfolio for all seasons.

■ Another option is to use software to build a portfolio or go to someone who can provide you with help. Pay them by the hour if you can. If you are ever going to get value for money in investing, going to someone with the skills to help you create a diverse portfolio that is right for you is it.

■ Remember that the use of further building blocks provides benefit at the margin, but can add complications to your investing life.

■ There are no right or wrong answers, only, hopefully, some better than others. Good luck!

A note on forecasting returns
As you can see, some basic and conservative estimates have been made of real returns, risk and correlations for bonds, equities and other portfolio-building blocks. However, you and I may get unlucky and have really stinking markets for the next thirty years. We cannot know for sure, but at least the probabilities of creating a successful portfolio are in our favour, which is as much as we can ask. These are my estimates; I am not an economist, nor pretend to be one. In any case, few people can predict with any much greater degree of certainty what long-term dimensions will look like either. You have a number of things that you can use to help you make your own mind up:

■ *Historic data:* Provides information on how markets have responded to a wide range of economic, political, social and market events. These events have tested the robustness or otherwise of our building blocks to a considerable degree. Monte Carlo simulations help too, and this is how the really important Figures 8.7 and 8.14 were created (flick back and take a look). You cannot be sure that events outside this experience will not happen. At least you have something to go on. Used wisely, within the context of the longer term, historic data is very useful.
■ *Simple forecasting guides:* Forecasting is a tricky area that has proven to be almost impossible to get right consistently, but we can use some simple rules to test the magnitude of our reasonable guesses for both bonds and equities for the next decade or so. The underlying rationale for each is covered in *Chapters 15 and 16* respectively. In summary:
■ *Equity returns = current dividend yield + expected growth in dividends*
■ *Bond returns = current yield on ten-year bonds*
■ *Reversion to the mean:* Bear in mind this powerful concept. Medium to longer term returns tend to fluctuate around the very long-term mean. Periods of returns well above the long-term average could be expected to return in line with the average through subsequent periods of lower returns. After the bull equity markets of the 1980s and 1990s, we may be in for a period of less than stellar performance starting with the period 2000–2002, as

▶

longer-term returns revert to mean levels. While this may be so, the timing of mean reversals is always hard to predict.

■ **Common sense:** This is probably your greatest asset, allowing you to make sense of and moderate what we see from the past and gazing into the future. Look carefully at the evidence. If an advisor tells you that they expect long-term returns to be in double digits make them explain why.

■ **Conservatism:** As an investor, it is generally better to adopt a 'hope for the best, prepare for the worst' attitude. If you are conservative with your reasonable estimates of return (lower), risk (higher) and correlation (higher) you may have to scale back your expectations or make higher contributions into your plan, but if things turn out better, you will be smiling. The other way around is far less palatable.

If you don't feel you can make your own reasonable estimates then there are worse fall-back positions that use the hundred years or so of return, risk and correlation numbers for domestic equities and bonds. While you can look at historic data and understand what has gone on before and make sensible guesses about what may happen in the future, you cannot be certain as to what the future has in store. Inevitably you have to make reasonable estimates of the magnitude and direction of these dimensions. As you have discovered, investing is about playing a probability game, but always cognisant of the fact that there are well documented instances where the probabilities do not work out, even over quite long periods of time. As Edward Bulwer-Lytton once said:

'Fate laughs at probabilities.'

References

Bernstein, W. J. (2001) *The intelligent asset allocator.* New York: McGraw Hill.

Bogle, J. C. (1999) *Common sense on mutual funds: New imperatives for the intelligent investor.* New York: Wiley.

Markovitz, H. (1952) Portfolio selection, *Journal of Finance,* vol. VII, no.1, 77–91.

Swenson, D. F. (2000) *Pioneering portfolio management.* New York: The Free Press.

11

Fancy tools – getting technical

Understanding the benefits and flaws in some of the fancy software tools that are used by the industry to help decide what building blocks makes sense for you, puts you in a position to evaluate and where necessary challenge the advice you are given.

The process of allocating money between different building blocks, in a combination that gives you the highest chance of success, becomes quite complicated if you have more than two. In the previous chapter, we used rules of thumb but there are software packages that will allow you to do this in a more technical way. If you decide to follow this route, you have an interesting and valuable learning process ahead. You will quickly realise that asset allocation is not a science and that the effective use of un-thinking software depends on a sensible, rational and conservative approach, if you want to get a meaningful output when you crank the handle.

Two common approaches are used in the industry. The first is portfolio optimisation, where the object is to try and find the best trade-off between risk and return for portfolios along the risk spectrum. The second approach is probability-based and focuses on evaluating your chances of achieving your hoped-for purchasing power outcome. Used together they can help to find a better mix of blocks to reach your goals.

11.1 Using optimisation to define 'efficient' portfolios

Portfolio optimisation sounds grand but it is merely the process for finding portfolios that provide the best balance between risk and return, either for a given level of return, or for a given level of risk. This process is based on mean-variance optimisation (MVO), a term that some private banker, broker or investment consultant is bound to use it at some point because it sounds so technical and impressive. Just remember it is the mathematics of working out how risk and return are affected when different building blocks are combined together, each with different patterns of zig and zag in their returns.

Lots of models exist today, with various whistles and bells attached, but at the end of the day they all do much the same thing. They take the inputs for the three dimensions of risk, return and correlation to every building block potentially in the mix, plug them into Harry Markovitz's equation and calculate the mixes that provide the best trade-off between risk and return along the risk-spectrum. It can all be done pretty much in an instant. The hypothetical line that they fall on is known as the efficient frontier. Commonly, the output will be an efficient frontier something like that in Figure 11.1. Theoretically, there are no portfolios more efficient than those on the frontier.

Reflect on this comment (Loeper, 2003) if you are tempted by the sexiness and seemingly sophisticated nature of optimisation software, and advisors that use it:

'Despite the mysticism many perceive in these tools, understand that all these tools do is to solve a mathematical equation. They do not know what you are

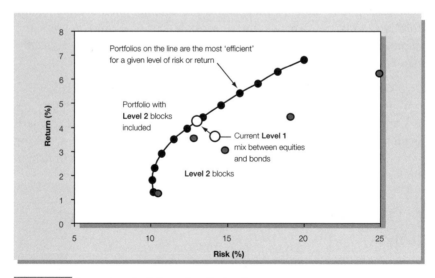

figure 11.1 Generic principles of optimisation

inputting into them and will calculate whatever you ask them to. These tools don't even know they are solving financial problems (or creating them).'

The elusive frontier

You may have seen these type of graphs produced by your portfolio manager, advisor, or private banker pointing out where on the curve you should be invested. It can all look so compelling when they point to a level of risk and say 'voila' your portfolio should have 35.5 per cent in A, 54.5 per cent in B, 3 per cent in C and D and 4 per cent in E.'

Remember though, the efficient frontier does not exist in real life because risk, return and correlations are constantly changing and your initial inputs are prone to error. It is probably best to think in terms of a broad area where portfolio characteristics are better – generally up and to the left on Figure 11.1 where returns are higher and risks are lower. In reality, a number of statistically similar portfolios made up of different building block mixes will lie somewhere in the region of the curve. Perhaps imagine that you used a can of spray paint, instead of a pencil, to draw the line.

William Bernstein in his book *The Intelligent Asset Allocator* (2001) provides the caution you need undertaking this process. He states that trying to define the efficient frontier, and portfolios on it, is akin to:

'Trying to generate electrical power by placing a battery and a lightning rod at the place you last saw lightning strike.'

He continues the analogy suggesting that optimisation does, however, provide value to investors, despite its limitations:

'Still, if you are trying to capture lightning in a jar, you are better off in Texas than in Alaska. There are certain asset combinations and portfolios which are likely (but not certain) to do reasonably well.'

The use and abuse of optimisation

MVO is a useful tool in the right hands. It forces you to make sensible estimates of the relative levels of return, risk and correlation for each building block that you are considering using in your portfolio and allows you to study the effect of changes to these inputs. However, MVO is not without its critics and drawbacks.

Garbage In – Garbage Out

This old adage has never applied more aptly to anything than it does to MVO modelling by poorly educated advisors with a laptop full of software. Estimating what you think is an appropriate level of return, risk and correlation between different building blocks is a tough task and at best is only an informed guesstimate. If what you put into the software is nonsense, your output won't be worth the paper it is printed on. Always think hard about the inputs.

Estimation error maximisation

Optimisation is sensitive to inputs. Small and seemingly insignificant differences can alter suggested allocations dramatically and outputs may appear unreasonable and extreme. Richard Michaud, a highly respected industry student of asset allocation, describes this phenomenon aptly as 'estimation error maximisation' (1989). Unconstrained portfolios (i.e. ones which you don't put any limits on how much should be allocated to each building block) tend to default to those with apparent high levels of return per unit of risk such as hedge funds with 'equity like returns and bond like risk'.

The one path process does not reflect life

These models look at a single time-period and provide suggested portfolio mixes in response to your single life inputs. In real life, we know that things are not so straightforward and the chances of this single life being the one you end up with is remote. This falls into the straight-line compounding problem discussed earlier.

It underemphasises returns and overemphasises risk

The outputs from the software tend to underemphasise the real value to you of the differences in return between one choice and another, as the axis appear, to equate return and risk on the same scale. The difference between 4 per cent and 5 per cent compounded over thirty years is huge in terms of wealth foregone; yet does a marginally wider range of annual returns, described by 16 per cent and 19 per cent risk really matter that much over thirty years? The answer is 'no' and you should always remember that increasing returns by 1 per cent is far more valuable to the long-term investor than reducing the volatility of short-term returns risk by 1 per cent. Don't confuse the value of the two.

Common-sense constraints and adjusting outputs

You will be tempted to place constraints on the portfolios to control allocations that seem too odd from your personal perspective. These
common-sense constraints on the different asset levels are probably similar
to our common-sense approach give or take a few, possibly statistically
immaterial, percentage points. You need to be pretty skilled (or recklessly
brave) to use unconstrained optimisation. Some investors subconsciously
manipulate their inputs to try and generate what they perceive to be sensible portfolios. At some point you have to decide how meaningful the
process really is.

It's difficult to decide which portfolio is best

If I asked you whether you wanted the portfolio that gave you 8 per cent
return with 7 per cent risk or one that gave you 9 per cent with 11 per cent
risk to meet your goals, would you know which to choose? Probably not,
because we don't think in percentage risk terms or have the mental ability
to translate this into something more meaningful. Efficient frontiers
provide few clues to the chances of success and risks to your end goals that
you will face.

What optimisation does well is to make you think about the process and
provide guidance as to which portfolio structures you should look at more
closely. Figure 11.2 shows the advice process generally used by those who
use optimisation as their main asset allocation tool.

By and large, anyone who tries to provide you with advice on portfolio
choice using optimisation alone should be questioned, as they aren't
focusing on your long-term goals.

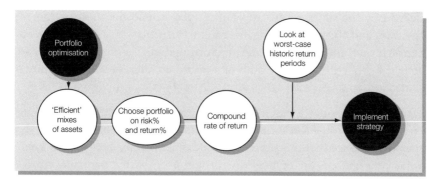

figure 11.2 Create good mixes and see what return characteristics they
have

11.2 Using probability-based models

The next level is a bit more sophisticated and begins to try and quantify your chances of success, thereby allowing you to make informed portfolio choices. It focuses on answering the real questions that most investors want answered.

Answering the right questions

As an investor, you should be interested in questions that relate to the chances of achieving your investment goals. These might include questions such as:

- How sure can I be that my retirement fund will be big enough when I retire?
- What level of income can I take from my portfolio without eroding the purchasing power of my investment pool during my retirement?
- How confident can I be that I won't run out of money before I die?

Instead of looking at compounding a single lifetime return as optimisation does, a probability-based approach generates a large number of possible lifetime outcomes that could theoretically occur, given the risk and return profile of a certain portfolio. This allows you to get a feel for the chances of being successful with one portfolio mix compared with another and forms the basis on which you can decide what mix is best for you. This is the approach that underlies the analysis provided in the 'Understanding your chances of a success' sections in *Chapter 9*.

Each lifetime return is calculated by randomly generating the first year's return from within the expected distribution of returns for the portfolio (as defined by the standard deviation of returns around the mean return for the mix) and then randomly generating returns from this distribution for the next year, and so on, over the investing period. In simple terms, you are rolling a dice with the same odds of a return coming up that your chosen portfolio has, to get each year's return figure over each investment life.

Figure 11.3 provides a graphical representation of just four lifetime outcomes to give you a feel for the process. Imagine 10,000 lifetimes and you may begin to see that this process provides you with the ability to estimate what your chances are of achieving certain goals with a particular mix of assets. In practice, this methodology can be used to answer questions where you set the parameters that you are comfortable with such as: 'I need to be

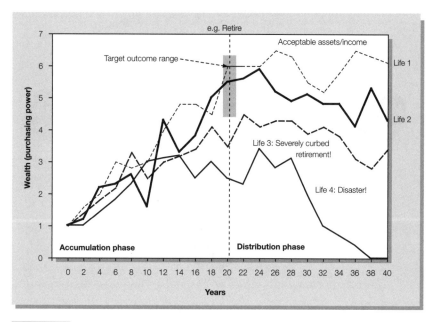

figure 11.3 **Assessing the chances of success using multiple lifetimes**

90 per cent certain that I will have at least £600,000 in my pension pool by the time I retire, and certainly no less than £450,000'. As with any tool, garbage in – garbage out, is always a risk. The value lies in testing different scenarios and seeing where the risk to your long-term purchasing power goals lies.

As you can see, two of the four lives are in the target outcome range. Life 3 has significant consequences because income in retirement is being generated from a smaller pool and is thus lower; Life 4 is a disaster because you run out of money before you die. This analysis is a little tenuous on four lives but simulating 10,000 lives or more and you can get a fair estimate of your chances of being successful.

This is a Monte Carlo simulation and if you want to test your advisor or private banker, just ask them if they use stochastic (probability-based) models to assist with their asset allocation. If they stare blankly at you the chances are they don't use one and haven't thought why they might be useful. But how else will they be able to reassure you (and be confident themselves) that you will meet your purchasing power goals?

Any advisor worth their salt should adopt a process that incorporates a balance between: finding an optimal (efficient) mix of assets: evaluating

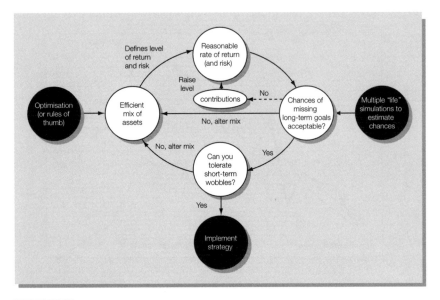

figure 11.4 **Focusing on the chances of a successful outcome**

your chances of a hoped-for outcome in terms of your long-term purchasing power goals; and your comfort with the likely range of shorter-term fluctuations to your portfolio during the time you are invested. Figure 11.4 summarises the process adopted by more enlightened investors.

More sophisticated software takes the output from the optimisation and then tests different portfolios along the curve against your purchasing power lifetime cash flow, to come up with a portfolio that provides you with the greatest chance of meeting them. Figure 11.5 shows the increased value to an investor of employing this type of software as the question being answered evolves from 'what risk do you want to take in your portfolio?' to 'what are the chances that you will meet your purchasing power goals?'

If you are interested in going down this road, there are a number of software packages available. They are easy to buy and relatively cheap. The details of one programme, *Portfolio Pathfinder*, can be found in the Bibliography. Dick Purcell, the brains behind this model, is an ardent and intelligent believer in user-friendly asset allocation models that answer investors' portfolio choices in this way, thereby helping them to meet their 'lifetime purchasing power needs and goals', to coin one of his phrases.

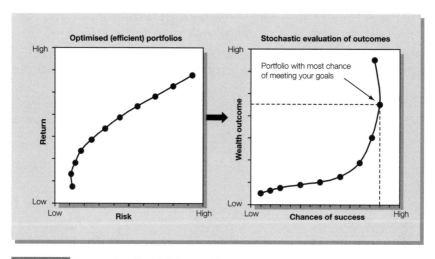

figure 11.5 Answering the right questions

Most models are US-orientated but can be adapted for other markets. Playing with them provides an education in itself and can stimulate some interesting thinking.

11.3 Summary: getting technical

■ Optimisation is a useful tool, but should be viewed as a starting point in the process of trying to decide which mix of assets makes most sense for you. Some form of Monte Carlo simulation adds significant insight.

■ While a purely rule-of-thumb approach is a little loose, being seduced by a seemingly sophisticated and complex mechanistic approach to choosing your mix of building blocks is naive and likely to damage your wealth.

■ Always remember that these programs are only as good as the input and the operator: garbage in – garbage out. Don't be fooled by fancy computer programs – good investing was around long before the software!

References

Bernstein, W. J. (2001) *The intelligent asset allocator.* New York: McGraw Hill.

Loeper, D. B. (2003) *The alternative to alternative classes.* Financeware,

Wealthcare Capital Management White Paper. Available from: http://www.financeware.com/ruminations/WP_alternativeclasses.pdf

Michaud, R. O. (1989) The Markowitz Optimization Enigma: Is optimized optimal? *Financial Analysts Journal*, vol. 45, no. 1, January/February, 31–42.

4

Smarter implementation

Hopefully, you have a good idea of what mix of building blocks to use in your portfolio. Now, you need to turn this plan into reality. Unfortunately, many investors fail to follow through, blinded and confused by the plethora of choice. Here is some guidance on pulling the trigger.

Chapter 12: Six steps to a smarter portfolio

Here you will find guidance on selecting the best products in the marketplace, the questions to ask providers, how best to purchase your investments and how to set up a simple system for tracking a portfolio to determine how you are doing against your goals. This practical focus is taken down to website level and identifies providers.

Chapter 13: Costs – what a drag

If you sat down and work out how much of your money was being siphoned off by the investment industry, you would be amazed. Costs matter, as John Bogle would say. Gaining a real understanding of what your all-in costs are and the effect they may have on the success of your investment programme, is time well spent for a lose-the-fewest-points investor.

Chapter 14: Standing your ground on index funds

One of the challenges as you try and put an investment plan into action is that as soon as you speak to anyone in the industry, the chances are that they will try and persuade you that they can beat the markets. Their argument often ends up as an attempt to malign index funds and persuade you that by buying them you are consigning your investment programme to mediocrity. Identifying and refuting the common put-downs will help you to have the confidence to stand your ground.

12

Six steps to a smarter portfolio

It is no good getting to this point in the book, thinking 'what do I do now?' then shutting the book and entering a state of investment inertia. You need to work out how you are going to implement your portfolio strategy. The temptation is to put your investment in the mental 'To be dealt with later' pile; but resist the temptation. Dealing with it now allows you to sit back and relax in the future.

You are ready to go: you know your Level 1 mix of assets and you may have chosen some additional building blocks to use as well. Now all you need to do is to work out what products to buy, how to buy them, how to keep track of them and how to give your portfolio a regular check-up. We will focus on the UK market but the same general principles apply wherever you are.

12.1 Step 1: Choosing your market benchmarks

For each building block chosen, you have to decide what benchmark you are going to set and try to replicate, such as the broad UK equity market. It needs to reflect fully the building block characteristics that you want in your portfolio and provide the basis for reviewing how well each product is doing in capturing these characteristics. In most cases this benchmark will be a published market index, such as the FTSE All-Share index, which covers a specified group of securities tracked in accordance with some clear and consistent rules. There are many indices to choose from and picking the right one is important. Below are some pointers for doing so.

Your Level 1 equity index choice

For your Level 1 equity allocation, the return benchmark should be the return of the whole domestic market, which provides a diversified and representative benchmark as it includes most public companies, be they large or small and weighted according to their market size. A few very small firms may be excluded.

The FTSE All-Share is the index of choice for the rational investor. The 'Footsie 100' on the other hand, which is commonly quoted in the media, represents only the biggest hundred companies out of about 2,800 companies listed on the main and the AIM stock markets (the latter tends to be small companies) and only around 80 per cent of the market in terms of capitalisation. A US broad market equivalent would be the Wilshire 5000 index, covering more than 7,000 companies. Most major stock markets around the world have a broad-based index. Figure 12.1 indicates the percentage capitalisation of the market that each of the major UK equity indices cover.

A school of thought does exist that argues that the FTSE All-Share index has become too concentrated in the largest stocks. In fact, the ten largest companies represent about half the value of the index and over half the index represents just four sectors: oil, banks, pharmaceuticals and telecoms. If you feel strongly about this, you could include an additional allocation to FTSE 250 stocks, i.e. the first 250 companies below the FTSE 100, to

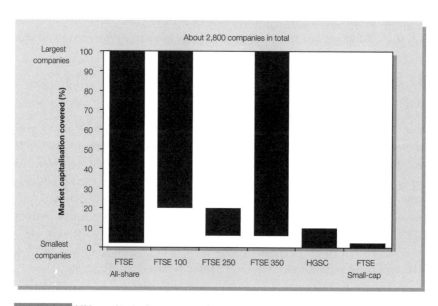

figure 12.1 UK equity index comparisons

balance this out a bit. The FTSE All-Share should deliver what you need – after all it does represent what is going on in the UK economy, which is what you are trying to capture. This is not a problem with indexing but of index construction.

Your Level 1 bonds index choice

Purists to the theme that the highest quality bonds provide the best market trauma protection may want to choose an index made up exclusively of government bonds (known as gilts in the UK), because they represent the ultimate flight to quality and liquidity destination in times of financial crisis. Again, any decision to move away from a British government securities (gilt) index is an active 'bet' away from this core position and should be made consciously and with due care.

Building-block benchmark choices

The benchmarks that you could use for other building blocks are set out in Table 12.1. In some cases you can see that for a couple of building blocks more than one suggestion has been made.

You should always seek to use *total return indices* where the income, in the form of dividends from equities and coupons from bonds, is reinvested in the market, as opposed to price indices where it is not, as a significant proportion of your long-term returns come from reinvesting income. This applies particularly to your accumulation phase, where you should be reinvesting all the income.

■ **Property:** The two indices listed in Table 12.1 reflect properties that are privately held (IPD) and property company shares listed on the stock exchange (FTSE). It really depends how you get your property exposure as to which is more appropriate.

■ **Hedge funds:** This benchmark is a universe of hedge funds tracked by CSFB/Tremont. There are others and if you are serious about investing in hedge funds you should research them for yourself. The absolute return target of deposits plus say 4 per cent is just a guess at what could be adequate compensation if you invest in a conservative and well-diversified fund of hedge funds, as opposed to cash.

■ **Commodities:** Either of these indices can be used, although the Goldman Sachs index has a higher exposure to energy commodities, such as oil and gas. Neither has exposure to timber.

table 12.1	Building blocks indices for the UK investor
Level 1: Domestic equity	
UK broad market	FTSE All-Share Index
Level 1: High-quality domestic bonds	
UK gilts	FTA British Government Securities Index
UK broad bond market	Lehman Brothers Sterling Aggregate Index
Level 2: Return smoothers	
UK index-linked gilts	FTA British Government Index Linked Index
UK property	IPD All UK Property Index (Private)
	FTSE Real Estate Index (Public)
Hedge funds	CSFB/Tremont Hedge Fund Index
	Absolute target, e.g. cash plus 4%
Commodities	Goldman Sachs Commodity Index
	Dow Jones AIG Commodity Index
International equities	FTSE World ex-UK Index
	FTSE All World ex-UK Index
	MSCI World ex-UK Index
Level 2: Return enhancers	
UK small cap equities	FTSE Small Cap Index
	Hoare Govett Smaller Companies Index
UK value equities	FTSE 350 Value Index
	MSCI UK Value Index
Emerging market equity	MSCI Emerging Markets Free Index
	FTSE All World All Emerging Index

■ **International equity:** These indices are well used. The FTSE All World includes a higher allocation to emerging markets than the FTSE World. Make sure it is priced in sterling.

■ **Small cap equity:** Both options can be used, although the Hoare Govett Smaller Companies Index covers a wider universe of smaller companies.

■ **Emerging market equities:** Both indices are well known and either can be used.

Products you buy should replicate your chosen index

When you select a fund, such as an index (tracker) fund, it is imperative to make sure that you are selecting a product that tracks the index you want it to track. Just because a fund is called a UK Index Tracker, it does not mean it is tracking the FTSE All-Share index, in fact many replicate the FTSE 100, thereby missing out the medium-sized and smaller companies. The same applies to exchange-traded funds; make sure you know what they are replicating. If you buy an active fund, check to see what the fund's benchmark is, either by looking at the prospectus or by asking the customer support team.

12.2 Step 2: Decide whether to go index or active

This decision is one of the easiest to make for the reasons covered extensively in Chapter 4. As Warren Buffett is reported to have said (Bogle, 2002):

'When the dumb investor realizes how dumb he is and invests in an index fund, he becomes smarter than the smartest investor.'

Play the game with the highest probability of success and invest in index-tracker products wherever possible. Choose the lose-the-fewest-points approach. The Dilbert cartoon by Scott Adams shown here sums up the situation perfectly. For those of you in the UK, a mutual fund is the equivalent of a unit trust or OEIC.

If you still need convincing, read Chapter 16, which should resolve any doubts you might have.

The serendipity of index-fund investing

If you decide to go down the market-replicating, rather than the market-beating route, you will achieve a number of really critical practical, as well as investment, benefits. These are consistent with your philosophy of losing the fewest points:

■ You are likely to beat the majority of actively managed funds over the long run, even if over short periods some active managers outperform.

■ If you choose a good fund you will probably never have to change managers during your investing lifetime.

■ You don't have to worry about whether your fund manager is destroying your investment strategy with bad decisions.

■ You immediately and dramatically reduce the number of providers and products that you need to consider. This makes your selection process simpler and improves the chances of selecting the best product.

Enough said.

Using an active manager

Do so only if they can prove to you with a great degree of confidence that they are going to add value through the exceptional people they employ and the proven process that they use. Remember that this is a relative game and the pool of fund managers has a very high level of talent in it, raising the average level of skill for all.

Reasons other than performance to use active managers

It may seem a little perverse to raise the issue of using an active manager to manage your money for any reason other than trying to beat the market. In reality there are a couple of reasons why you might consider employing one.

First, in the UK, some building blocks do not have index-fund equivalents. If you live in the USA or Australia, you are more fortunate, as most of the mainstream building blocks are available as index funds. In the UK, you may be forced to use an active manager simply to gain access to the building blocks that you choose. No problem – just make sure that you follow a few of the tips set out later in this Chapter. Fortunately, the situation is rapidly changing in the UK.

Second, despite having read this book, the thought of investing and managing your money may still fill you with dread. Managers can play a useful role in acting as subcontracted monitors and administrators; but be prepared to pay the price. In addition, you may not feel that you can trust yourself to stay the course and survive periods of market trauma without some sort of support; if this is the case, some solid and judicious advice at the appropriate moment may well protect you from the age-old problem of selling out at the bottom and changing your asset allocation in panic, at the cost of your long-term goals.

12.3 Step 3: Funds, separately managed accounts or brokers?

You need to decide the best structure for owing investments. Fortunately, the decisions that you face if you pursue a lose-the-fewest-points philosophy are relatively straightforward. It is only if you decide to use an active manager that things get tricky. My advice is to get smart, and win, by keeping things simple. You have three main options as in Figure 12.2.

Option 1: Funds

In the UK, funds are known as *unit trusts* or *open-ended investment companies* (OEICS), and in the USA they are referred to as *mutual funds*. In a fund, your money is pooled with other investors' money, but it remains yours and not part of the managing company's balance sheet, unlike when you make a deposit with a bank. Funds are a simple way to gain diversification across the whole market, which would be difficult for you to achieve cost-effectively on your own. You own units or shares in the fund, which are priced daily.

Index (tracker) funds

These are a significant development for investors and simplify good investing. Their aim is to track a specific benchmark as closely as possible, following a lose-the-fewest-points strategy. Index funds should have very low total expense ratios (TERs), e.g. around 0.3% per cent for a UK FTSE All-Share fund, with no initial fee. The way in which they work is covered in more detail below.

figure 12.2 Choosing the vehicle for your money

Exchange-traded funds (ETFs)

These should be considered alongside index funds as the vehicle of choice for a rational investor. Exchange-traded funds are similar to index funds but are shares listed on a stock exchange, which reflect the basket of securities that constitute a chosen index. Many of the world's major institutional investors use ETFs to help position their portfolios. Evidence from the USA indicates that the width and use of ETFs will grow substantially, once they become understood and accepted. Watch this space. ETFs tend to have low total expense ratios. One point to note is that they pay dividends, which you will need to reinvest yourself, unless your broker provides a dividend reinvestment plan (often referred to as a DRIP). Practical issues are covered later.

Actively managed funds

These are funds managed by active managers employing market timing and stock-picking to try and beat the market. What the fund manager can do with your money is defined in the fund's prospectus, but they are often so broad in scope, for the manager's protection, that it's hard to know what they will in fact be doing. Some companies do a better job than others in sticking to the spirit of the prospectus. Active management all-in costs are significantly higher than index funds and ETFs.

Investment trusts

Investment trusts share many of the properties of funds but are companies listed on the stock exchange and are, in some ways, like ETFs. Investment trusts are usually actively managed, but some replicate specific indexes like an index fund. They can be bought through brokers. A quirk of investment trusts is that they trade at either a premium or a discount to their net asset value or NAV (effectively the liquidation value of selling all the stocks). These arise through supply and demand mismatches and also the perception of the management of the investment trust and perhaps the leverage (borrowing) they are able to use. Somewhat surprisingly, index-replicating trust also seem to trade at discounts and premiums to the NAV. Costs can be lower than for OEIC and unit trusts. Some investors look to take advantage of the changes in discounts, but that is a secondary and difficult game. They may be worth a look.

Size issues

Using funds remains the primary option for you, irrespective of the size of your portfolio, particularly if you pursue a lose-the-fewest-points strategy. If

table 12.2 Summary of vehicle options

UK structural options	Fund			Separate account	
	Passive		Active		
Criteria	Fund	ETF	Fund	Passive	Active
Minimum size	£50	£50	£50	£10 million	£1 million
Maximum economic size	None	None	£1million	None	None
Management fees	<0.5%	<0.4%	1% to 2%	A few bp	1% to 2%
Initial fees	None	None	3%–5%	None	None
Average turnover	<5%	<5%	>60%	<5%	>50%
Cost of turnover*	0.1%	0.1%	0.9%	0.1%	0.8%
Performance certainty					
vs. index	High	High	Lower	High	Lower
Hand holding	Low	Low	Low	High	High

* Based on 1.5% p.a. for 100% portfolio turnover

you go the active route and have several million pounds to invest, you should weigh up the cost differential between funds and separately managed accounts.

Option 2: Separately managed accounts

A separately managed account is one set up with an investment manager in your name over which the manager has discretion to buy and sell investments that fall within a set of rules that you define with them. They are sometimes called *discretionary portfolios*.

Actively managed separate accounts

This is an option for investors with sufficient funds who are looking for a personalised service and some handholding. Traditionally in the UK, portfolio management for individuals was largely the preserve of the stockbroking community, who charged commissions on trades, encouraging the churning of portfolio. Fortunately, this is no longer the case, as other more disciplined and skilled managers have entered the marketplace, to whom you pay a fee based on the level of assets you have with them of 1 per cent to 2 per cent with brokerage and custody often on top. Minimum balances required to set up an individually managed portfolio range from £100,000 to about £2 million. Providers include private client portfolio managers, private banks and stock broking firms.

Tax considerations

If you are a UK investor and if your money falls outside of a tax shelter such as a pension plan, ISA or your capital gains are above the personal allowance you get each year, any activity by your manager that results in capital gains will result in you paying tax that could otherwise stay in your portfolio and compound over time. This cost is estimated at 1 per cent to 2 per cent a year, which is a big penalty to pay on top of their other costs. UK fund vehicles, on the other hand, do not incur capital gains on securities sold within the fund; you only incur capital gains on sale of your units.

Establishing portfolio guidelines

You need to think carefully about what your portfolio guidelines should be. They should include a statement of the objectives of the portfolio, the building block index mix against which it is to be judged, the countries and securities that it can invest in, and constraints on allocations to asset classes (building blocks), markets and issuers, that the manager can make, at their discretion. You also need to provide instructions as to when the portfolio should be rebalanced back to its original mix. One of the cardinal sins of an investment manager is to break the guidelines agreed with you for the management of your account, because this constitutes a breach of contract.

Generally, you are not locked into a contract for any specific period of time but it is worth making sure that an agreed timeframe and process for terminating the contract exists.

Indexing strategy (and tax-managed) in separate accounts

Straight indexing in a separate account vehicle tends to apply only to very substantial institutional investors. Generally, most providers require at least $10 million to manage your money effectively on a separate account basis. For most, sticking to funds or ETFs is the best route forwards.

As an aside, there is a small but increasingly popular use of separate account indexing, particularly for taxable investors. It allows your own unique tax circumstances to be managed more effectively and actively. Currently, interest seems to be coming from high-net-worth investors who understand the merits of indexing but have significant tax and portfolio issues that makes using an index fund or ETF less attractive. Only a few pioneers exist at present, predominantly in the USA, such as Parametric Portfolio Associates. Due to technology advances, separate account index management is available to investors with portfolios of $500,000 and above.

Option 3: Direct investing via a brokerage account

Some decades ago, owning individual securities directly through a brokerage account was the main method of investing. As you know, much evidence exists to show that even the professionals struggle to beat the market, either picking stocks or timing markets. Holding securities yourself demonstrates either overconfidence in your own ability to be right more times than you are wrong or implies that you believe you have superior insight and skills to the rest of the market. This route is likely to be suboptimal for the majority of individual investors. You will hear stories of individuals who have done well, but just accept that they are either exceptionally skilled or exceptionally lucky.

The 1990s 'rising tides raise all ships' climate encouraged many to believe that they could spend a few hours a month and beat the market and it is scary to think how many people opened brokerage accounts and got burned or held risks that they had no idea about and came unstuck.

Brokerage accounts do, however, have a role to play in the administration of your portfolio and can be used as a conduit through which to purchase your long-term building block fund and ETF positions, when you start your program, as you will see.

In summary

Table 12.2 summarises the criteria that differentiate the choices you have. You need to make your own mind up given your own circumstances, but my advice is to stick with index funds and ETFs.

12.4 Step 4: Selecting the best index funds

One of the great advantages of taking the index route, apart from giving yourself the best chance of achieving your goals, is that selecting a product is straightforward. Over the past couple of years, the choice and quality of index funds and ETFs have improved markedly, as Table 12.3 illustrates. Still, there are probably fewer than 100 UK-based index tracker funds and ETFs to choose from, across all building blocks, some of which you can discard quickly as they track inappropriate indices or building blocks. It's easier to choose from one hundred index funds/ETFs than from 3,000 active funds, and the process of choosing the best is far simpler.

table 12.3 Your access to index funds and ETFs is growing

Building block	Index fund	ETF	Comment
Level 1: domestic equity			
Broad market	■	Note 1	Index of choice
Large companies only			Too narrow
Level 1: high quality domestic bonds			
UK broad bond market	▨		Reasonable choice
Gilts	▨		For the purist
UK corporate bonds		▨	Not as high quality
Level 2: return smoothers			
Index linked gilts	Note 2		Hold to maturity
Property		Note 3	Choose an active fund
Hedge funds	Note 4		Watch this space – USA only
Commodities		Note 5	Watch this space
International equities		Note 6	Index of choice
Regional equities	■		Could use as a proxy for international
Level 2: return enhancers			
Small cap equities	▨		Limited to investment trusts
Value equities		Note 7	Choose active fund
Emerging market equities		▨	Newly launched

▨ Fewer than ten choices
■ More than ten choices

Notes to Table 12.3

Note 1: FTSE 100 and FTSE 250 ETFs exist so you could combine the two (85 per cent in the 100 and 15 per cent in the 250) to create a FTSE 350 index.

Note 2: Owning a fund could expose you to real interest rate risk resulting in fluctuations in your capital, although over time your capital should be reasonably protected against inflation.

Note 3: The first European property ETF was issued in 2005, which could provide some non-UK property exposure if that is something you want. Others should follow.

Note 4: The nearest thing so far to a passive approach to investing in hedge funds is investment in an investable index of hedge funds. Watch out for developments (see Chapter 17).

Note 5: Commodity ETFs are available in the USA (in $) and on the German stock market (in euros). You could own either.

Note 6: An MSCI World Index ETF was launched in 2005. This has around 12 per cent or so in the UK so remember to take this into account.

Note 7: An ETF reflecting higher-dividend-paying stocks in the FTSE 350 and weighted by dividend yield, as opposed to market capitalisation, has been developed that provides a proxy for value stocks because high dividends is one of the descriptors of a value stock. It's a start.

Tracking error is your critical selection criteria

The ultimate goal of using an index tracker fund, or ETF, is to gather as much of the market return as you can. The degree to which returns differ from the chosen index is known as *tracking error*, (i.e. the standard deviation of returns relative to the index). This can be caused by a number of factors, which we will look at below. Tracking error of 2 per cent is the outer limit of what is acceptable and the lower the better. Remember that even small differences can mount up over time due to the effects of compounding.

An established fund will be able to prove what its tracking error has been, demonstrate the consistency of its replication process and make you feel comfortable that it will be able to reproduce its strong results in the future. Some funds publish tracking error. If for some reason they don't, just compare the returns on a year-by-year and cumulative basis against the index, e.g. the FTSE All-Share index, or ask their customer service team for the data. If the differences are large, on the upside as well as the downside, the fund is not well managed, or is replicating a different index from the one you think it is. There is no reason to choose a new index fund, which is unproven in its ability successfully to track the index. Here are some of the ways in which tracking error occurs.

Replication methods affect tracking error

The way in which the investment manager chooses to copy the index is important. There are three common methods that are used.

■ **Full replication:** As its name suggests, each company in the index is purchased by the fund. This would give you zero tracking error in a world where transaction costs are zero, but it's not the world we live in. Inevitably, transaction costs will create some tracking error. In addition, smaller funds may suffer from having to buy odd lots of stock that cannot be split, as the amount being purchased is too small. Corporate actions and dividend payments also create activity that may generate tracking error.

■ **Sampling (or partial replication):** In this case, the manager takes the view that the cost of creating and maintaining a portfolio with all the securities in the index is greater than the tracking error risk of holding only some of the securities. The manager will use some form of optimisation model to put together a sample of securities that mimics the index as closely as possible.

■ **Derivatives:** This method is less common and places most of the funds in cash and purchases derivative instruments that mimic the market. Sometimes funds use both sampling and derivatives.

You should always check to see what type of process is used and ask why it makes sense for this kind of index. Take a look and see what other providers are doing.

Fees and costs contribute to tracking error

Fees always go a long way towards explaining tracking error, as not all index funds are made equal. Some charge very low fees of a few basis points (100ths of 1 per cent) and others as high as 1 per cent for domestic retail products. Better still; find out what the total expense ratio (TER) of the fund is. Never pay an initial fee for an index fund. Some index funds are taking the Mickey with high upfront fees and high TERs. Vote with your wallet and avoid them. Chapter 13 covers costs in detail.

Size may contribute to tracking error

This is important due to lot sizes explained above. It may affect the decision as to how the fund is replicated, which may not be the most effective method to use. Being in a small fund may expose you to additional tracking error if a large investor suddenly withdraws. Size may also imply limited manager experience.

Turnover may contribute to tracking error

In some jurisdictions, such as the USA, turnover is very important to the taxable investor and should be avoided as much as possible. Some funds may perform as well as other funds and have similar tracking error but after-tax returns may be lower as a result of portfolio turnover. In the UK, a unit trust or an OEIC does not pay capital gains tax, so turnover is less important, at least from a tax perspective.

table 12.4 Guidelines for selecting index funds	
Criteria	What to look out for
Index being tracked	■ Check it is tracking your chosen index ■ Remember – total return not price index
Tracking error	■ As low as possible, preferably less than 1% ■ Check cumulative returns versus index over five years ■ Avoid if significantly below (or above) index
Total expense ratio (TER)	■ Look for a very low TER. Less than 0.3% is good
Initial fee	■ Don't pay one
Fund size and age	■ Larger funds tend to be easier to manage ■ Avoids effects of a big investor pulling out ■ Five years' minimum record
Fund turnover	■ Less than 5% for Level 1 blocks
Replication process	■ Check what process is used ■ Ask why it makes sense for this fund
Manager experience	■ Always look for a team that has done its job well ■ Stability is a plus, as experience counts
Redemption fee	■ Fine if it is short term (one year)

Manager experience will affect tracking error

Index investing is not a just a 'plug it into the computer and sit back' process. Skilled index managers are aware of each of the elements of their process where tracking error can occur and manage them very tightly. There is no substitute for experience and success. We will look briefly at the most respected index investor in the industry later.

Table 12.4 summarises the guidelines for choosing an index fund.

There are enough high-quality index funds and ETFs for you not to have to stray outside of these parameters for your Level 1 or most Level 2 building blocks in the UK. Currently, index bond funds and ETFs are a bit limited in the UK. Over time, index fund fees are expected to fall and more managers will enter the market. It is likely that your choice of building blocks will also increase.

Getting it right upfront is very important as you don't want to have to switch later on, particularly if you are a taxable investor.

Index fund providers

There are several index fund providers in the UK, whom you may wish to contact to get hold of some literature and prospectuses to review. This is not a definitive list or in any way a recommendation – it just helps to steer you to some of the longer-established firms with the widest choice of building blocks. Some are omitted, not by implication but for the sake of simplicity. The onus is on you to work out which is most suitable for you.

These providers include: Legal & General (*www.legalandgeneral.co.uk*), HSBC (*www.hsbc.com*), Gartmore (*www.gartmore.co.uk*), M&G (*www.mandg.co.uk*), Norwich Union (*www.norwichunion.co.uk*) and Scottish Widows (*www.scottishwidows.co.uk*). In the USA, Vanguard is a leading provider of index funds. For institutional investors, Barclays Global Investors and State Street Global Advisors are the two leading providers.

Selecting exchange-traded funds

When selecting an exchange-traded fund (ETF), a similar focus exists: check the total expense ratio and see how closely the ETF tracks its chosen index. See how much money is invested in the ETF you are looking at – bigger is generally better. Start with a provider such as Barclays 'iShares' (*www.ishares.net*), which is the predominant choice in the UK; but look too at what is available on other exchanges particularly the Deutsche Bourse (*www.deutsche-boerse.com*), which has a number of ETFs (including a commodity ETF). Keep a look out for new products. Be prepared to reinvest dividends.

12.5 Step 5: Administering your investments

At this point you need to think about how you are going to go about administering your portfolio, with the least fuss and bother. Few of us like paperwork; in fact, for some people the feeling of anxiety about investing is as much to do with handling the administration as it is to do with living with a portfolio. Fortunately today, there are efficient and simple ways to hold, monitor and administer a portfolio, particularly if you are a rational long-term, buy-and-hold investor using index tracker funds and/or exchange-traded funds.

Setting up your administration system

When setting up a portfolio you will have some initial administration to do as well as some regular maintenance work, which can be kept to a minimum. When you buy a building-block product, you will need to keep a record of your ownership of it including: its exact description and any fund code that identifies it; the number of units/shares you own in each fund (active or index) or ETF; any buying and selling of these investments, including how many units/shares were traded and the date and the price at which the transaction took place; and any dividends from equities or coupon payments from bonds that you received.

In the case of income, you should check if the fund can automatically reinvest it for you to save time and effort. Remember, if you receive cash, you need to put this to work as soon as possible. This class of shares is often called *accumulation shares.* In the UK you may be liable for tax on any income, if you are a taxable investor, even if it is immediately reinvested.

You will need this information to fill out your tax return declaring the income received and capital gains that you have realised during the fiscal year if this pot of money is taxable. Fortunately, most of these items are all produced either by brokers, fund companies, or can be collated by you using some sort of personal financial planning software.

Minimising your administration

The degree to which you can minimise administration will be a function of the number of building blocks you have decided upon for your mix, the products you have chosen, and how they are aggregated together into a portfolio. Remember, though, that your investment needs should drive your decision-making and not your desire to reduce the administrative hassle.

As an example, you may decide to select an index fund you want to use with one fund company. While it may be easier to select another fund from within its product range, say a bond fund, this may not be the best option. Resist the temptation to take the easy route by using the same provider. Buy what is right for you, but take a little time to think about the method through which you purchase them. There are three main ways.

Route 1: Buy funds direct from providers

Taking this route you will end up with different accounts with each fund company you deal with and will be sent different reports at different times and with different formats. You will need to consolidate your portfolio so that you can keep track of it easily. You could use a portfolio software package such as Quicken (*www.quicken.co.uk*) or Microsoft Money (*www.microsoft.com*). You can find reviews online that may help you to narrow down which is best for you. Also, there are websites where you can set up dummy portfolios, entering all your transaction details, and getting regularly updated prices on your holdings; generally, though, this is limited to UK funds, most UK equities, bonds, gilts and ETFs. An example is MoneyExtra (*www.moneyextra.co.uk*). This is only likely to grow in the future.

If you use an actively managed fund to replicate a building block, the chances are that you will have to pay the full initial fee, which is often as high as 5 per cent, if you buy it direct from the fund company, irrespective of the fact that you have received no advice from them. Look at buying through a discount broker or a fund supermarket to avoid some or all of the fee.

Route 2: Purchase via fund supermarkets

Fund supermarkets are a simple and effective way to buy and administer funds; the online shelves are stacked with products provided by range of managers. Two supermarkets are Cofunds and FundsNetwork, offering several hundred funds from the majority of managers. To a large extent they overlap. FundsNetwork is sponsored by Fidelity and can be accessed directly via its website (*www.fidelity.co.uk*). Cofunds (*www.cofunds.com*) is backed by some of the UK's major managers and a leading fund administrator but can only be accessed if you use an adviser. Both allow you to set up a monthly investment program. Only FundsNetwork has a facility for phasing in a lump sum investment over six months, a process known as *pound-cost averaging*.

Route 3: Purchase by execution only using a broker/IFA

Many independent financial advisors (IFAs) and brokers provide an execution-only service, which includes access either to one of the big supermarkets or their own proprietary supermarket. If you intend to buy ETFs and perhaps index-linked gilts, as well as funds, you will need to use a broker who can trade this broader range of investments for you.

IFA websites include firms such as Bestinvest (*www.bestinvest.co.uk*), and Hargreaves Lansdown (*www.hargreaveslansdown.co.uk*), being a couple amongst many. Brokerage firms, where you can not only buy funds, but also ETFs and index-linked gilts, at low transaction costs, include Squaregain (*www.squaregain.co.uk*), American Express (*www.sharepeople.com*) and TD Waterhouse (*www.tdwaterhouse.co.uk*). Banks have online brokerage options as well. There is no shortage of choice; again, you need to decide which firm is best for you.

Generally, if you invest in funds via a fund supermarket you will not pay transaction fees – but check first. Remember if you are investing regularly in a number of ETFs, brokerage transaction costs will add up. Work out how much it will cost you as a percentage of your monthly investment – a penny saved is a penny earned. A £10 commission per trade on a £1,000 monthly investment split between four ETFs is 4 per cent of your capital needlessly given up. This route is probably best for investing larger sums or where the annual expense ratio of an ETF is substantially below that of comparable index funds and offsets the commissions.

Figure 12.3 illustrates how you can use a brokerage account (or IFA) to consolidate your investments. Some brokerage firms have charges for inactivity (something you will be aiming for), so look out.

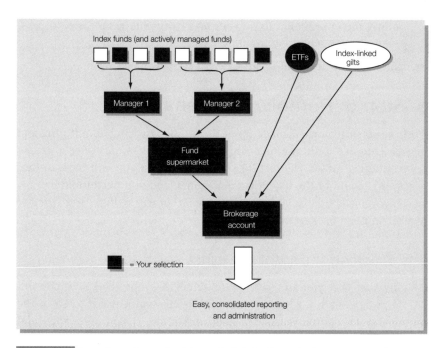

figure 12.3 Investment needs drive administration choices

Conclusions about administration

How you administer your investments will depend upon your own individual circumstances and the vehicles that you use. Time spent thinking about what administrative issues are going to arise from your portfolio and how you are going to handle them will save a lot of time and angst down the road. Here are some pointers that you should bear in mind.

■ Choosing the right investments is your primary decision, which may dictate the administrative process. Remember that the same products may be sold through a variety of channels and one may be more administratively effective and/or cost-effective than another. Try to keep things as simple and as cheap as possible.

■ When you receive information from your broker, fund company or portfolio manager, deal with it immediately. It won't take long. Otherwise, the temptation is to throw it onto the 'I'll do it later' pile and the hurdle of dealing with it becomes greater with each envelope that arrives.

■ If you are a keen technology user, keep as much information online as possible.

■ Careful record-keeping is essential and if your filing system is working, finding the information to do your tax return will be far easier for you or anyone you employ to do it.

■ Don't avoid admin. Set up an efficient system to control it.

12.6 Step 6: Portfolio maintenance

Portfolio maintenance is made up of three tasks: tracking, monitoring and rebalancing. It should not take you more than a few hours once a year to keep things in order. Figure 12.4 summarises what you will have to deal with. At the end of the day, it is your money and you need to know how much you have, how anyone managing your money is doing and whether your plan is on track to meet your goals.

Task 1: Tracking a portfolio against your goals

Making sure that you are on track to achieving your goals is important. Working out roughly where your accumulated wealth needs to be in the future, say every five years, is a good discipline. If you are retired and drawing an income, your goal may be to make sure that your purchasing power pool remains intact.

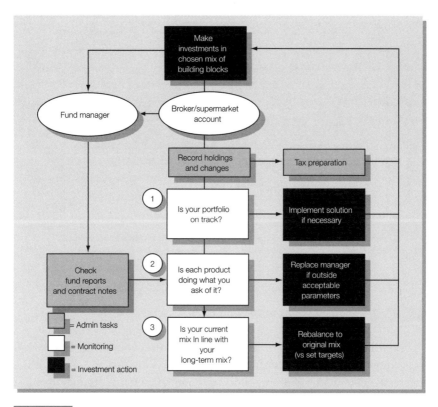

figure 12.4 Continual tracking, monitoring and rebalancing

You can use the tables (or formulae) in Chapter 6 to calculate rough figures in real terms for target points along the way. Remember that the amount you see in your actual portfolio will be in tomorrow's money, reflecting the nominal returns you have made. To get back to real terms, you need to keep a note of inflation each year and use this to turn it back into today's money (i.e. what its purchasing power is). Inflation data can be easily obtained from the Bank of England website. To make the conversion:

■ create an index for inflation. Start with 100 and multiply this by 1 plus the rate of inflation, e.g. 5 per cent inflation will be 1+0.05. The inflation index in year one becomes 105. Say in year 2 inflation is 7 per cent, you multiply 105 by 1.07 to give 112.4.

■ To calculate your portfolio's purchasing power, divide whatever your portfolio is worth, say £125,000, by the inflation index divided by 100 = 125,000/1.124 = £111,210.

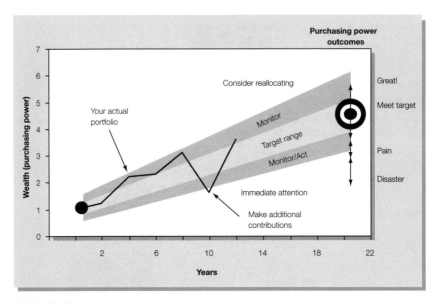

figure 12.5 **Keeping your portfolio on track**

If you find that the portfolio value is falling behind your goals, at least you will know and you can: contribute more; take a chance and increase the aggressiveness of the building-block mix (an inadvisable strategy in most cases as you increase the chances of missing your goal); or rein in your expectations. It is possible you get lucky and returns surpass expectations; in which case, you can either reallocate assets elsewhere or expect a better standard of living later.

You should only look at your portfolio annually at most; any more frequently, and you will probably shock yourself with the inevitable ups and downs. Time does a good job at smoothing out the bumps. Check whether your portfolio falls within the ranges that you predicted when you set up your plan as Figure 12.5 illustrates.

Perhaps every three years or so, you should ask yourself if returns have been abnormal or prolonged in terms of their deviation from the long-term returns that you anticipated. If so, and you are worried, consider whether you need to take some action, particularly increasing the rate at which you are contributing to the pool. Don't be tempted into making rash decisions with your portfolio structure based on one or two years; after all, what is one, two, or even five years in thirty? Contribute too much and you will be happy if things get better.

Task 2: Monitoring the performance of the building blocks

Each year, take a look at how your investments have done, building block by building block against their chosen index. Say, for example, you own a FTSE All-Share index fund – take a look and see what the total expense ratio is now, how closely the fund has tracked the index, how large it is and if there have been any changes in strategy or personnel.

In the event that performance is out of line with the market, then you may have to take remedial action by replacing the manager or at least keep them under close scrutiny. This is a rare event if you have chosen an index fund carefully. Remember that 'out of line with expectations' means both above and below the benchmark index you have chosen. A manager whose results are better than expected may well be taking more risks than you want him to – beware.

Task 3: Rebalancing your mix of building blocks

Rebalancing is the process of returning your portfolio back to its original mix, as over time building blocks will generate different levels of return, and the assets in the mix will become skewed in favour of the better-performing asset, which is usually the riskier asset.

If you believe that markets revert to their long-run average – not a bad assumption to believe in and you would be in good company, then by rebalancing your portfolio, i.e. selling some of the building blocks that have outperformed and buying those that have underperformed, you may be positioning the portfolio appropriately to avoid/capture any mean reversion. It provides a discipline of buying low and selling high. However, there are no certainties that this will pay off over the timeframe you are investing over. As such, you should primarily view rebalancing as trying to maintain the risk/reward profile of your portfolio over the time you are invested for and which you chose in the first place. You just have to ignore the fact that, over some time periods and with the benefit of hindsight, it may turn out that it could have been better not to rebalance at all.

Perhaps the most succinct statement on rebalancing comes from David Swensen, who invests for Yale University in the USA:

'Over long periods of time, portfolios allowed to drift tend to contain ever-increasing allocations to risky assets, as higher returns cause riskier positions to crowd out other holdings. The fundamental purpose of rebalancing lies in

controlling risk, not enhancing return. Rebalancing trades keep portfolios at long-term policy targets by reversing deviations resulting from asset class performance differentials. Disciplined rebalancing activity requires a strong stomach and serious staying power.'

He makes the point that in a severe bear market such as 1973–1974 the rebalancing investor was forced to buy more equities as markets continued to fall. Equally, rising equity prices needs a strong stomach as selling equities as part of a rebalance appears, at the time, to be a loser's strategy.

When should you rebalance?

Some investors rebalance every year, which may be reasonable in steady markets. However, it probably makes sense to set a target for rebalancing, for example, when your Level 1 assets have changed by 10 per cent or more. Too low a target and you will be forever tinkering with the portfolio and incurring transaction and tax costs. In any case, small deviations are probably statistically insignificant, given all the assumptions that you have made to get to that allocation in the first place. Too high a target and you will expose your portfolio to too much risk, which could be costly. An example of a sensible rebalancing strategy for say a 50 per cent bond and 50 per cent equity mix would be to allow the portfolio to run to 60 per cent in equities and 40 per cent in bonds and vice versa, before rebalancing back towards a 50:50 long-term mix.

Rebalancing issues

The tax consequences of rebalancing a portfolio need to be taken into consideration. If you sell equities that have gone up in price, then you may incur significant capital gains, which may outweigh the added risk of holding a higher proportion of equities than intended. Remember that if you are making regular contributions to an investment plan, you can allocate new contributions into the building block that is underweight. By doing so you can avoid having to crystallise any capital gains in the outperforming building block. Even if you are not contributing regularly, your portfolio will be throwing off cash in the form of dividends from your shares and coupons from your bonds, which you could use.

That's it! It really is not too difficult to turn your theoretical portfolio into reality. In the rest of this chapter you can find some tips to help you to find the information you need and to make the decisions that you face.

12.7 Market valuation levels and lump sum investing

As you approach the point of pulling the trigger and investing your money, there is one final point for you to consider if you are looking to invest a lump sum, as opposed to making regular contributions. Throughout this book, conservative estimates have been made of long-term expected rates of return on building blocks, but we have never tried to place a sense of current valuation levels on them, as it takes you down the market-timing road. Yet markets do seem to experience periods when their valuation levels are extreme compared with long-term averages.

The danger for a lump sum investor

If you are a investing a lump sum you face a dilemma: what happens if equity markets crash after you put your money into them or returns are particularly weak over a long period of time? It's a real problem, as any investor putting money into equities at the end of 1999 quickly found out. Imagine that you have £1 million to invest from an inheritance and you decide to put it all into equities; you would be pretty upset if you invested it and within a year or two it was worth only £500,000. Let's do some simple maths: Remember that 50 per cent down requires your portfolio to rise by 100 per cent, not 50 per cent, to get back to where it was; also, if your portfolio delivered 5 per cent in real terms a year from that point forwards (our estimate of average real returns), it would take you almost fifteen years to get back to its initial level of purchasing power. This is a very real risk that could damage the outcome of your investing programme. How can you avoid getting hit in this way?

Sensible approaches for limiting your risks

The first thing you can do is own a diverse portfolio where your eggs are spread between a number of baskets including Level 1 bonds and Level 2 investments such as property, commodities and possibly a hedge fund of funds. As such, you will have some protection, provided all these investments don't fall at once.

Second, you could try and gauge whether you think that equities look attractive relative to their long-term levels. That sounds a bit like market timing, but there may be some merit in taking what is a somewhat contrarian stance. To do this you need to have some measure of valuation that you can use and compare current valuation levels to the historic average.

You can so this in a crude way by using what is known as the price to earnings ratio (or P/E ratio), which describes what the market is prepared to pay for each £1 of corporate earnings. The higher the P/E ratio, the more optimistic people are about future earnings growth. The long-term average P/E ratio in the UK is in the region of 12–14 times earnings, yet at times it has risen (and fallen) well beyond this. In 2000 the P/E for the market was in the high 20s. In the USA at that time it was around 40 times, compared with a long-run average of 15. When prices (and P/E ratios) end up well above or below their historic levels, you might expect that they will revert towards more normal levels to bring them back in line, given that long-term earnings are likely to be reasonably stable. This is known as mean reversion and it is explored in more detail in Chapter 15 (see Figure 15.2). To quote Robert Shiller, who predicted the crash in 2000:

'Metaphorically, when one is mountaineering, one can enjoy the exhilarating view from up high on a mountain, and may look forward to the possibility of discovering a way up to a much higher level. But one will reflect that, realistically, at a random date years from now, one will probably be back at ground level.'

The problem for you is that while this may be true, you simply don't know when that random date is. While it makes sense theoretically, in practice there are no hard and fast rules: sometimes markets revert quickly, other times it can take decades. For example, deciding that the previous ten years of returns up to 1989 of 16 per cent were well above the long-run average of 5.4 per cent and underweighting your exposure to equities could have resulted in you missing out on the 12 per cent a year that investors made in the 1990s. There is no certain answer to this one. Throughout this book, we have used 5 per cent real returns as an expected figure for equities, which is pretty conservative. Better that way around.

Average your way in if it really concerns you

If you are particularly concerned about current valuation levels, you have two choices, above that of holding a diverse portfolio. The first is more strategic: reduce the allocation you make to equities (or to whatever building block appears grossly overvalued) and make allowances for the reduction in returns that you may expect. If at a later point prices fall and valuations become more favourable, you could increase your exposure up to your original long-term strategic mix, by selling other assets.

Alternatively, and more tactically, you could average your way into the allocation by investing a set amount regularly over a period of time. This is known as *pound-cost averaging*, where you are reducing the risk of a short-term fall in markets. If it happens, you will regularly be buying shares as the market falls, thus lowering the average price at which you bought your equities. As you are investing a set amount, the lower the price, the more shares you own. The maths behind it means that the average price at which you get your equity exposure is lower than the average price of the shares over that period.

With either of these strategies, you could lose out if the markets forge ahead. It is a risk management issue and one that only you can resolve. In short, own a diverse portfolio and be contrarian in your outlook when it comes to extreme market valuation levels. Fortunately, it is not so much of a problem if you are building a portfolio using monthly contributions, as you will be averaging in across the whole of your investment lifetime.

12.8 Tip 1: Selecting the best active managers

I know that some of you will still be tempted! The hope of beating the markets over the certainty of underperforming the market by costs of an index fund is a strong, if somewhat irrational emotion. You may have to choose an actively managed fund if an ETF or index fund does not exist. Sifting out the fact from the fiction is not easy in the actively managed fund world as marketing departments have plenty of scope to paint a rosy picture as to why their firm is the one that will win. The fact that they all claim to beat the market is a bit of a clue as to what you are up against!

A few tips for picking active funds

Past performance has been the driver for advertising campaigns and the sale of funds around the world. Yet you know that past performance says little about future outperformance. It's true that a few truly talented managers are out there – the problem is sorting the wheat from the chaff. Picking truly talented managers is as difficult as picking stocks. There are two steps: the first is to find the right sort of manager, and the second is to find the right sort of fund.

Locating the right type of manager

Picking the right manager is difficult, given that performance is of little help. As a result, you need to make a qualitative assessment of a manager who you will never get to meet and on whom you will get precious little information other than a glossy marketing biography. There are, however, some underlying characteristics to look for. They don't define a good manager, but such a person is likely to be found in this subset. In short, the few managers who you want managing your money tend to have a passion for investing, bordering on obsession, have integrity and put your best interests at the forefront of whatever they do. Here are some things to look out for:

- **Independence** Independent private firms tend to have longer-term motivations based around quality and reputation rather than gathering assets to deliver profits to a parent company's bottom line, above all else.

- **Aligned interests** It is always good to see a fund manager who has a direct and significant stake in the funds he or she manages. Look at websites closely – those that do are likely to tell you. In addition, firms that are focused on investment quality tend to restrict the size of their funds, closing them to new money rather than just see them balloon into unmanageable beasts with diluted excess return potential.

- **Longevity** Too many managers jump ship for money. You should be looking for someone with the conviction that what his or her firm is doing is the best way to be doing it, and it is worth staying with. Remember that if you are a taxable investor, cashing out and reinvesting to follow a manager could be very costly. Remember, you need them to stick around for twenty to thirty years. Unfortunately for you, only seventeen fund managers in the UK have been managing their fund for more than fifteen years!

- **Process** Some fund management firms have disciplined, quantitative processes that seek to take the emotion out of investing, which helps them to be a little more contrarian in their approach. Disciplined processes that can be demonstrated to work, with strong proof statements, are worth considering and provide an alternative option to concentrating of future performance in the hands of a single manager who may retire or move funds.

Locating the right type of fund

- **Index choice** Make sure you only look at funds that are trying to beat your chosen benchmark index.

- **Screening** Narrow the universe of funds further by screening out persistently poor performers, particularly those with high costs.

- **Costs** Always check fee levels and total expense ratios. Pick funds at the lower end of the expense spectrum. There is no evidence that higher fees lead to better performance, except in the cars that the managers drive. Avoid initial fees, and funds with high turnover. Costs mean greater hurdles to success.

▩ ***Information ratio*** In plain English this tells you how much return a manager creates through their skill, rather than that from the market, for the additional risk (tracking error) that their decisions incur, relative to the market. The higher this ratio the better. Information ratios, after fees, of 0.5 and above, over a reasonable time frame, are considered good. It is worth noting that Berkshire Hathaway's information ratio (a proxy for Warren Buffet) is 0.48 over 30 years (Siegel, 2003). Yet even with a ratio of 0.5, you need at least fifteen years to know whether this is generated by skill or luck. As a simple rule of thumb, to see if a track record is long enough to judge whether it is down to skill or luck (with 95 per cent confidence) you divide 2 by the information ratio, and then square the outcome (i.e. multiply it by itself). So, an information ratio of 0.5 requires $(2/0.5)^2 = 16$ years of track record.

▩ ***Up and down markets*** It is worth taking a look at how the manager has performed in both up and down markets. Hopefully, a good manager will be able to demonstrate skill in most conditions. Many managers in the late 1990s did well in the bull market by overexposing their clients' money to technology stocks, but looked woeful when this gamble came home to roost. It is always worth asking what the worst period has been, why that was and how they responded.

▩ ***Cash balances*** Look for funds where cash balances are and have been low. Cash, over the long run, will always be a drag on performance.

▩ ***Limit the number of funds you own*** While many investors are seduced by the prospect of beating the market over the long run, many inherently understand that the risk of a manager underperforming exists, and own several similar funds. Unfortunately, your investments will resemble the broad market pretty closely, and you now own an index-like fund but with active fees.

One particular problem you face is that if you find a manager you like and they move, you will have to sell-up, crystallise capital gains, perhaps need to pay tax that could still be in your portfolio, and probably pay additional fees to get into his, or her, new fund. These costs could seriously erode much of the good work they are doing.

Fund of funds (or managers of managers)

Recently, the concept of *funds of funds* (or *managers of managers* who allocate separately managed accounts to managers as opposed to investing in funds) have become popular, based on the premise that employing a professional to pick a pool of funds makes sense. This adds another layer of fees (another hurdle) and few have any real track record to test their efficacy. In addition they are being set up all over the industry and you will have to become a skilled selector of managers of managers. Keep an eye out on this, but don't expect too much, for all the reasons we have covered.

All in all, this advice may not seem very helpful, but there is no easy way to select good active funds that will outperform over the long run. If you find one let me know. If you can't, you know what to do.

12.9 Tip 2: Where to find information on indices

As part of your research into different building blocks and as part of your monitoring once you have established a portfolio, it is useful to get your hands on historic index data. Unfortunately, the very long-term data used in this book can only be accessed under license at great expense, which is a pity. Some free data is available, though, that can be used for personal use. This includes the following websites: *www.mscidata.com* for global equity markets (in US$ and local currencies), *www.dowjones.com* for their commodities index (in US$), *www.hedgeindex.com* for Hedge Fund returns and *www.ipdindex.co.uk* for UK property. The hardest index time series to find are the FTSE Indices and they generally have to be paid for. Organisations, particularly in the USA, tend to be less proprietorial with index data than those in the UK, if it is for personal use. In terms of monitoring your portfolio, index returns for each building block should be provided; if not, ask the product provider for them. You have a right to know. Some books containing data can be found in the Bibliography.

12.10 Tip 3: Where to find useful information on funds

The easiest place to access information is online. If you are familiar and comfortable with the web, you can access a wealth of information that can help reduce the number of possible funds needed to replicate your building block mix. In the UK, progress has been slow, relative to that in the USA, in providing good information to investors. Things are improving, but no single website is perfect. Below are brief descriptions of some of the leading providers of information on funds in the UK, and in some cases globally. These are free sites at the basic level. Some charge fees for additional research.

Investment Management Association (IMA): www.investmentfunds.org.uk

This is the trade body for the UK's investment management industry. It provides good background information. The site has a Investor menu and an option called Find a Fund. This allows you to search funds available to UK investors in a number of ways including by total expense ratio and index tracker. Search and find the bulk of index funds available. It's a good start but you will need to use other sites to gain a better insight into the detail of each fund.

Trustnet: www.trustnet.com

Trustnet's site covers all of the UK's unit trusts, OEICs and some exchange-traded funds. It also provides charts and annualised return data information on the FTSE indices. If you go to the Databases menu, pick Unit Trusts & OIECs and then Prices & Performance you can screen all the funds. If you are looking for index funds go to the Databases menu and in the All Sector box you can choose the option Indexed Funds. This provides a list of index funds. Similarly, you can click on the Exchange-Traded Fund option. You will need to look more closely at each fund by clicking through the link on the fund name. Some firms provide information, whereas others don't. For those funds that provide information you can compare the fund's performance versus the index and get a feel for its tracking error, size and fees. Expense ratios can be obtained by cross-referencing to the IMA site. Do some investigation yourself.

Standard & Poor's: www.funds-sp.com

This is another firm that provides good fund information. It also covers funds from overseas providers, not just UK-based funds, as in the IMA database. You may wish to register. After completing the formalities, use the Find a Fund navigator to get around. You can find some good information on funds identified on other sites.

You will also see that S&P provide stars (1 lowest to 5 highest) and fund ratings (A to AAA). If funds don't make the grade they are not rated (NR) or if they have insufficient data they are un-rated (UR). The stars are based on statistical performance, whereas the ratings are based both on quantitative performance analysis as well as in-depth interviews with the fund management group, the portfolio manager and team, and also about fund specifics such as age, size, turnover, etc. You can buy these detailed reports. This is a possible way to go if you are selecting active funds, and have narrowed your options, which you want to explore in more depth. This is a well designed and thought out site that can be used in combination with others to obtain expense ratios and more fund information.

FT Funds: http://funds.ft.com/funds

The Financial Times has established a fund rating service, which uses a similar database of funds to some of the other sites and provides a search mechanism based on its own classifications of fund risk. The site provides total expense ratios on each fund from Fitzrovia, the leading provider of such data. This is a useful site and can again be used with the other sites.

Morningstar: www.morningstar.co.uk

This is a global group that provides information on the universe of funds available to UK investors and provides a rating system for funds based on stars. This is a widely used service in the USA. Some investors use the rating system as some sort of endorsement of future market-beating performance for higher-rated funds, which it is not.

On the website, go to the Fund Selector button on the home page and choose the relevant category that you want a list of funds for, which for Level 1 assets are: UK Large Cap Equity, Sterling Government Bond and Sterling Diversified Bond. Level 2: UK Small Cap Equity Property Sector Equity and Global Emerging Markets Equity. Use the IMA category if you prefer. Again, you have to sift out the index funds for yourself. If you click on the fund name you get a brief summary.

Funds in each category are rated from 1-star (poorest) to 5-star (strongest), based on risk-adjusted performance. The bottom 10 per cent are given 1 star, the next 22.5 per cent get 2 stars, the next 35 per cent 3 stars, the following 22.5 per cent 4 stars and the top 10 per cent get 5 stars. Remember, though, in most cases past performance tells us little about the chances of future good performance, except for index funds.

A word on the US experience of Morningstar ratings

In the USA, investors have latched on to Morningstar ratings with gusto. Let's face it; most of us want to spend as little time as possible selecting funds. High Morningstar ratings drive very large flows of assets into these funds. In some periods 95 per cent of all investment flows into US equity mutual funds went into 4 and 5-star funds (Blake and Morey, 2000). Another study (Del Guerico and Tkac, 2001) revealed that getting a 5-star fund rating increased flows into a fund by more than half. Conversely, downgrades resulted in fund stars caused a larger-than-normal outflow of funds. To be fair to Morningstar, it makes no claims to the predictive power of its star ratings.

Caveat

This brief review of a few independent fund information websites, represents my own personal opinions. Use and evaluate them yourself. At the end of the day, you need to be comfortable with the information that you have to hand before you commit your money. You should take advice if you feel you need it. Using these sites, you should be able to come up with a short-list of funds. You can request literature from these by phone or online and get answers to any questions that you may have.

12.11 Tip 4: Don't forget about tax

Managing your tax situation well is a very important component of successful investing. As an investor, it makes sense to use any legal tax breaks that you are given. In most countries there are tax incentives designed to encourage you to invest more for your future and to rely less on the state. Remember that legally paying the taxman at a future date instead of today, or even altogether, can have a significant beneficial effect on portfolio returns over the long run. Tax breaks come in a number of forms.

Retirement (pension) savings

In the UK, retirement saving is tax-efficient because you are given a tax break for saving into a pension plan. A top-rate tax payer investing £60 of their pay will get the benefit of £100 in their plan as their contribution is exempt from tax. Apart from these contributions receiving favourable tax treatment, capital gains and some forms of income are largely exempt from tax, although this changes depending on the chancellor's whim. Pension funds are tax-exempt in many jurisdictions.

Personal tax shelters

In some jurisdictions, individual investors are provided with tax-deferred or tax-free investment structures. In the UK, for example, you can invest, with taxed income, up to £7,000 a year in an ISA, which effectively shields you from most income or capital gains tax in the future. You should seriously consider taking advantage of this tax break.

Personal allowances

Again, some jurisdictions have allowances for some capital gains that are free of tax. The base cost of your investments, i.e. the price you bought them at, may also be increased over the years, thereby reducing any gains that you must pay tax on later. This is the case in the UK. Remember that these can be used if you find you have to rebalance your portfolio at some time. With a buy and hold index fund/ETF strategy, you should have little need to crystallize capital gains, particularly when you are accumulating wealth. The Inland Revenue website *www.hmrc.gov.uk* provides the latest allowances. It makes sense to use up your capital gains allowances as it means the level of unrealised capital gains in your portfolio will be lower over time with less tax to pay if and when you liquidate your portfolio.

Sliding scales

In some countries, capital gains tax rates vary depending on how long the investments are held for, and what type of assets are held. Take advice from your accountant or phone the Inland Revenue, if you are a UK taxpayer, as they are remarkably helpful and efficient.

Harvesting and offsetting losses

Many jurisdictions allow you to offset capital losses that you make against capital gains. The magnitude and time scale over which losses can be carried forward varies from country to country. Some jurisdictions have rules to stop you from simultaneously selling and repurchasing stocks known as bed-and-breakfasting. The harvesting, i.e. realising, of tax losses can be a significant source of improved returns for a taxable investor as they can be offset against capital gains. However, the UK industry is at present not as focused as it could be on tax-efficient investing and thinking about after-tax returns. Keep an eye on what develops.

Different treatment of income and capital

Some places treat these two differently. In some cases investment decisions may be influenced by tax treatment.

In general, there are three points to be made here if you are a taxable investor:

■ First, maximise the tax breaks that are legally afforded to you by your government. It will make a significant difference to your wealth in the long run.

■ Second, if you are unsure about what breaks are available to you for each pool of money you are investing and exactly how you can take advantage of these breaks, seek advice. Planning ahead to maximise the tax-efficiency of your investment plan is worthwhile and if you are going to spend money on advice, this is a good place to do so.

■ Finally, your building-block mix needs to be driven by your investment needs, not by tax planning. Being tax efficient within the context of your long-term building block mix makes sense.

12.12 Ten tips for smarter practical investing

Turning your theoretical investment plan into reality needs a little thought, but is not a difficult thing to do. Here are the tips to help you through the process:

1 Decide which blocks you will use index funds (or ETFs) for to replicate your chosen market benchmarks.

2 Review funds available for each building block (index first, active second) using the information websites available.

3 Gather data on fund size, tracking error, expense ratios and manager for index funds. Use similar criteria to review active funds where index funds are not available. In case of the latter, possibly read S&P and Morningstar fund reports. Make a short-list.

4 Obtain brochures and prospectuses for short-listed funds either online or by telephone, and ring and ask any questions that you may have.

5 Choose funds once you are satisfied with the information you have been given.

6 Review manager, supermarket and broker websites to see where and at what cost the funds are available. Review their administrative capabilities, transaction costs, dividend reinvestment capabilities and monthly investment programme capabilities.

7 Open an appropriate account and pull the trigger. Set up regular savings plans if necessary and transfer existing holdings into the new platform (provided you don't have to crystallise any gains on which you will have to pay tax).

8 Use all available tax shelters.

9 Review your portfolio and its constituent parts once a year. Take action if you are worried that you are off-track in terms of meeting your purchasing power goals – which usually means contributing more. Deal with managers performing outside of expectations. Rebalance when your Level 1 mix is more than 10 per cent out of line.

10 Sit back and relax!

References

Blake, C. R. and Morey, M. R. (2000) Morningstar ratings and mutual fund performance. *Journal of Financial and Quantitative Analysis*, vol. 35, no. 3.

Bogle, J. C. (2002) The investment dilemma of the philanthropic investor. Bogle Financial Markets Research Center. Available from: http://www.vanguard.com

Campbell, J. Y. and Shiller, R. J. (2001) *Valuation ratios and the long-run market outlook: an update*. Cowles Foundation discussion paper no: 1295, 1–19.

Del Guerico, D. and Tkac, P. A. (2001) *Star power: the effect of Morningstar ratings on mutual fund flows*. Federal Reserve Bank of Atlanta, Working Paper 2001–15.

Siegel, L. (2003) *Dimensions of active management*. Presentation to the Society of Quantitative Analysts, September. Available from: http://www.sqa-us.org

Swenson, D. F. (2000) *Pioneering portfolio management*. New York: The Free Press.

13

Costs – what a drag

A book that places a **lose-the-fewest-points** philosophy at its core
would be incomplete without taking a good look at the effect of costs on
an investment programme.

13.1 Why do we throw our money away?

The adage 'a penny saved is a penny earned' has never been more apt than
when investing. Yet investors tend to be poor at understanding the true
effect of costs on their wealth; surprising, given that in other walks of life
they would be indignant about similar usurious levels of costs. Costs make
a significant difference to your lifestyle in the future. After setting your
long-term investment policy, controlling them is the most important factor
in investment success, although controlling your emotions is right up there
too.

To get your attention, on what sounds like a boring subject, take a look at
the bullet points below. To quote research by the FSA:

*'One must invest about £1.50 in an actively managed unit trust . . . in order to
obtain the market rate of return on £1; and that . . .*

*Obtaining the market rate of return on £1 requires an investment of about
£1.10 to £1.25 in an index tracker.'*

Now that is a worrying statistic for every investor. The industry croupier is
stealing from your pocket. Costs are also higher in the UK than the USA
where these levels are closer to $1.30 for active funds and $1.10 for index
funds. Yet as investors we seem unconcerned with costs for some strange
reason; only 14 per cent of respondents to a survey in the UK (Autif, 1998)

said that reasonable charges were the main reason that they chose a fund. Most buy on past performance, which you now know to be a lottery. There seem to be number of reasons for this:

■ We don't have to pay cash to settle the bills – it all comes out of performance, and thus feels painless.

■ We are used to paying for professional services such as accountants and lawyers, where we get something for our money, so why not investment managers?

■ We have an innate feeling that in a competitive market higher costs will result in higher quality. That's simply not the case.

■ We underestimate the long-term effects that small differences in annual costs make to the result of investing. Exponential effects over time are hard to calculate in our heads.

■ We fail to identify just who has their hands in our pockets.

Let's run through an example of the costs that you will incur as an investor. These are much more than just the annual management fees that a fund manager will charge. To understand the effect of costs we will look at two hypothetical actively managed funds – High Cost Fund and Low Cost Fund – towards the end of this chapter.

13.2 More than just management fees

Funds incur a wide range of seen and unseen costs. Let's start at the beginning:

Cost 1: Management fees

This represents the direct remuneration that the fund manager gets from you in return for managing the fund and which is calculated as an annual percentage of assets managed. As a brief aside, some funds that focus on paying income may take management fees from your capital so that they can pay a higher level of income – watch out, as your capital will be quickly eroded by this practice and inflation, our second cost.

Cost 2: Inflation

This is the one unavoidable cost. You can only spend *real returns*. All annual fees eat away heavily, in percentage terms, at your real returns. For example, 2 per cent costs from a 10 per cent return before inflation means that 20 per

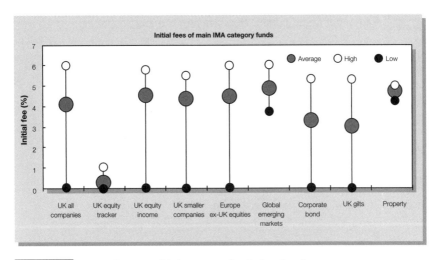

figure 13.1 **Initial fees are high except for index trackers**

Source: Lipper Fitzrovia data from investment Management Association website

cent of your returns are eaten up by costs. But 2 per cent costs after inflation of 3 per cent leaves you with only half of your nominal return. Always think of the effect of costs on real returns.

Cost 3: Initial fees

Initial fees, sometimes known as upfront fees, sales fees, or loads, are taken from you at the outset, purportedly to cover the cost of advice (Figure 13.1). Your advisor, if you use one, may get some or all of this fee as payment from the fund company, for channelling business its way. If you purchase funds

table 13.1 **Initial fees are too expensive to pay**

Initial fee	Amount invested of initial £10,000	10 years	20 years	30 years
0.0%	£10,000	£16,289	£26,533	£43,219
1.0%	£9,900	£16,126	£26,268	£42,787
2.0%	£9,800	£15,963	£26,002	£42,355
3.0%	£9,700	£15,800	£25,737	£41,923
4.0%	£9,600	£15,637	£25,472	£41,491
5.0%	£9,500	£15,474	£25,206	£41,058
6.0%	£9,400	£15,312	£24,941	£40,626
Difference: 0% to 6%	**−£600**	**−£977**	**−£1,592**	**−£2,593**

Assumes a 5% real (after inflation) annual rate of return.

table 13.2 Annual management fees are just the start

Fee category	Annual cost	As %
Management fees	**£316,000**	**1.30%**
Registrar's fees	£30,000	
Marketing fees	£41,000	
Secretarial fees	£58,000	
Custodian's fees	£28,000	
Audit fees	£7,000	
Professional fees	£15,000	
Directors' fees	£31,000	
Other expenses	£27,000	
Total expense ratio	**£553,000**	**2.27%**

Average net assets over 365 days £24,336,692
Source: Lipper Fitzrovia

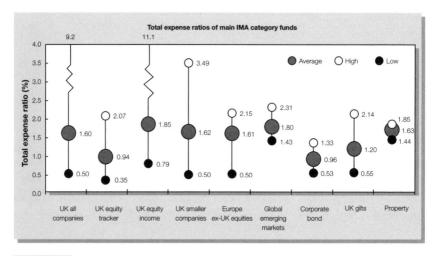

figure 13.2 TERs are surprisingly high in the UK

Source: Lipper Fitzrovia data from investment Management Association website, December 2002

through a discount broker or fund supermarket you can usually get a reduction. Ironically, if you buy direct from the firm managing the fund they will charge you full-whack, which is ridiculous for delivering nothing. High upfront fees are the norm in the UK except for index trackers; yet even some of those have the audacity to charge initial fees – avoid them if they do.

It's common to accept blindly that initial fees are an inevitable sunk cost, but that attitude will cost you dear. Take a look at Table 13.1 to see the damage they can do to your future wealth. If you pay an upfront fee of 6 per cent on a £10,000 investment, over thirty years this would be equivalent to almost £3,000 of your future purchasing power given up. General advice is to avoid paying initial fees wherever possible.

Cost 4: Total expense ratio (TER)

The fund manager will be paid an annual management fee calculated as a percentage of your assets; but that's only the start of the annual cost story. Several additional costs are charged annually to the fund, reducing the overall performance of your investments. In aggregate, these annual costs are known as a fund's *total expense ratio* (TER). Fortunately, Fitzrovia (*www.fitzrovia.com*) provides excellent industry-wide coverage of fund TERs and these can be accessed on websites described in Chapter 12. Fitzrovia's TER calculation is defined as:

'*The annual percentage reduction in investor returns that would result from largely fixed operating costs if markets were to remain flat and the fund's portfolio were to be held **and not traded** during a period.*'

We will come to the issue of costs associated with trading a portfolio in a moment. First, take a look at Table 13.2, which illustrates the TER of a specific fund using data from Fitzrovia. You can see that the total costs are far more than just the management fees. In this case, annual management fees are 1.3 per cent a year, yet the TER of the fund is actually 2.27 per cent, a whole 1 per cent higher.

Furthermore, as you can see, from Figure 13.2, average TER levels are high – too high for the rational investor. Index tracker funds have the lowest average TER, which is still far higher than in the USA, where the best are around 10 basis points, or 0.1 per cent. Put simply, the UK investor deserves better. Careful screening for funds, in particular index funds, that control costs and thus have low TERs, will pay rich dividends for you.

Cost 5: Portfolio turnover

As you can see from the definition above, the TER is based on a scenario where 'the fund's portfolio were to be held and not traded during a period'. Yet this is not realistic, because an active fund manager will be making decisions all the time to try and beat the market, buying and selling investments regularly. This activity is known as *turnover* on the portfolio, which is usually measured as a percentage of the value of the total portfolio that is sold and bought each year.

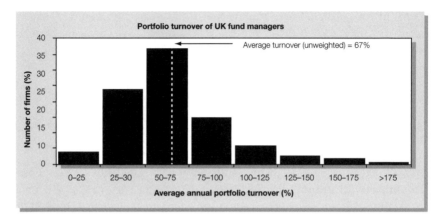

Portfolio turnover of UK fund managers

Average turnover (unweighted) = 67%

Number of firms (%)

Average annual portfolio turnover (%)

figure 13.3 Investment managers are busy people

Source: Lipper Fitzrovia, December 2002

Levels of turnover have risen significantly over the past couple of decades with portfolios in some cases looking more like speculative short-term trading strategies rather than longer-term investments. In the USA, around forty years ago, turnover was about 15 per cent, meaning that a portfolio's holdings turned over once every six years or so. Today, with turnover of 100 per cent on average, portfolios are changed completely every year.

It appears that today's managers believe that they can spot undervalued securities, which then achieve a price that reflects their value in under a year. Wow, they must be good! Turnover costs. A recent study in the UK, again by Fitzrovia, looked at portfolio turnover for UK fund managers. On average, it is pretty high, as you can see in Figure 13.3, at around 67 per cent of the portfolio every year.

There are several components to the cost of turnover:

■ **Broker's commission:** Fund managers sell and buy shares through brokers who get paid a commission for each trade they make. Ideally these arrangements should ensure best execution, i.e. the best price, for the client. Unfortunately an issue called 'soft dollars' has, in the past, meant that trades have been directed towards certain brokers and in return managers have received things such as research and software systems, at the cost of best execution. This costs you money.

■ **Bid/offer spread:** This is the difference between the cost of buying and selling a share. A broker will buy shares at below the mid-point price of the shares in the market and sell you shares above the mid

table 13.3 **Turnover is costly**

Cost of a round-trip trade (selling and buying)

Commission	30 basis points
Bid/offer spread	75 basis points
Price impact	25 basis points
Stamp Duty	50 basis points
Total	**180 basis points = 1.8%**

Source: James (2000)

point. So, in the course of trade you will suffer the bid (buy) /offer (sell) spread.

■ ***Price effects****:* This is a cost that arises if large blocks of shares are either being bought or sold. Market makers, who set prices, will move the price during the trade. Demand for shares, i.e. a buy, will push the price of shares up before the completed purchase is made. Big fund management group insist on secrecy when they trade to avoid moving the price against themselves too far.

■ ***The taxman****:* Of course, he gets his hand in the pie. This is amazing given the fact that large portions of money invested represents assets that people are trying hard to accumulate to provide for themselves in their retirement, an activity so encouraged by the government. Stamp duty is paid on the purchase of shares.

So what does turnover cost? The answer is that it probably costs somewhere in the region of 1.5 per cent to 1.8 per cent for a round-trip in the UK market, i.e. selling a share and replacing it with another as you can see from Table 13.3. You can therefore calculate the cost that a fund manager incurs by multiplying 1.8 per cent by the level of turnover activity they create on the fund. In some cases the costs may be higher, in others lower, depending on the firm's relationship with its brokers, the shares being traded and the size of trade. This figure is good enough for our purposes. With turnover of 67 per cent for the average fund, the cost associated with it is 1.2 per cent a year. The hurdle for the active manager grows.

Cost 6: Taxes

In the UK, unit trusts and OEICs do not incur capital gains tax on sales of securities held within them, although they may pay income tax on some forms of income. If you own such a fund, as far as you are concerned, you will pay capital gains tax between the cost of buying a fund, indexed up according to the chancellor's latest rules, and the value you sold it for. So, turnover has no effect from a tax perspective within the fund. Other structures such as pension plans, PEPs and ISAs are tax-free for most income and all capital gains. Check with your tax advisor if you want details.

If your assets fall outside tax-efficient structures you will incur capital gains tax once you have used up your annual allowance, paying cash to the chancellor that could otherwise have been compounding in your portfolio. Some estimates put this tax cost at somewhere between 1 per cent and 2 per cent a year with turnover of 50 per cent. It is evident that for a taxable investor, portfolios with low turnover are better than portfolios with high turnover. By and large, well-managed index funds have a turnover below 5 per cent, for Level 1 building blocks.

Assessing the effect of your 'all-in' costs

All-in, you have upfront fees, everything that goes into TERs, turnover costs and possible tax consequences to suffer. Controlling costs is important. The best way of demonstrating just how much of your return pie the industry will take is to consider two hypothetical funds: High Cost Fund and Low Cost Fund.

Let's assume that these are both good active managers who can produce an annualised return of 10 per cent before factoring in any costs. With inflation at, say, 3 per cent, the annualised increase in the purchasing power of your money, or in other words your real return, is 7 per cent. High Cost Fund has an investment process that turns over the portfolio 100 per cent

table 13.4 The effect of costs and fee structures

Cost	Low-cost fund	High-cost fund
Initial charge	**0%**	**5%**
Initial amount invested (£10,000)	£10,000	£9,500
Annual management fee	0.75%	1.50%
Other expenses	0.10%	0.30%
Total expense ratio (TER)	**0.85%**	**1.80%**
Turnover	20%	100%
Turnover costs*	0.30%	1.50%
Total annual costs	**1.15%**	**3.30%**
Nominal return	10.00%	10.00%
Real return before costs	7.00%	7.00%
Real return after costs	**5.85%**	**3.70%**

Estimated conservatively at 1.5%

table 13.5	Costs matter, as John Bogle would say			
Fund	Amount invested after initial fee	10 years	20 years	30 years
Low-cost fund	£10,000	£17,657	£31,176	£55,046
High-cost fund	£9,500	£13,662	£19,647	£28,254
Difference	**£500**	**£3,995**	**£11,529**	**£26,792**

every year. Low Cost Fund turns over 20 per cent of the value of the portfolio. Not only are their investment styles different but also their marketing departments have created different fee structures (Table 13.4).

As you can see there is 2.15 per cent absolute difference between the two managers. High Cost Fund's manager has to be considerably better at beating the market to beat Low Cost Fund's manager, simply because of its turnover strategy and pricing policies. Taking an initial investment of £10,000 we can work out just what a difference these two different approaches make to your long-term wealth accumulation. With High Cost Fund you head to Bognor and with Low Cost Fund the Bahamas beckons. Over thirty years you give up around about 50 per cent of your future purchasing power (Table 13.5). The choice is yours.

Scale down Low Cost Fund's TER to 0.3 per cent and reduce turnover to 5 per cent and you can see why an index fund is such a compelling proposition; the hurdle that high cost funds set themselves is very high, requiring significant market-beating decisions, simply to catch up.

13.3 Summary: costs – what a drag

■ You need to get a handle on costs because they really will make a significant difference to your investment programme.

■ In the UK, costs remain ludicrously high for most products.

■ Avoid paying initial fees wherever you can; they add nothing to your investment programme. Never pay an initial fee for an index fund or an actively managed bond fund. Get discounts by shopping around on active funds.

■ Costs are far more than just annual management fees. Always look at total expense ratios. Avoid paying over 0.5 per cent TER for your Level 1 assets – aims for lower.

- Find out what turnover any active manager incurs. On average turnover costs UK investors over 1 per cent per year.

- If you are a taxable investor turnover may have tax consequences for you, which could be as high as 1 per cent to 2 per cent per year.

- All in all, know who is dipping their hands in your pocket, give them a sharp slap on the wrist, and avoid dealing with them in future. Keep as much in your pocket as you can. After all, it is your money, you are taking the risks with it and it is your future that is being affected.

References

Autif (1998) as quoted in FSA (2001) *Comparative tables: Bulletin No.1*. London: FSA, Annex A, p.5. Available from: http://www.fsa.gov.uk

James, K. R. (2000) *The price of retail investing in the UK*. London: FSA, FSA Occasional Paper.

14

Standing firm on index funds

In an industry dominated by managers trying to beat the markets for a living and advisors who rely on the fees and commissions that active investment products provide, you should not be too surprised if you come across resistance to accepting the validity of the index fund and its rightful place as the default vehicle at the core of a portfolio. A number of arguments are used to dissuade investors from using index funds. Have the confidence to know that you are right and stand your ground.

14.1 Common arguments used to put down index funds

The common arguments that you will face are easy to refute. Remember that just because they may be able to find isolated cases to support their arguments, as a smarter investor, you are playing a game of probabilities, which always lie in favour of using index funds unless an active manager can really demonstrate their superior and sustainable skills.

Argument 1: You don't want all that rubbish in your portfolio

Telling you that you shouldn't be forced to hold rubbish in your portfolios simply because it is in the index is a common put-down. The argument suggests that active managers can avoid this rubbish and choose to own only 'good' stocks.

At one level you may find yourself agreeing with this – after all, why would you want to hold the stock of a company that has a poor outlook?

Remember, though, that markets appear to be quite efficient and the price of each company's shares should reflect all available public information about it. There is a big difference between a good company and a good investment, as many astute investors have pointed out. Perhaps the rubbish is priced appropriately; owning rubbish is therefore not a problem if the price reflects its outlook.

The empirical evidence tells us that the majority of active managers are beaten by index funds in the long run, suggesting that it is hard to pick the good investments from the supposed rubbish to a degree that covers their all-in costs.

Argument 2: Active managers can hold cash in falling markets

Active managers have an advantage over index funds because they can move into cash when markets are overvalued, and then shift back into equities once markets are set to rise; or that at least is how the argument goes.

If active managers can pick these market turning points before they happen, you would expect to see cash levels in funds to be at their highest at market peaks, in anticipation of market falls and at their lowest at the bottom of the markets. This seems like a reasonable case, but the evidence again suggests otherwise.

In 1973 cash held in US equity funds was around 4 per cent at the height of the market and 10 per cent at its lows in 1974 (Malkiel, 1999). Before markets began to fall in 2000 cash was 4 per cent of US equity funds but increased to 6 per cent a year later after equities had fallen substantially. In fact this is borne out in almost every market fall – 1987, 1990, 1998. Simon Keane, professor of finance at Glasgow University comes to the following conclusion (Keane, 2000):

'There is no way of anticipating the phases of a bear market except by luck or with the advantage of hindsight. The notion that active fund managers can systematically anticipate the start or duration of a bear market with sufficient accuracy to give them an advantage over index funds is insupportable.

'Even if it could be shown that all active managers outperformed all index funds during a bear market, it would still not follow that investors would be better off in an active fund. It would only be valid if investors were better off in an active fund under normal growth conditions – but the evidence is clear that this is not

table 14.1 The market tends to beat active managers				
Fund category	Comparison index	2002	3 years	5 years
All domestic funds	S&P SuperComposite 1500	59%	53%	60%
All large-cap funds	S&P 500	61%	54%	62%
All mid-cap funds	S&P Mid Cap 400	70%	77%	91%
All small-cap funds	S&P Small Cap 600	74%	72%	66%

Source: *Standard & Poor's Indices Versus Active Funds Scorecards (SPIVA™): Fourth Quarter 2002*

so. Holding a bank deposit is the ultimate defensive strategy but overall it is a relatively poor investment.'

Keane's research demonstrated that in 1998, when equity markets around the world fell, US active managers underperformed the market by 2.5 per cent on the downturn and by 5 per cent on the upturn. He postulates that the accumulated evidence indicates clearly that bear markets are by and large unpredictable and that investors are better rewarded by adopting a buy-and-hold-policy than trying to establish defensive positions.

Table 14.1 gives the percentage of active funds in the USA that were beaten by the equivalent S&P market index. The period under review is 2002, the year of the big sell-off and the three-year market fall 2000–2002. The evidence seems convincing to me. Could you truly have picked in advance those that beat the index? If you could, you have a great future as an investment consultant.

Argument 3: Indexing creates inefficiencies to be exploited

As more people index, and research into the true or intrinsic value of companies by both buy and sell side analysts declines, then inefficiencies will appear, which the astute active manager can exploit to beat the market. Again, at first glance, this argument seems reasonable, but if we look a little deeper, it appears to be a little shallow. First, indexing represents only around 20 per cent of all institutional equity assets and 10 per cent of retail equity assets in the UK. Very few index bond funds exist in the UK. As such, we are a very long way from the stage of such inefficiencies being pronounced.

Remember, too, that active managers, analysts and market makers play an important role in setting the fair price of stocks and providing liquidity. I have no idea at what level between indexed assets and actively managed

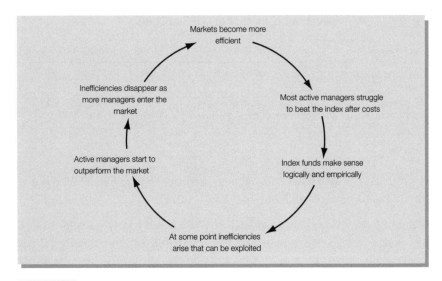

figure 14.1 **The cycle of efficiency**   *Source: WM Company*

assets that these inefficiencies begin to creep in, but I am pretty certain that the markets in the UK and USA are today scoured pretty thoroughly for inefficiencies. If inefficiencies increase then active managers will exploit them and outperform. More money and resources will flow into active funds and the inefficiencies will disappear, again favouring index investing. And so the cycle continues, as Figure 14.1 illustrates.

Argument 4: Active managers win in inefficient markets

When markets are inefficient, or to put it another way, when information is unevenly available to investors, possibly due to a lack or reduced level of market coverage by analysts, those investors who seek out and use information wisely may be able to outperform the market. This argument suggests that active managers are a better option in less efficient markets such as smaller company stocks, international and emerging markets.

You might think this reasonable too, but recall the logic we used earlier. All investors are the market and the average investor will be the market before costs. After costs, which tend to be significantly higher in these markets, the average manager will by definition underperform the index by these costs. As index funds have lower costs, they will beat the majority of active funds. Maybe a few managers, with their insight, will end up with skill-based performance that persists.

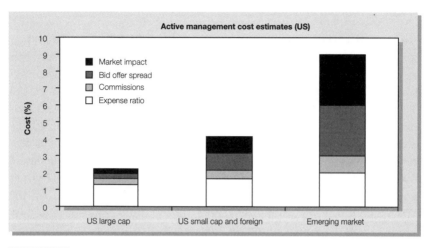

figure 14.2 **Hurdles for active managers are high**

Source: Bernstein, W.J., *The Intelligent Asset Allocator* © 2001, McGraw-Hill, reproduced with permission of the
McGraw Hill Companies

It seems that the significantly higher costs of playing in these markets mops up most of the skill-based gains that may be achieved by smart professional managers. In inefficient markets transaction costs are often far higher due to wider bid-offer spreads (the difference between the price you can buy a share at versus the price you can sell it at) and other brokerage costs. This is true for small-cap stocks, some international stocks and emerging market stocks. In addition, management fees are usually higher. Less liquid stocks, more common is smaller, less heavily traded, markets, may also incur a higher price effect cost. Figure 14.2 outlines the increased cost hurdles faced by active managers between efficient large-cap markets and other supposedly inefficient markets. In the UK, expense ratios are generally a little higher.

A closer look at small-cap funds

Research by Garrett Quigley and Rex Sinquefield looked at UK unit trusts between 1987 and 1998, and reached the following conclusion:

'Contrary to the notion that small-company shares offer abundant "beat the market" opportunities, we find that small company unit trusts are the worst performers. In fact their performance failure is persistent and reliable.'

'Overall, this study, like all mutual fund studies, does not enlighten us about what kinds of market failures [inefficiencies] *occur. It does say that if there are any, UK equity managers do not exploit them.'*

You saw in Table 14.1 that the market beat the majority of managers.

A closer look at international equity funds

On pure logic, the average international equity index funds should outperform the average active fund by around 3 per cent over the long run, this being the differential between active costs and index fund costs. The empirical data tells a different story: for example, international (world ex-US) actively managed funds have in the majority outperformed passive funds over the past decade. This has been largely due to the fall and sustained low level of the Japanese market, which at one point in the early 1990s represented around 60 per cent of the most common international benchmark the MSCI EAFE index. Active managers have under-weighted Japan in their portfolios, and have been right. If you strip out Japan and look at, say, the MSCI EASEA (i.e. the world ex-US and ex-Japan) index funds have outperformed the average active fund. In Europe the same applies.

Despite this data, the logic underlying index funds remains. Active managers have in the past decade or so called Japan right. As you personally have to make a decision today as to whether active or passive management makes most sense, for international equities, you have to ask yourself whether managers have the skills to make effective market timing decisions going forward. Japan has been much harder to call in the past couple of years. Can you afford to choose a manager who calls it wrong?

Argument 5: Index funds success is self-fulfilling

During the bull market of the late 1990s, some commentators claimed that the flow of funds appeared to push the prices of a handful of large companies up just because they were included in the index. However, this would seem to suggest that somehow passive index funds are dictating prices to the market, which seems a little absurd. The vast majority of funds are still managed in an active way and active managers must dictate prices of stocks. The buying of large company stocks by index funds probably represents less than 5 per cent of trading volumes. Surely this passive voice, that does not attempt to price the stock, merely to buy it, can't be dictating to the 95 per cent of active money trading the stock. In addition, if this were the case, then wouldn't all stocks in the index have risen by the same amount during this period? They evidently did not. Any effect would be likely to be short lived.

Argument 6: Why accept certain failure?

Finally, an argument that plays on your emotions is often used: the suggestion is made that either you miserably accept that you are guaranteed to underperform the market, by costs, if you invest in an index fund or you can have the hope and chance of beating the market. No one likes to be a loser and the manager will play on your emotions by showing you a fund with a few years of good returns, and hoping that you will forget about performance persistence, luck, efficient markets, manager costs and reversion to the mean.

Don't be a loser and play the loser's game. Stand up to this emotional pressure, confident in your understanding of where the chances of success really lie long term.

14.2 Bond investing: active or index?

In the great active versus index debate, the arguments and research largely revolve around equity investment. However, you should not overlook the efficacy of index investing for bonds, which up to now has been whispered rather than shouted from the rooftops. The evidence is compelling and comes down firmly in favour of investing in index funds, and exchange-traded funds. Gradually, index bond funds or ETFs are increasing in the UK, but only a handful exist today.

According to Morningstar, over the ten-year period 1988–1998, US bond index funds returned 8.9 per cent a year against 8.2 per cent for actively managed bond funds. Because bond returns are more closely grouped than equities, this translated into index funds beating 85 per cent of all active funds. This differential is largely due to fees.

As a caveat, there are some excellent active bond managers and some appear to have consistently strong performance. To date, bond index funds only represent around 3 per cent of all US mutual fund assets and much of this is institutional money. Outside the USA, bond index investing is either non-existent or at a very rudimentary stage, and this applies in the UK.

14.3 Summary: the active versus index debate

■ Over longer periods of time index investments have generally beaten a majority of actively managed funds. The logic that the average index funds will outperform the majority of actively managed funds due to differences in cost is borne out by a mounting pile of empirical evidence.

■ Index funds are likely to float towards the top and many of today's winning managers will sink back as their performance fails to persist. Some will beat index funds in the long run – picking them today is the challenge.

■ This result is largely expected and widely known for more efficient markets where it is harder for active managers to find value-adding opportunities such as UK large cap stocks.

■ Surprisingly, though, index fund vehicles tend to outperform a majority of actively managed funds in less-efficient markets including small-cap stocks, and non-domestic markets. This is generally a consequence of the higher fees charged and the significantly higher transaction costs associated with these markets, negating the potentially larger gains from exploiting inefficiencies.

■ Active managers have had more success in beating international equity index funds, largely due to active managers under-weighting Japan, which has been a really poor performer for a decade. This will be harder to call going forwards.

■ The claim that active managers will outperform index funds in bear markets has been shown to be lacking in supporting evidence. What research there is points to the fact that active managers have a poor record, as a group, in anticipating downturns and subsequent upswings in markets. A buy-and-hold strategy is in all likelihood a better option.

■ Much of the empirical data does not take into account the problem of survivorship bias or the effect of the high turnover, and thus tax costs, for taxable investors, which would significantly improve the efficacy of index investment vehicles over active vehicles, in some countries such as the USA.

■ While index funds have outperformed a majority of active funds, some active funds do and will outperform them over different periods. The evidence would seem to suggest that short-term outperformance is rarely sustained. The very small number of active funds that outperform over longer periods could in many cases be attributed to luck. However, it is possible that it may in some cases be down to exceptional manager skill.

■ Any material evidence of performance persistence usually relates to persistent underperformance caused by high fees, rather than any persistence in outperformance. Any persistence is generally too limited actually to act on.

■ There is no useful methodology for selecting them in advance. Past performance is no guarantee or predictor of future returns.

■ Statistically, even the best active managers need to provide fifteen to twenty years of data for you to know whether they have outperformed by luck or judgement.

■ Many managers move around so frequently that it is hard to know whose performance you are actually looking at.

As we have seen earlier, good investing is about maximising the probability of reaching your goals and index funds are the best practical way for most investors to attain performance that captures the bulk of the characteristics that you want from each of your building blocks.

References

Keane, S. (2000) *Index funds in a bear market.* A monograph published by Glasgow University in association with Virgin Direct: as quoted by Anon (2003) *Active fund managers add to market misery.* Virgin Direct, March. Available from: http://www.virginmoney.com.

Malkiel, B. G. (1999) *A random walk down Wall Street.* New York: W. W. Norton, 188–189.

Quigley, G. and Sinquefield, R. (2000) Performance of UK equity unit trusts, *Journal of Asset Management*, vol. 1, no 1. 72–92.

5

Smarter building block insights

So far in this book, we have avoided getting into too much detail when talking about the building blocks that you can use. It is useful though to understand a little more about the two Level 1 building blocks that will form the backbone of your investment portfolio, as well as the Level 2 building blocks you may call upon. These important ideas are covered in a non-technical manner.

Chapter 15: The thrills and spills of equities

Making sure that you understand where equity returns come from and that in the shorter term they are not always based on economics, but on sentiment, is key in beginning to understand both the thrills and the spills of equity market investing. Understanding history provides some good lessons for the future and a few warning markers.

Chapter 16: The ins and outs of bonds

Taking a closer look at bonds will help you to understand both the value that they bring to your portfolio as a return smoother, but also the limitations that they have, particularly when the effects of inflation are taken into account. Understanding how they work is vital to understanding how you can use them effectively.

Chapter 17: Spotlight on return smoothers

Here, you will get a little more insight into each of the main return smoother blocks that are available to use in your portfolio, the role that they can play in your portfolio and some of the practical issues associated with them.

Chapter 18: Spotlight on return enhancers

You will be able to gain an insight into those building blocks that provide you with the scope to enhance your portfolio's returns and to explore some of the hotly debated issues that surround them.

15

The thrills and spills of equities

If human beings weren't so emotional, investing would be so much easier and investing in equities, in particular, would be less of a roller-coaster ride and more of a stroll through the Devon hills – but there we are. Understanding the thrills and, just as importantly, the spills of being an owner of equities is central to understanding the challenges in both building and preserving wealth.

There are two emotional extremes that afflict equity investors: on the one hand, particularly in rising markets, it's easy to begin to believe that they are a route to quick wealth creation, and aren't that risky; after all, from 1980 to 1999, eighteen of the twenty years generated positive returns, and half of those generated after-inflation returns of more than 20 per cent a year. A sum of £1,000 invested over this period grew to £12,000 – now that was thrilling! If you flick back to Figure 8.7, you will see that the twenty-year bull market that multiplied your wealth more than tenfold was a rare event.

On the other hand, the 40 per cent fall from 2000 to the end of 2002 was quite a spill, destroying large amounts of wealth for those drawn into the delusion that equities were a risk-free route to riches, particularly those drawn in at what turned out to be the top of the market. That's quite a spill, but far from the worst that has happened in the UK, let alone in other markets.

To become a smarter investor, you need to get a handle on the thrills and spill of equities and how you can use them to drive your wealth accumulation, protect your wealth from the ravages of inflation, and why it is so important to make sure that you hold sufficient insurance, by owing *return smoothers*, to protect you if the worst happens.

15.1 Why the thrills and spills?

To get to the root of the issues that you face as an equity investor, you need to think about why equities can deliver long-term, mid-single digit real returns, and why from time to time returns are simply so far away, both on the upside and the downside, from this long-run average. Let's perhaps start unravelling this issue with a 1934 quote from Benjamin Graham, one of the founding fathers of today's investment management industry. He stated (Graham and Dodd, 1996) that:

'In the short run the market is a voting machine; in the long run, it is a weighing machine.'

Spend a bit of time thinking about this statement, as it elegantly defines the fundamental difference between what investors are willing to pay for shares in a company at a point in time, as opposed to what their true value is given the state of their company in the real world. When investors disconnect the relationship between real life and markets, problems arise.

The short-term voting machine

As a holder of equities, you become part-owner in real businesses, either in the UK or overseas, depending on what building block you are using. In the UK, there are about 2,600 public companies listed on the London Stock Exchange, AIM and Techmark exchanges, which you have the ability both to own and, through your rights as a shareholder, to have some say in how they are run. In return for investing capital, your reward comes in two distinct forms: the regular *dividends* that you get paid in cash; and the *capital appreciation*, or otherwise, reflected in changes in the share price. Together, these give you the *total market return* from your investment.

However, this total market return does not necessarily reflect the underlying value of companies and markets in the real world, but investors' emotional perceptions of what they are worth and these change with market sentiment. Some of the increases in share prices you experience may reflect a speculative change in perceptions, creating gains as it waxes and losses as it wanes. This is the market operating as a voting machine, as Graham puts it.

As seen in Chapter 12, the amount investors are willing to pay for each £1 of future earnings depends on sentiment prevailing at the time and it is reflected in the ratio of the price of a share to its earnings, otherwise known as its price/earnings ratio. Higher ratios reflect the increased optimism that investors feel, reflected in the higher amount that investors will pay for future earnings. Changes in price that reflect changes in perception, and an increased willingness to pay up for earnings reflected in changes in P/E, are speculative returns.

Playing the game of capturing these shorter-term changes in sentiment is more akin to gambling than investing. A classic case is the technology boom and bust, of the late 1990s and early 2000s, when investors paid high prices for non-existent or unlikely future earnings. John Bogle, a wise and rational investor, summed up investing as opposed to speculating most eloquently as follows (Bogle, 2002):

'If there was a single dominant failing of the recent bubble, it was the market's overbearing focus on the momentary precision of the price of a stock rather than on the eternal vagueness of the intrinsic value of a corporation. Nonetheless, the price of a stock is perception, and acting on that perception is speculation. The value of a corporation is reality and acting on that reality is investment.'

Always beware of so-called experts who says *'it's different this time'* and that a re-evaluation of earnings is required to explain why you should pay so much for earnings. This is probably a pretty good signal that a bubble is about to burst! Stock prices will fall when these above-normal earnings fail to materialise, which has always proved to be the outcome in investment bubbles.

The long-term weighing machine

In reality, the profits (earnings) of a company grow through increased sales and improved profit margins; improved sales come from good product development, focused marketing, well-chosen segments in which to compete, motivated sales teams, and taking care of existing clients. Better profit margins come from improved productivity through better skilled employees, better processes, strong corporate governance and technological efficiencies. Value is created in the real world by hard work, not wishful thinking. This true value is sometimes referred to as *intrinsic value*, a phrase coined by Benjamin Graham.

Returns from equities come from the dividends that companies pay (and in aggregate the market pays) and the capitalisation of their profits (earnings), resulting in a change in the price of stocks and in aggregate the market. These dividends plus your capital gains equate to the total market return that you receive. However, only some of the price change is due to the underlying economics of each company, represented by their changing profitability and thus growth (or decline) in earnings per share, the rest comes from changes in investor sentiment.

Imagine that a company managed to increase its profits so that its earnings per share rose from £1.00 to £1.05, a growth rate in earnings of 5 per cent over a year. At the start of the year the P/E ratio was 15 and thus the price of the shares was £15 (i.e. £1.00 × 15). At the end of the year, if the P/E ratio remained constant at 15, the price of the shares would rise from £15 to £15.75 (£1.05 × 15), in other words a 5 per cent rise in price or capital gain and the company also paid a dividend of 3 per cent, giving you a return from the endeavours of the company of 8 per cent. The dividends that you receive and the capitalisation of earnings growth, at a constant P/E are sometimes referred to as *investment returns* and represents the return from the endeavours of the company.

Imagine, though, that in this same year, investors began to feel bullish about the economy, the market in general and the firm in particular and were now willing to pay 16 times earnings for the shares, instead of 15. This would result in a price rise from £15 to £16.8 (16 × £1.05) or a 12 per cent increase in price. Your total market return would be:

3% dividend + 12% price change = 15%

So, the difference between *investment returns* and *market returns*, in this case 7 per cent, is due to investors' changing perceptions affecting the level of the P/E ratio. This difference is sometimes referred to as the *speculative return* (Figure 15.1).

The magnitude and longevity of these differences tell us that evaluating the intrinsic value of a company, or a market as a whole, is difficult and that

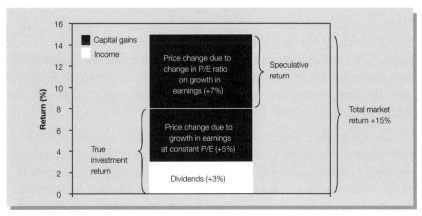

figure 15.1 **The elements of market returns**

emotions seem to cloud investment judgement, sometimes significantly. Strong growth in an economy tends to reinforce investor behaviours such as over-confidence, over-optimism and unwarranted self-belief, which, at extremes, leads to bubbles and subsequent busts. As Warren Buffett (1996) said:

'Nothing sedates rationality like large doses of effortless money.'

In the long run, speculation zeros out

In the end, though, the link between investment returns and market returns must reflect what is really happening in the underlying economy and business world, a point well worth remembering. Put another way, long run returns are attributable to *investment returns* and not short-term speculative excesses. In fact, in the USA, since 1872, real market returns and investment returns were comparable at around 6.5 per cent. Buffett again makes the point succinctly about investors in his company Berkshire Hathaway (Buffett, 1997):

'The longer a shareholder holds his shares, the more bearing Berkshire's business results will have on his financial experience – and the less it will matter what premium or discount to intrinsic value prevails when he buys or sells his stock.'

Estimating the intrinsic value of an enterprise is not easy for most of us without the insight, experience and enthusiasm of the likes of Buffet.

Equity returns tend to return towards the mean

Early in my career I was given the insightful piece of wisdom that markets were like rubber bands stretched between two long-term points in time. At times, they are pulled away from their relatively relaxed norms to points at which they become stretched by the force of the hand of the speculative markets. The further from the norm they go, the greater the force trying to return them to their unstressed position. At some point, which is hard to pick, they will spring back, sometimes overshooting dramatically for a time. Not a bad word picture to bear in mind.

Periods when markets have been overvalued (i.e. P/Es have been higher than average) have tended to be followed by periods of lower-than-average returns as markets *return to mean* levels of value, and vice versa (Figure 15.2). The fallibility of this approach is that the magnitude and longevity of periods of outperformance can be extremely extended, and the market turning points and speed of mean reversion cannot be judged with any

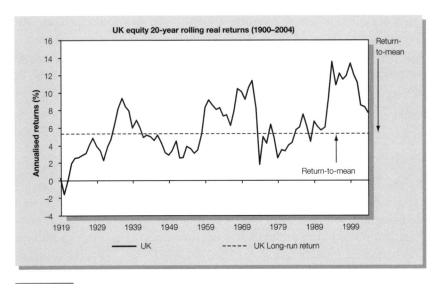

figure 15.2 Equity markets seem to revert to their mean over time

Source: DMS Global Data (Ibbotson) © 2006 E Dimson, P Marsh and M Staunton

accuracy. This is one of the dilemmas you face in investing a lump sum in the markets that we explored in Chapter 12. If it were easy, investment professionals would prove it in outperformance – something we simply do not see en masse.

There are many documented instances of rational investors holding out against the opportunity to make speculative returns because it was felt that the market had moved away from fundamental economic reality. Two examples are Buffett and his 'not getting' the tech-stock thing, and Philips & Drew Fund Management, one of the UK's biggest pension managers at the start of the 1990s, who were underweight equities during the mid-to-late 1990s. Both in their own way were proved right but PDFM's business was severely eroded as it stuck to its guns. Even the Sage of Omaha came in for some serious, but ultimately unwarranted, stick from his critics.

15.2 The thrills of equity investing

As you have read, equities are the engines of portfolio growth, delivering on average around 5 per cent after inflation per year, in the UK. That means doubling your purchasing power once every fourteen years or so – that in itself should be quite a thrill, in return for having the stomach to hold them, although you may not think so; however, over thirty-five years, each

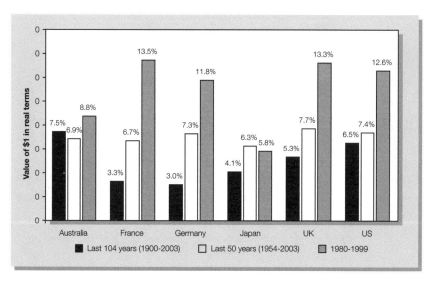

figure 15.3 Long-term annualised real returns from global equity markets
(1900–2003) Source: DMS Global Data (Ibbotson) © 2006 E Dimson, P Marsh and M Staunton

£1 of spending power invested would buy over five times as much as the money you put in. At times, you may get an even bigger thrill, but don't bank on it. Be happy if you achieve the long-run average return you are hoping for. In fact, in investing, generating positive real returns of any sort over the period that you are investing is a bonus and reaching your target rate of return especially pleasing.

Around the world, people have generally fared well in real terms by being investors in equities over the long run. The 'weighing machine' that Benjamin Graham refers to is in effect weighing all of the effort, hard work, innovation, creativity, productivity and determination of managers and employees day in, day out, which have contributed to the growth of capitalist economies over the past century.

As you can see in Figure 15.3, returns above inflation have ranged from around 3 per cent to 7 per cent. Returns for Japan, Germany and France over the 104 years period were more muted than for the others due to very high inflation at times earlier in the century. Over the past fifty years and during the bull market from 1980 to 1999, returns were well above the long-run average. These rates of return, particularly the latter, where in the UK your purchasing power would have doubled every five to six years, were clearly unsustainable. While we would all like to see this repeated, it is probably unlikely in the near future.

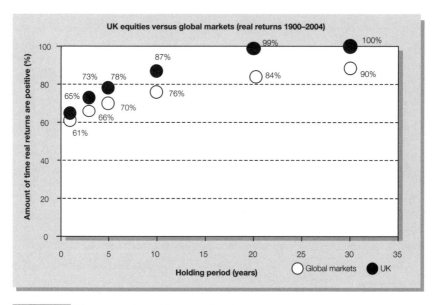

figure 15.4 Chances of positive purchasing power outcomes

Source: DMS Global Data (Ibbotson) © 2006 E Dimson, P Marsh and M Staunton

It's all very well looking at long-run returns, but what you really need to know is what the chances are that you will see positive real returns and hopefully returns similar to your reasonable estimates over a certain time.

You have a good chance of positive returns, but there's no guarantee

Let's start then by looking at the proportion of times that real returns have been positive over different investment horizons, which will give you an insight into likely outcomes for your own investment horizon. You can see from Figure 15.4 that UK equities have generated positive returns about two-thirds of the time over any one-year period. If you held them for twenty years or more, you would have had positive returns on nearly every occasion, but not quite.

As for global markets (in this case sixteen global equity markets covering around 85 per cent of the world's equity market capitalisation) you can see that around 15 per cent of the time, if you held them for twenty years, your wealth might actually have decreased; for thirty-year periods, globally, returns have been negative around 10 per cent of the time. In some individual cases, the instance of negative returns has been considerably higher. The message here is that perhaps it pays to be a little cautious with the UK

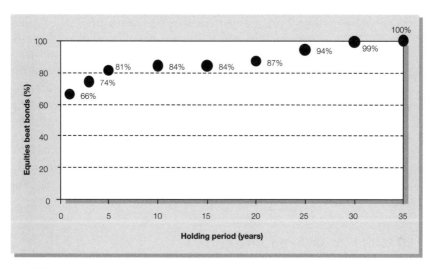

figure 15.5 **UK equities generally outperform bonds (real returns 1900–2004)**   *Source: DMS Global Data (Ibbotson) © 2006 E Dimson, P Marsh and M Staunton*

data and to be aware that a risk does exist to your purchasing power over extended periods of time. Interestingly, these numbers are in a similar range to the estimated chances of losses calculated by Monte Carlo simulation (Figure 8.7).

Why you should get more reward than for owning bonds

You should earn a reward for the additional risks that you incur from investing in equities as opposed to bonds; you could lose your money, you have no certainty that dividends will be paid, or any certainty that your shares will appreciate. In the pecking order of claims on a company's assets, equities are at the bottom of the pile below secured bankers, bondholders and other creditors; this more risky position demands greater reward for investors. This premium is known as the *equity risk premium*. Measuring it in the past is simple enough; however, like many arguments in investing, not only are there short-term exceptions to long-run averages, but different time frames tell different stories. Academics and economists argue ad infinitum about the level of the equity risk premium but as the Economist succinctly put it in 2003:

'Yes, over long periods equities have done better than bonds. But there is no equity "premium" – in the sense of a fairly predictable excess over bond returns on which investors can rely ... Searching for a consistent, God-given premium is a fool's errand.'

All I can say, as a practitioner rather than an academic, is that over the long run a premium appears to exist and should do so in the future, otherwise we would simply invest in bonds with lower risks. As you can see from Figure 15.5, while some shorter-term periods exist where bonds outperform equities, over the longer-term equities are the better return bet. These short-term periods give hope to active investors that they can benefit by switching their mix around.

As the objective of good, simple, long-term investing is giving yourself the greatest chance of success, and equities have a greater chance of delivering long-term real returns than either bonds or cash, if you are a long-term investor you should have a natural bias towards equities.

A good defence against inflation

Understanding how equities have protected investors from the ravages of inflation over different periods can provide some useful insights. In an inflationary environment, companies put their prices up and revenues and earnings rise in nominal terms. In addition, the nominal value of their assets such as land, stock and building also increases. You would logically expect that equities would therefore have an inherent capability to protect against inflation as they lay claim to the 'price-level-sensitive residual value

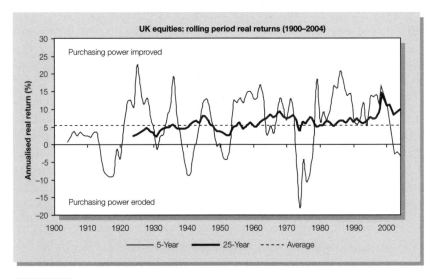

figure 15.6 **In the long run equities provide strong protection against inflation**   *Source: DMS Global Data (Ibbotson) © 2006 E Dimson, P Marsh and M Staunton*

of a corporation' as David Swensen (2000) puts it, at least in the medium to long term.

Comparing how equities have performed in real terms over the shorter term, five years, and over the longer term, 25 years, you can see that despite performing poorly when inflation rises rapidly, over time they would have been a pretty good means of protecting your wealth from the ravages of inflation. An inherent logic suggests that they should, and in practice its appears that they have done a reasonable job (Figure 15.6).

I once worked with colleagues in Sao Paulo, Brazil and remember them talking about the times of hyperinflation in the early 1990s when everyone in the office spent the day managing their own cash, moving it from one inflation-protected bank account to another, or into foreign assets, rather than managing their business. You can perhaps see the logic in using other diversifying building blocks that provide inflation-hedging, such as property, commodities and inflation-protected bonds, despite equities' seemingly robust defence against inflation.

An aside: Spend dividends at your peril

You should note at this point that a significant proportion of returns come from the dividends you receive from your equity investments. This may be contrary to the belief that has grown up over the past couple of decades

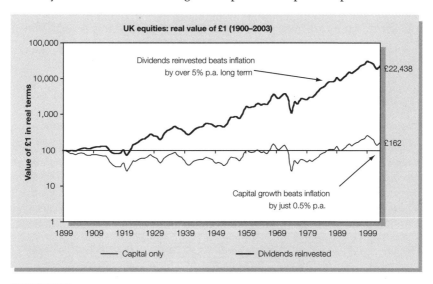

figure 15.7 **Reinvesting dividends is vital for equity returns**

Source: DMS Global Data (Ibbotson) © 2006 E Dimson, P Marsh and M Staunton; Barclays Equity Gilt Study (yields)

where changes in price seemed to contribute far more to returns than dividends. In the long run, that simply is not the case. Take a look at Figure 15.7, which demonstrates this for the UK. I have used a log scale to help to make it easier to see that there have been times when capital gains alone have been insufficient to generate positive purchasing power gains.

15.3 The spills of equity investing

However much you should be trying to focus on long-term goals, the latent fear of periods of serious market trauma should lurk in the back of your mind; markets can and do crash. The surprising thing is, not that they do, but just how frequent, traumatic and prolonged they can be both in the UK and around the world. You need to understand the potential frequency, magnitude and longevity of these crashes if you are to give the markets the due respect that they deserve. Owning a diverse portfolio is the only real protection.

Equity market crashes occur relatively frequently

Let's take a look at the UK first and see what crashes investors have experienced since 1900. Table 15.1 shows times when UK equity markets have fallen by more than 10 per cent in real terms; it reveals the cumulative falls from top to bottom of the market and how long it would have taken for your wealth to return to a level where it could buy as much as when the market was at its previous peak. The data is for year-end to year-end, which may to some extent mask the true high to low of the market, but it is good

table 15.1 Periods of UK equity market trauma (in real terms): 1900–2004

Peak date	Decline (%)	Decline duration	Trough date	Recovery duration
December 1913	−46%	7 years	December 1920	2 years
December 1928	−31%	3 years	December 1931	2 years
December 1936	−44%	4 years	December 1940	6 years
December 1946	−21%	6 years	December 1952	2 years
December 1956	−10%	1 year	December 1957	1 year
December 1968	−26%	2 years	December 1970	2 years
December 1972	−71%	2 years	December 1974	9 years
December 1989	−18%	1 year	December 1990	2 years
December 1999	−40%	3 years	December 2002	?

Source: DMS Global Data (Ibbotson) © 2006 E Dimson, P Marsh and M Staunton

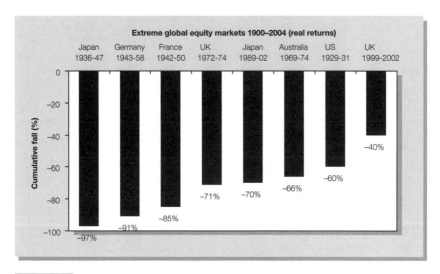

figure 15.8 **Globally, equity market trauma can be severe**

Source: DMS Global Data (Ibbotson) © 2006 E Dimson, P Marsh and M Staunton

enough for our purposes. Markets have the potential to destroy significant wealth.

As you can see, equity market crashes are relatively frequent occurrences. While it may appear from these numbers that equity markets tend to bounce back reasonably quickly, don't be deceived. Figure 15.8 gives a sample of equity market falls around the globe. Look out.

A vivid and hopefully extreme example of a long-lived decline can be found in Japan where in 1989 the Nikkei index (for equities) stood at over 40,000. Fifteen years later, it still languished at only 10,000. The really extreme declines are generally the effect of war, but 70 per cent or so, as experienced in the UK in 1972–4, are very severe.

Markets can take longer to recover than you may realise

In fact, across the sixteen biggest global markets, when there has been a fall of 10 per cent or more, we find that in some cases it can be many years before an investor's purchasing power recovers to the level it was before the market fell. Since 1900, these sixteen markets have experienced over two hundred occasions between them in which their markets have fallen and over 140 times by more than 10 per cent. Figure 15.9 shows the distribution of the years it has taken to recover purchasing power back to its pre-fall level. As an investor, you need to decide whether your investment horizon is long

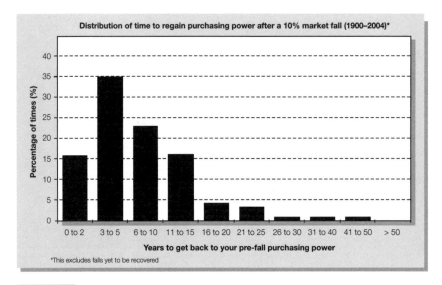

Distribution of time to regain purchasing power after a 10% market fall (1900–2004)*

Years to get back to your pre-fall purchasing power

*This excludes falls yet to be recovered

figure 15.9 **It may take longer than you imagine to get back to where you started**   *Source: DMS Global Data (Ibbotson) © 2006 E Dimson, P Marsh and M Staunton*

enough to sit out these periods, whether you are willing to take the chance that this happens to you and how you can mitigate the risk by sensibly diversifying your portfolio. You can see that around 50 per cent of the time markets bounce back within five years from a fall of 10 per cent or more.

The fact that I am writing this book in 2006 means that I probably have to emphasise the effects of equity market trauma less to you than I would have needed to in 1999. Investors who believe that markets usually bounce back quickly, taking their experience as the crashes of 1987 and 1998, should take heed of these numbers. Regaining purchasing power losses, from global experience, may take longer than anticipated. Your conclusion on market trauma should be: it happens; it happens frequently; in all markets; and can be very painful and sometimes long-lived when it does. Caveat emptor.

Equities have more extreme surprises than statistics suggest

If returns truly fell in a binomially, or a bell-shaped, distribution, as assumed by the industry, then you would expect that the poor returns of 1974 would be expected, statistically, once in 1,400 years and the great returns of 1975 to happen every 33,000 years. Statistics don't fully capture the nature of true markets. In fact, equity markets have a greater chance of larger extreme returns than those anticipated by a normal distribution. Evidence bears this out.

Perhaps the best known case of investors being caught out by market extremes was the fall of Long Term Capital Management, a hedge fund that blew itself up despite the presence of two exceptional Nobel Prize winning economists, and leading market traders. Their models said that what happened couldn't happen; it did, they lost 90 per cent of their capital in a month and effectively went bust. Expect the unexpected might be a good motto to adopt.

15.4 What about future equity returns?

As investors, we should be reasonably confident that companies operating in free capitalist economies should be able to continue to pay dividends and to increase their profits and collectively generate real growth in a nation's economy over the long term. They have done so in the past over reasonable periods of time and human nature, as it is, in the environment of an open capitalist society, should ensure that this is so. In the long run, we can be therefore be reasonably confident that eventually *investment returns* and *market returns* will be similar – they have to be.

The concept of 'return to mean' of markets that are over-or undervalued implies that periods of time, may be extremely prolonged periods, when market returns will be distinctly different from the underlying economic reality. As such, we need to take into account what has happened before our investing and be conservative in what we think may happen in the future. When markets returns have been above investment returns over a period of time such as the 1980s and 1990s, it is perhaps prudent to assume that reversion to mean will result in a subsequent period when returns are below the long-run averages. It would not be unreasonable to expect that returns in the coming couple of decades to be less exciting than the past couple of decades.

In the long run, you would expect the return from equities to be related to the growth in dividends as higher corporate profits (i.e. earnings) are generally assumed to lead to higher dividends. At the end of the day, equity returns have to reflect economic reality. That provides us with a simple model for coming up with future long-term rates of returns from equities. In terms of potential levels of returns over the next decade, assuming a dividend yield of 3 per cent in the UK and a not unreasonable assumption of dividend growth of 5 per cent in nominal terms and inflation at 3 per cent,

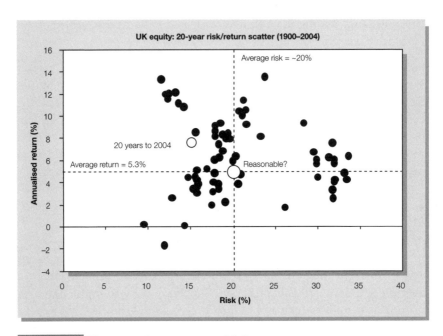

figure 15.10 **What constitutes reasonable?**

Source: DMS Global Data (Ibbotson) © 2006 E Dimson, P Marsh and M Staunton

and assuming a constant P/E ratio, we get the following estimate of real expected equity return:

3% dividends + 5% dividend growth − 3% inflation = 5% real return

If you believe that the P/E ratio will contract from this point forwards (it would not have been a bad assumption to make by the dispassionate investor in 2000 for example), returns will be lower.

The reasonableness of risk and return estimates used

The problem you are up against as an investor, as you have seen on many occasions throughout this book, is that you have little idea what your own investment path will look like within all the range of possible outcomes that could exist. History gives a feel for what they are, and Figure 15.10 will perhaps attest to the reasonableness of the 5 per cent return and 20 per cent risk figures used for equities throughout this book. Using this rate of return for the Monte Carlo simulations in this book allows you to explore the chances that other investment lives occur.

15.5 Summary: the thrills and spills of equities

You should be able to come to some conclusions about equities. These are summarised below:

■ Equities are the drivers of real portfolio returns for longer-term investors, beating both bonds and cash. In the UK they have beaten inflation by around 5 per cent a year. Returns in the long run reflect economic reality. You can estimate the future real returns for equities by adding the current dividend yield to the projected growth in dividends (earnings).

■ In any year, you have about a two in three chance that returns will be positive. You also have a two in three chance that returns will be better than bonds.

■ Over twenty years, there is a very good chance that you will have positive growth in purchasing power, although global market evidence and Monte Carlo simulation urges caution. Let's say a one in ten or so chance exists that you will lose purchasing power over this time frame, is not overly pessimistic.

■ Equities have nearly always beaten bonds over any thirty-year period in the UK.

■ Equity returns are volatile and their risk is somewhere in the region of 20 per cent for developed markets, giving a wide range of annual returns around the mean return. Thus, your short-term ride is bumpier to a loftier long-term level of purchasing power, compared with bonds. Real life shows that extreme returns tend to be larger and more frequent than estimated using binomial distribution statistics.

■ Markets in the shorter term tend to become overvalued or undervalued due to speculative returns reflecting changes in the willingness of investors to pay for future earnings of companies, and collectively the market. The measure of this willingness is reflected in the P/E ratio. The difference between price and value is an important one to make.

■ Markets have a tendency to revert to the mean level of long-run returns. However, the timing and pace of this reversion appears to be impossible to predict. Periods of above-average returns are often, but not always, followed by less-exciting returns and vice versa.

■ If you are investing a lump sum, it is worth assessing whether markets appear overvalued according to the somewhat crude method of comparing current P/E with this historic average, or by comparing the last ten or twenty years of returns with the long-run average. If it concerns you: diversify; scale back your equities and expectations; average your way in.

- Equities provide a good hedge of inflation in the medium to long term. However, in periods of high inflation, short-term erosion of purchasing power may occur. It may be useful to include other inflation hedges in a portfolio such as property, or index-linked bonds.

- Investors should take a prudent approach: be conservative when estimating future returns; be prepared for large extremes from time to time; expect markets falls to occur, with reasonable frequency and not to be fooled into thinking that markets will necessarily bounce back quickly – sometimes they do, sometimes they don't.

References

Bogle, J. C. (2002) *The investment dilemma of the philanthropic investor.* Bogle Financial Markets Research Center. Available from: http://www.vanguard.com

Buffett, W. (1997) *1996 Annual Report: Chairman's Letter.* Berkshire Hathaway Inc. Available from: http://www.berkshirehathaway.com/1996ar/1996.html.

Buffett, W. (2001) *2000 Annual Report: Chairman's Letter.* Berkshire Hathaway Inc.

Economist (2003) Taking stock, *Economist,* June 6.

Graham, B. and Dodd, D. (1996) *Security analysis: The classic 1934 edition.* New York: McGraw-Hill.

Swensen, D. F. (2000) *Pioneering portfolio management.* New York: The Free Press.

16

The ins and outs of bonds

'Bonds' is a catch-all term that too many investors assume to be synonymous with safety. The reality is somewhat less clear as it covers a broad range of opportunities with different risk and return characteristics. It simply identifies a type of security that pays a fixed rate of interest for the money that you lend to its issuer. It's important to understand the difference between treasury bills issued by governments that are like cash, to bonds maturing some years in the future, issued by companies that are in extreme cases struggling to survive or governments around the world with poor economic track records. These latter assets can act more like equities. Understanding the ins and outs of bonds will allow you to be certain that you own the right sort and that you are at least aware of the fact that they are not infallible in all circumstances.

16.1 The ins and outs of bonds

Perhaps the best place to start is by recapping on the definition of bonds; simply put, bonds are IOUs issued by companies and governments to investors, which pay a fixed rate of interest to the lender, known as the *coupon*, and promise that their principal will be returned at a set date in the future, the *maturity date*. Simple – well almost! Bonds are sometimes known as fixed-income investments. Unlike equities, you are not participating in the wealth-generation of a company directly, but merely collecting monies that are owed to you, with adequate compensation, hopefully, for the risks you are taking on.

As you are aware, bonds play an important role in many investors' portfolios by dampening return volatility in normal market conditions and the prospect of potentially significant protection at times of equity market trauma, as money flows to safe havens and as the outlook for inflation becomes benign. To understand the true nature of bonds, you need to grasp a few simple concepts, which we explore below.

How bonds work – in a nutshell

Let's look very quickly at how bonds work; as a rational investor you need to be compensated adequately for lending your money to a company or a government. Over time, after the bond is issued, the market's perception of the risk to your money is likely to change and the yield, i.e. the compensation that you require for taking these risks, will change too. Perhaps it's because inflation is expected to rise in the future or because the business environment is becoming increasingly difficult and bankruptcies are on the rise; whatever the reason, a bond needs to offer this new level of compensation or else investors would simply buy newly issued bonds that did. Because its coupon is fixed throughout its life, the only way in which a change in yield can be delivered is through the change in the bond's price. If yields rise, bond prices fall; if yields fall, bond prices rise (Figure 16.1).

In general, bonds are issued at a price of 100 referred to as *par*. At the maturity date of the bond, if you invested £100 when a bond is issued, you will receive back £100 at maturity. In the interim, though, the price of the bond, and so the value of your capital invested, may move either up or down as yields change.

A bit more on bond yields

When a company or government wants to borrow money from you, they need to design a bond that will both match their financing requirements

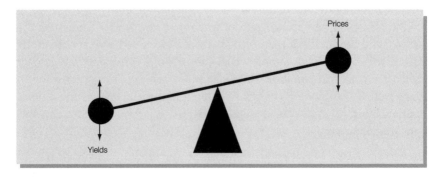

figure 16.1 The bond seesaw

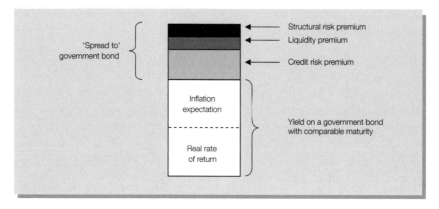

figure 16.2 Components of a bond's yield

and meet your needs. The coupon that the bond will pay will need to be attractive and reward you for the risks you are taking, which may relate to the market as a whole or may be specific to the borrower.

A bond's yield is made up of various things: the general market level of yield required by investors usually defined by a comparable maturity government bond; the risk of default on the bond by the issuer, otherwise known as credit risk; the degree of liquidity of the bond, i.e. how easy it is to sell at a fair price; and certain structural features that may be more attractive to the borrower than to the investor, for which the investor needs to be compensated. These components of yield are illustrated in Figure 16.2.

The general market yield

You can think of the general market yield as having two components: the real yield that an investor demands for lending money and the current outlook for inflation. The real yield is the adequate compensation, after inflation, you expect for investing in a very high quality, liquid and simple bond structure such as a UK government gilt. This will include compensation for tying your money up, known as the maturity premium (otherwise you would only invest in cash) and other perceived risks you face. Real yields move up and down for a wide variety of reasons, such as supply and demand and global crisis.

The component of a bond's yield that reflects the current inflation expectation is the main driver of the bond markets – a rising inflation expectation is bad for bond prices as yields rise and vice versa. Periods when an economy grows rapidly relative to long-run averages (booms) often tend to lead to higher inflation expectations, increasing bond yields and so a fall in prices. Tough economic times tend to create a more positive outlook for inflation and bond yields fall and prices rise.

Generally, the least risky bond is the shortest-dated government issued bond of an economically powerful nation; the least risky is perceived to be the US government. US government bonds are known as treasuries; UK government bonds are known as gilts. If the UK government issued a bond (gilt) on the same day as a corporate issuer, with the same maturity date, the UK government bond would have a lower coupon, as an investor's money is safer and more liquid than the corporate issue. When you move beyond gilts, you assume a number of other risks.

Credit risk needs to be rewarded adequately

Credit risk is the risk that a borrower may be unable to pay you back. A very financially strong company has a good chance of repaying, so you won't need that much additional yield. On the other hand, a weak company has a far greater chance of folding and if you lend to it, you will need a far higher level of compensation. Rating agencies assign credit quality ratings to companies. You may well have heard the term 'triple A rated', which refers to the strongest company and is often used in everyday conversation. Ratings from AAA to BBB are known as *investment grade* and BB and below are known as *sub-investment grade, high yield* or *junk*.

You may have noticed a significant interest in corporate bond funds in the early 2000s. In part, their rapid rise to prominence was due to a combination of the fall in equities during this period, as investors fled from higher risk assets and the more benign outlook for inflation that ensued. The result was a strong upward price movement in bonds, as yields in general and credit spreads narrowed, as the industry would say. To you or me that means that the chances of a company going broke fell and so the level of compensation required for this risk also fell. It was also a grab for higher yields, in a generally low yield environment, that many investor thought to be attractive; but how many really know what they are risking and whether they are being adequately compensated, particularly those in more risky *high income* or *high yield* funds?

Liquidity premium

Some bonds are not freely traded and if you are forced to sell them before maturity, you may find it difficult to get anyone to buy them at a reasonable price. Investors demand additional yield to compensate for the risk of holding illiquid bonds. For some investors this is not an issue and they can reap the benefits of their illiquid investments, taking the premium on offer.

Structural risk

The structure of some bonds may include features that provide additional risks to those holding them; an example would be the issuer's ability to repay you before maturity, a likely event likely if interest rates fall substantially. This is obviously advantageous to the borrower as its financing costs will be reduced, but it won't be for you, as you have to give up the higher yield you were getting and reinvest in other bonds that now deliver a lower rate of return. This is known as a *call option*.

The sensitivity of a bond's price to changes in yields

The bond seesaw of Figure 16.1 explains the generic relationship between yields and prices but only tells us that as yields rise, bond prices fall and vice versa. In reality, some bonds are more sensitive to changes in yield than others. This sensitivity of a bond's price to a change in yields is known as its *duration* and is a measure described in years. In general, a bond's duration is broadly related to its time to maturity, but the level of its coupon will also affect this sensitivity. The longer the duration, the more sensitive the price is to a movement in yields. The risk associated with movements in bond yields, that is to say bond price movements, is often referred to as *interest rate risk*.

Think of it this way: a bond represents a series of cash flows from the regular coupon payments you receive and your principal back at maturity. Duration is the measure of the average maturity of these cash flows payments, discounted into today's money, where each payment is weighted by its value. Put simply, it is the average time in which a bondholder is paid back. The level of coupon makes a difference; if you own a bond with a high coupon, e.g. 10 per cent a year, you will get the benefit of your money back sooner than from bond that pays a 3 per cent coupon. A bond's duration is less that its maturity except in the case of bonds that pay no coupon (zero coupon bonds) where you buy them at a discount and at maturity you get the full par value back. In this case their duration is equal to their maturity.

Also, you can think of duration as being a point of indifference where the fall in price of a bond (due to a rise in yields) is compensated by the fact that the coupons can now be reinvested at the higher yield. The duration of the bond is the time it takes to reach this break-even point. From this perspective, the bond seesaw becomes less relevant if you have a longer-term investment horizon. Generally, you should not own bonds that have a duration beyond the point at which you wish to liquidate your portfolio, such as to buy an annuity in retirement.

Rule to calculate gains or losses

There is some complicated maths to do to calculate a bond's duration, but don't worry, you'll never have to do it! What you do need to know is how sensitive prices are to movements in yields for bonds with different durations. A useful rule of thumb exists that allows you to understand the effect of a change in yields on the price of a bond (or fund made up of many bonds).

Duration × rise (fall) in yield = capital loss (gain)

Remember to add the coupon you receive into the calculation to see whether the total return is a gain or a loss. From Table 16.1 you can see clearly that the longer the duration of a bond, or a portfolio of bonds, the greater the change in price for a given movement in yields. This is important. Remember why you should use high-quality domestic bonds as equity market trauma protection. When markets fall, many investors will seek safe havens for their money and the resultant demand for high-quality domestic bonds will force yields lower and prices will rise, providing a strong diversifying effect to your equity losses. Longer duration bonds of high quality magnify this effect.

Always find out what the *weighted average duration* of your portfolio or fund is. Duration figures should be readily available for any bond fund and if they are not then ask for them from the company selling you a fund. Once you know the fund's duration you can work out how volatile it is likely to be for a given rise in bond yields. Never buy any form of bond investment without knowing its duration and average credit rating. How many owners of corporate bond fund have any idea of how far the price of their fund could fall if the credit and inflationary outlook worsened and yields rose?

table 16.1 Using a rule of thumb to calculate gains or losses

	Duration					
Yield rise	*1 year*	*2 years*	*3 years*	*4 years*	*5 years*	*10 years*
1%	(1%)	(2%)	(3%)	(4%)	(5%)	(10%)
2%	(2%)	(4%)	(6%)	(8%)	(10%)	(20%)
3%	(3%)	(6%)	(9%)	(12%)	(15%)	(30%)

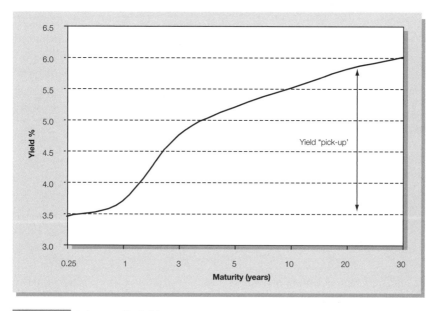

figure 16.3 A 'normal' yield curve

Yield curves

The yields on different maturity bonds with the same credit rating are often compared by way of a *yield curve,* which is a snapshot in time. This concept is also known as the *term structure of interest rates.* Figure 16.3 portrays what is known as a normal yield curve. However, from time to time longer-dated bonds may yield less than short-dated bonds (known in the trade as a negative yield curve). A number of theories exist to explain the yield curve, which we will not get into here. What you need to know is that, by and large, you are compensated for owning longer-dated bonds, compared with cash, but they have a greater sensitivity to changes in yields. However, this can theoretically work to your advantage when you use bonds as a diversifier of equity market trauma, as seen above.

Not all bonds are equal

As was mentioned at the start of this chapter, you need to ensure that you aren't deceived into believing that all bonds are safe investments and, except for differences in yields and maturities, much the same across the board. They actually span the investment spectrum from cash-like characteristics to highly risky equity-like investments. Advice like 'own a bond

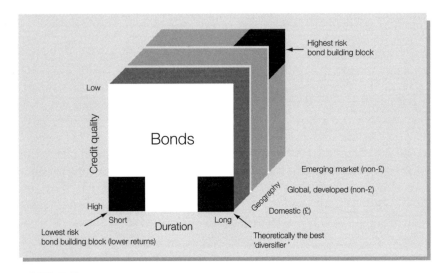

Low

Credit quality

Bonds

Highest risk
bond building block

Emerging market (non-£)

Geography

Global, developed (non-£)

Domestic (£)

High

Short

Duration

Long

Lowest risk
bond building block (lower returns)

Theoretically the best
'diversifier '

figure 16.4 **Not all bonds are equal**

fund' is as useful as throwing a dart at the investment spectrum, unless it is more clearly defined.

Figure 16.4 provides an insight into the factors that describe the wide range of investments that fall under the all-encompassing label of bonds. These include: duration, as covered above; *credit*, describing how likely you are to get paid a coupon and get your cash back at maturity; and finally, what I have termed *geography*. If you move outside the UK, in terms of bond ownership, you will incur exchange rate (currency) risk on your bonds and outside the big, developed economies, you will own bonds of companies and governments in less stable economies and political environments. These are often referred to as emerging markets.

Your Level 1 allocation

Your Level 1 bond allocations should be very high-quality domestic bonds with longer duration (i.e. have a higher sensitivity to interest rate movements) issued by the UK government and very strong, large companies. This is because at times of financial market crisis, you benefit most from these sensitivities, both because the inflation outlook generally becomes more favourable and their role as a safe haven.

Bond opportunities outside of this are generally *Level 3* decisions, with the exception of index-linked bonds, which we will cover in a moment. Domestic high yield bonds, i.e. those issued by less strong companies and emerging market bonds, tend to have quite high correlations to equities. The point here is just be certain what you are buying for your portfolio.

Leave any active management aspirations to others

Opportunities do exist to make capital gains through holding longer duration bonds when yields are anticipated to fall and shorter duration bonds when yields are expected to rise, for those of you who believe that you can judge the magnitude and direction of interest rates. If you also fancy your chances at analysing and monitoring bond credit better than the agencies and bond analysts then you can also try and time the changes in credit spreads. My advice is don't try; in reality, only a few professional managers seem to be able to demonstrate the ability to do so over time – stick to an index fund (or ETF) approach and own either a long-dated gilt fund or broad market fund that covers both gilts and investment grade corporate bonds.

16.2 Taking a closer look at bond returns

Over the long term, bonds have produced returns significantly below those of equities. It is tempting to look at short-term bond rallies such as the period 2000–2003 and believe that bonds are a significant and constant source of stable returns. In the long run, holding bonds in your portfolio

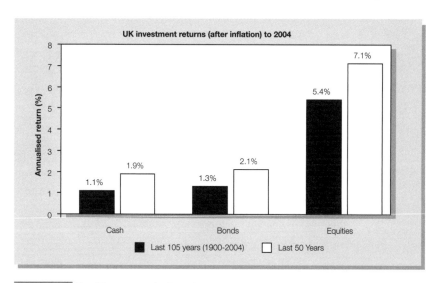

figure 16.5 Equities outstrip bonds and cash in building purchasing power   *Source: DMS Global Data (Ibbotson) © 2006 E Dimson, P Marsh and M Staunton*

contributes to increased portfolio stability with some potential marginal contribution to building purchasing power. Equities remain the return engines of portfolios, as you can see from Figure 16.5, and as explored in Chapter 15.

UK bond returns over different time periods

Looking at holding periods of five and thirty years, you can see that bonds are quite variable in terms of the returns that they generate (Figure 16.6). This may be a revelation to some who see bonds as an income-generating haven. Quite a few periods exist where bonds have eroded purchasing power not only over five years but also over thirty years. Remember that these are annualised return numbers and do not illustrate the severe cumulative effect on your money. The real investing world is cruel and there is virtually nowhere to guarantee the growth of your wealth. The safest option is to hold index-linked bonds to maturity, but you will probably only double your money every thirty-six years of more – the price you pay for such protection.

Real returns over the recent past have been significantly higher than the long-run averages of 1–2 per cent a year but don't mindlessly extrapolate that into the future. During the 1970s and 1980s yields on bonds were very

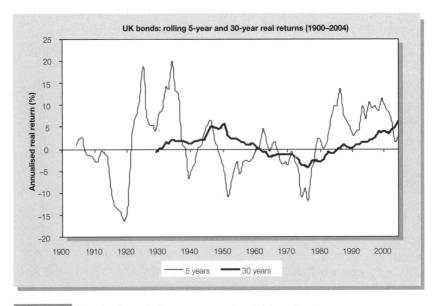

figure 16.6 Bonds do not always generate stable returns

Source: DMS Global Data (Ibbotson) © 2006 E Dimson, P Marsh and M Staunton

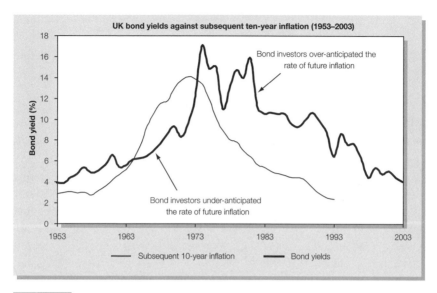

figure 16.7 **Bond markets have not been too good at predicting inflation**

Source: DMS Global Data (Ibbotson) © 2006 E Dimson, P Marsh and M Staunton; Barclays Equity Gilt Study

high to compensate for the high levels of inflation in the UK. Yields have fallen dramatically to low levels, as successive UK governments appear to have got inflation under control. As a consequence, bond returns have been unusually strong due to a combination of the initially high coupons that generated high real yields as inflation fell to levels lower than anticipated when the bonds were issued, and the fall in yield required by the market, which has lead to capital gains on bonds, resulting in rising prices.

If you compare bond yields at a given time against the subsequent ten-year average inflation figure you can get an approximate picture of how well the bond market is at judging future inflation. The answer is not too good (Figure 16.7).

Inflation appears in better control these days and the late 1990s and early 2000s have seen yields at record lows. Bond returns may not be as spectacular going forwards, which we will look at later in this chapter.

16.3 Bond markets crash too!

The twenty-year bull market, with the exception of 1994, has shaped most of our collective memories. Any safe haven imagined by investors is an illusion. In the main this is to do with the confusion between nominal and real returns that exist in many investors' minds. If you consider crashes to be

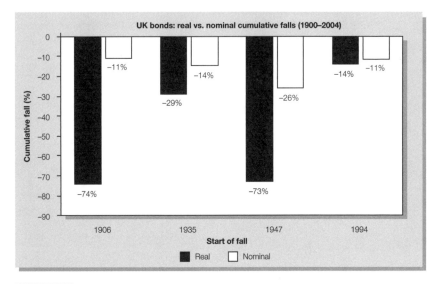

figure 16.8 Bond market crashes

Source: DMS Global Data (Ibbotson) © 2006 E Dimson, P Marsh and M Staunton

falls in your purchasing power, which you should, bond markets suffer periods of significant crashes too. Figure 16.8 below illustrates some of the market crashes in the UK. As you can see, nominal falls have been considerably lower than the actual fall in purchasing power and flatter to deceive the true picture of the risk to your capital of bonds in periods when inflation is higher than anticipated.

Recovery from crashes is significantly slower in real terms

Unlike owning equities, where the underlying companies can raise prices in line with inflation, real bond losses can only recover through the real yield that they generate. Nominal losses can recover far more quickly as coupon interest works to recoup nominal capital losses. Figure 16.9 shows the bond market recovery in both nominal and real terms for a bond market fall starting in 1947. You can see that in nominal terms, you would have got your money back in sixteen years, which is long enough in any case. In fact, in real terms, purchasing power crumbled over twenty-eight years and it took another nineteen years to get back to your original purchasing power.

Bonds are not as safe as some investors think. Always keep the thought in the back of your mind that bonds and unanticipated rises in inflation can be an ugly combination.

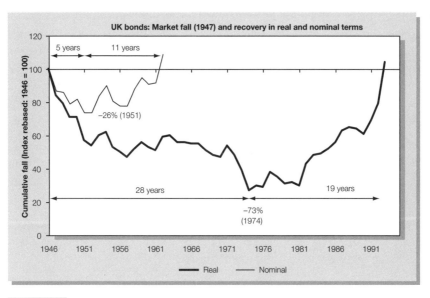

figure 16.9 Recovery of purchasing power is a slow process

Source: DMS Global Data (Ibbotson) © 2006 E Dimson, P Marsh and M Staunton

Generalisations on bond returns

Figure 16.10 summarises the return characteristics of bonds in a number of different economic environments.

16.4 The outlook for bond returns

All of the above may leave you questioning why you would want to invest in bonds at all. Well there are some valid reasons. The first is that you are predominantly owning them to dampen the bumpiness of your portfolio's

Deflation	Financial crisis	Normal	Inflation
Strong returns: yields fall and nominal coupon and principal payments now buy more than before.	Investors seek to place funds into liquid and safe investments – the best of which are government bonds	Provide low single digit real returns. Nominal returns approximate to coupon. High premium paid by long-term investors	Tend to do badly when inflation surges as yields rise and bond prices fall – coupons are insufficient to match inflation

figure 16.10 Bond returns in different economic environments

returns because they are less volatile than equities and for protection on those occasions when equity markets falls abruptly. The second is that if you believe the government has got a handle on inflation, so allowing the bond markets a higher chance of successfully guessing what inflation will be, then you could expect bonds to keep pace with inflation and provide a low-digit real return over time. A big 'if' perhaps, given past government failings.

There is, however, a reasonably effective and simple way of predicting future nominal bond returns, provided by John Bogle in one of his excellent books (1999). It is a useful tool at least to give you a sense of future bond return magnitude. He states:

'The initial interest rate at the start of a given decade is by far the preponderant force governing subsequent returns,' which he concludes, *'is a remarkably efficient but imperfect, indicator of future returns.'*

As you can see from Figure 16.11, there is a reasonably strong relationship between the bond yield prevailing at a point in time and the subsequent ten-year annualised return. In a sense, this is saying that over a ten-year period, the interim capital gains and losses largely even out, although we know this not to be true in some cases.

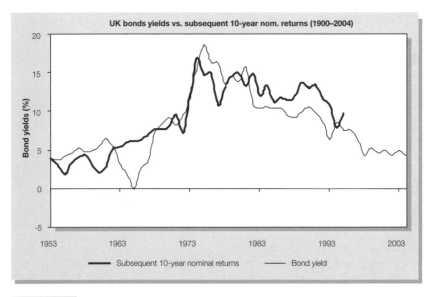

figure 16.11 **Today's bond yield is a reasonable predictor of nominal returns**

Source: DMS Global Data (Ibbotson) © 2006 E Dimson, P Marsh and M Staunton; Barclays Equity Gilt Study

On that basis and as a rough proxy, the nominal return for the next ten years is similar to the yield today. At the time of writing this is around 5 per cent in the UK. If you believe that we are in low inflation environment with inflation at 3 per cent then real returns may be around 2 per cent. This is the level of return used throughout this book and in the Monte Carlo simulations.

16.5 Summary: bonds

- In the short term, bonds generally, but not always, underperform equities. In any one year bonds have about a one-in-three chance of beating equities.

- Over the longer term, though, real equity returns significantly outstrip real bond returns.

- The predominant role of bonds is one of smoothing portfolio returns both by dampening returns and through the diversification benefits they hold, creating a greater certainty of outcome at the cost of some long-term purchasing power. Getting your long-term mix right is critical.

- Bonds come into their own at periods of equity market trauma, particularly high-quality domestic bonds such as those issued by the UK government (gilts). Scared investors retreat from equity markets and the increased demand for gilts pushes prices up and yields down. These periods are often accompanied by increased worries about the economy, which tend to result in an improved inflation outlook, which is good for bonds too.

- Longer-dated bonds are more sensitive to movements in yields, which may be beneficial in this role.

- The main risk that bond investors face is one of unanticipated rises in inflation, at which point yields rise and prices fall.

- Some bond markets have suffered severe and prolonged erosion of investor purchasing power, which is masked by the more rapid recovery of nominal losses through coupon payments. Beware.

- Bonds are expected to return around 5 per cent in nominal terms and 2 per cent in real terms over the next ten years or so. But who am I to say?

- If you are particularly worried about inflation in the future, read up on index linked bonds in Chapter 17.

References

Bogle, J. C. (1999) *Common sense on mutual funds: New imperatives for the intelligent investor.* New York: Wiley, 48–49.

17

Spotlight on return smoothers

By now, you have probably picked up a reasonable idea of the portfolio building blocks, what they bring to the table and a general sense of how much you should own of each. As with all investment matters, the more you know, the better chance you have of knowing what both the upside and the downside can be. Understanding and preparation is the key to good investing; and to that end, this chapter helps you to delve a little deeper into each of the return smoother blocks we have covered.

This chapter is not designed to give you all the facts and figures, but to provide insight into what you may be letting yourself in for, if and when you include them in a portfolio. When you move outside of the more mainstream building blocks, particularly into property and hedge funds, practical issues make decisions more difficult. They are covered here in a balanced way, to give you an insight into the challenges, as well as the benefits, in owning them.

17.1 Index-linked gilts – 'linkers'

Index-linked gilts are an interesting and potentially exceedingly useful building block in your armoury. They are bonds issued by governments where the capital value you invest and the interest you receive are linked to a measure of consumer inflation, the retail price index, or RPI, as it is often called. This example illustrates how they work. Say you invest £1,000 in an index-linked gilt that pays a 2 per cent coupon (that is the yield it will deliver after the effects of inflation), maturing after ten years. Imagine that inflation ends up being 2 per cent throughout the investment period. When the bond matures and the government returns your capital, you will get £1,219 back. In fact, your capital will increase each year to keep pace with inflation and your 2 per cent coupon paid during the time you own the bond will pay you 2 per cent of the increased capital amount calculated each year, so maintaining its purchasing power. In truth, there is a slight lag of eight months over which inflation is calculated that could lead to small differences, but by and large you are protected.

You may be wondering if you should invest in index-linked gilts or normal gilts. Well, the simple answer is that if you are worried about the prospect of rising inflation, you should seriously consider the former. If on the other hand you think that inflation will remain low, or even that deflation will occur, you should consider normal gilts. Remember that because your capital is linked to the RPI, if this falls in a deflationary environment, then the value of your capital will fall too. In some countries, governments protect your capital in such circumstances. By and large, governments have a poor record of keeping inflation in control. You will need to decide for yourself. The difference between the yield on *linkers* and conventional gilts is known as the *breakeven inflation rate*. Ask your broker what this is if you are thinking of buying them. This is effectively the rate of inflation that the market anticipates in the long term. If you think it will be higher, buy linkers, if you think it will be lower then buy conventional gilts or other high-quality domestic bonds. Figure 17.1 plots the yield for both since the early 1980s when the first linkers were issued. You can see that early on, they were a great investment.

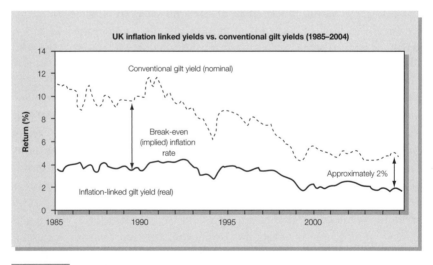

figure 17.1 **Real yields and inflation expectations**

Source: Bank of England

Using them in a portfolio

Not surprisingly, given their structure, linkers have a high correlation to inflation, and as we know, conventional bonds tend to fare badly when inflation unexpectedly rises, and so have a low to negative correlation with it. Now, given that you are well versed in the game that you should be playing, you will have spotted that linkers are likely to contribute to Markovitz's free lunch if included in your portfolio. In fact, inflation-linked bonds are uncorrelated with conventional bonds and have a low correlation to equities. That's good news for investors.

As a long-term investor, you may feel comfortable using equities, commodities and real estate as protection against inflation and the low level of bonds that you hold may be high-quality conventional bonds, which provide shorter-term protection from equity market trauma. Depending on your view on inflation and for further diversification, you could hold some index-linked bonds as well. If your investment horizon is shorter, then you could even use linkers for your entire bond holding, as they are pretty certain to protect you from inflation, without the volatility that will come with owning commodities. Circumstances when it may be prudent to use index-linked bonds would be when you are approaching retirement and need cash at that point perhaps to buy an annuity, pay off the mortgage or buy a holiday home. You should be reducing your exposure to equities and protecting your capital from unexpected inflation.

Owning exposure to linkers

There are two ways to own index-linked bonds: directly by buying them through a broker; or by owning a fund. There are a couple of things you need to consider: First, during the time that you own an index-linked bond, your capital will fluctuate as the factors influencing real yields fluctuate. Just like conventional bonds, index-linked bonds prices will go down as real yields go up and vice versa. So, if you are going to own them directly, you need to pick one that matures around the time that you need the money, e.g. your retirement date in order for you to avoid having to sell it at a time when the price has fallen. This is a *buy-and-hold* strategy. There are only a few issues to choose from, so it should not be too difficult. You will need to open a brokerage account to do so.

You could on the other hand buy an index-linked bond fund, which holds a basket of index-linked gilts, either actively managed, or in an index fund. While a basket of linkers will provide inflation protection over time, when you go to sell your fund holding, you are at risk that this will be when prices have fallen. Remember, because your real yield is low to start with, to keep an eye on the level of fees you will be paying. If you intend to hold this allocation for a long period of time, for example throughout your retirement, you don't have to worry about this so much and funds may be a good option.

Owning gilts directly will require a brokerage account and you will need to reinvest your coupons in an inflation-protected way. Most funds, on the other hand, provide accumulation shares, which mean you can avoid having to do this yourself and is an easier route for many.

17.2 Property – the misunderstood asset class

For many people, property has always been an integral part of their investment portfolios. This is hardly surprising given that it is the world's largest asset class. In the UK especially, people have become obsessed with property, in some cases almost to the exclusion of everything else, evidenced by the substitution of conventional pensions with a buy-to-let property strategy, by an increasing number of investors.

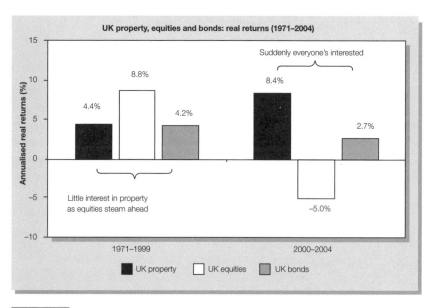

figure 17.2 **Property is back on investors' radar screens**

Source: IPD UK All Property Index

Somewhat surprisingly, the allocations to property by institutional investors have been falling; in the 1970s UK pension funds had 20 per cent allocated to property, which by the start of 2000 had fallen to 5 per cent – how they must have rued that decision, having let risky equity assets overpower their portfolio mix. Since the equity market fall starting in 2000, property has remerged as one of the darlings of investors looking for a portfolio for all seasons (Figure 17.2). Property investing should not be a market-timing play but a long-term diversifier of equity market trauma and a hedge for unanticipated inflation in the medium to long term. Investors would do well to treat it strategically in the future. Market timing is a tough game to play, as you know from this book.

By the end of this section you will hopefully have a rounded view of property investing, rather than the dinner party approach of 'The flat we bought in London as an investment has doubled in value in a year'. You should be able to decide whether, given some of the practical issues that you face, you want to include it in your portfolio.

Individuals tend to hold high exposure to property

Homeownership is a fundamental emotional as well as financial goal of many, although I'm not sure how many of us really sit down and do the mathematics behind it – after all, it is hard to quantify intangible benefits such as 'a feeling of comfort' or 'belonging' on top of the rent or own decision we face. As individuals, we tend to like property; it's tangible; it will go up if inflation goes up; we can get pretty highly leveraged, at times, relatively cheaply (at least in the short term); and pay back today's borrowing in tomorrow's debased money.

From an investing point of view, some people struggle to decide whether their home should be considered as part of their investment programme or not. Not being an economist, I take the simple approach that if you intend to live in it, or a house of similar value until you die, then it's not. You have to have somewhere to live, and it is either rent or mortgage payments for most. If, on the other hand, it is a second home, or if you intend to trade down and use some of the capital to fund your retirement, or other needs, then this part is an investment.

Reasons for owning property investments

Using property in your building block mix makes sense. You might do well to consider spreading this exposure away from residential property into commercial, industrial and retail investments. There are many ways this can be done, increasingly in an indirect manner, which we will explore later. There are two main reasons why real estate should hold an inherent appeal.

Reason 1: Property has a low correlation to your equity/bond portfolio

Property generally exhibits a pattern of returns that is not closely related to any strong degree to bonds or equities. On the upside, it contributes to the free lunch of reducing risk, but the price you pay is that, in the longer term, returns from property would be expected to be lower than those from equities, although above bonds, as you can see below.

Reason 2: Property provides a long-term hedge against unanticipated inflation

As a long-term investor, inflation remains your greatest scourge. Canny investors use a combination of real estate, linkers and commodities to hedge portfolios from periods of unanticipated inflation. It has provided a strong degree of protection from inflation over the medium to long term, which intuitively makes sense given the ability to raise rents and selling prices to rise with inflation. After all, a building is a building; but as you can see in Figure 17.3, over short-term periods, e.g. three years, property may

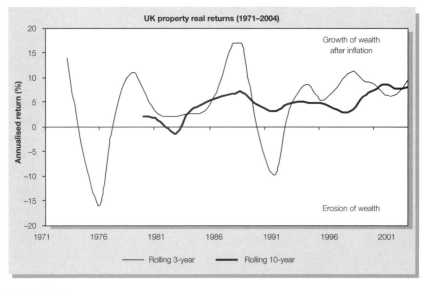

figure 17.3 **Property has provided a good longer-term hedge against inflation**   *Source: IPD UK All Property Index*

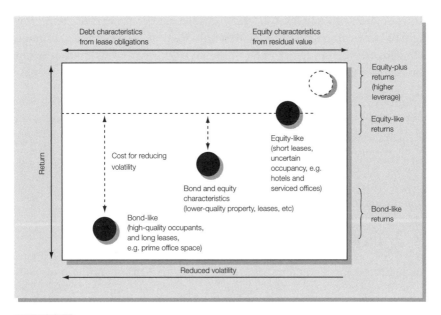

figure 17.4 **Property characteristics – a blend between bonds and equities**

not keep pace with inflation, but over longer periods it generally does, as you can see from the rolling ten-year line.

Returns should fall between bonds and equities

Property represents a series of cash flows like a bond, made up of the regular payment of rent and the residual value of the building; the surer the occupancy and length of rental lease, and the quality of the renter, the lower the volatility of the capital value of the building. As such, buildings with high-quality tenants on long-term leases tend to act more like bonds and are less volatile because income dominates returns. On the other hand, properties with short tenancies, the ultimate being hotels, tend to have more equity-like volatility in their capital value. In the long term, therefore, property returns should fall between bonds and equities depending upon the underlying characteristics (Figure 17.4). In the short term, sentiment and supply and demand will affect capital values; when these turn around, property prices can, and do, fall in value.

Leverage is commonplace in property investments

Property is often a leveraged investment, thereby magnifying returns; for example, if you put £50,000 capital into a £500,000 property, and borrow the rest, and it goes up by £50,000, you have made 100 per cent (before the cost of borrowing) on a property that only went up 10 per cent. You should view investing in property as an unleveraged play; after all, leverage is not unique to property, it's just that we are familiar with it.

You can easily borrow to buy equities, or any other building block for that matter, but you wouldn't necessarily want to do so. Just because you can, does not mean that you should. You need to separate leverage mentally from the underlying returns of the building block, in this case property. Always remember that a property investment that appears to offer equity-plus returns is going to be taking on considerable risk and probably using significant leverage to achieve these returns.

A look at historic returns

As indicated above, income plays a very large part in generating returns; if you had invested in an unleveraged a mix of offices, industrial and retail properties such as shopping centres in 1970, but spent all the income you received up to the start of 2005, you would have turned £100 of spending power into only £64. If you had reinvested all your income in property, you would have turned £100 into £515. Income drives property investing. The doubling of house prices in the early 2000s appears somewhat anomalous in this context, and it would be prudent to be cautious about the outlook for residential property in the next few years. Don't bank your retirement on it!

Annual returns can vary significantly and property markets crash too

While you should be concerned with the range of returns that a diversified pool of property can deliver over your investment horizon, it does help to understand how volatile property returns can be. In fact, if you calculate the standard deviation of returns, which the industry calls risk, property comes out a little above bonds, at 11 per cent. A word of caution here: the pricing mechanism for the properties that makes up the index is prone to *stale pricing*, where property prices tend to get smoothed out rather than reflecting true current market values.

The effect of stale pricing is illustrated nicely in a simple but revealing piece of analysis in which two stocks from the S&P 500 equity index were priced at one month and three-month intervals over a fifty-year period (Gompers and Lerner, 2001). Their correlations to the S&P500 index were computed monthly using these two different price data, revealing that using monthly

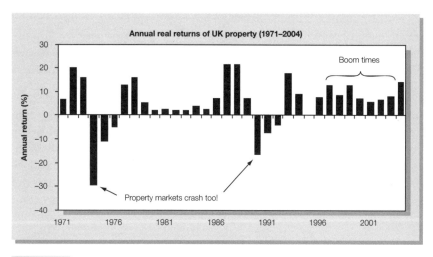

figure 17.5 **Property markets go down as well as up**

Source: IPD UK All Property Index

prices the correlations were 0.74 and 0.58, whereas using quarterly prices their correlation to the market dropped dramatically to 0.33 and 0.25 respectively – same stocks but different apparent correlation benefits. Figure 17.5 plots the annual real returns of UK property.

Forward-looking returns

Again, we face the task of estimating future returns. Intuitively, property falls between bonds and equities, for which we estimated real annualised returns of around 2 per cent for the former and 5 per cent for the latter. Therefore, unleveraged real returns for property would conservatively fall in the 3 per cent to 4 per cent region. With leverage, this may be a little higher.

Getting some property exposure

Today, the choice of investment opportunities in property covers the risk/return spectrum from bond-like income generating investments acting as return smoothers to opportunistic and often highly leveraged investments in global markets and distressed real estate situations, acting predominantly as return enhancers. Such product proliferation means that you need to think what makes most sense for you. What you should be looking for, as part of your Level 2 allocation, is a property investment that will help to generate steadier returns for your portfolio and provide another means of protecting your wealth from inflation.

It probably makes sense to diversify between commercial, industrial and retail – you may feel that you have sufficient exposure to residential property through your own home. Such investment would provide further diversification as filling office space in the City is different from leasing a shop in Glasgow.

In practice there are three main options. Remember that these are just different vehicles that may all range across the bond-like to equity-like spectrum depending upon their underlying investments. Read all literature and prospectuses carefully to get a feel for what the fund will be investing in, how much leverage it will use, and just how much they are going to cream off the top. Property funds have a reputation as rapacious fee takers.

Route 1: Funds that invest in property company shares

You could choose a unit trust that invests in the publicly listed shares of property companies. In the UK these are companies that focus predominantly on property and pay corporation tax like any other company on profits. If a property company diversifies its business into, say, security services, you will be getting a less than pure property market exposure. By investing in a fund you will own a diversified portfolio of real estate companies and thus properties. At last count, only a handful of funds exist in the UK. Returns from real estate publicly listed companies tend to be more volatile and have a slightly higher correlation to equities. Always look closely at the mix of property exposure the fund will have and the (usually considerable) fees you are being charged.

In the USA (and Australia, Japan, Hong Kong and Singapore) a specific type of listed property company known as a real estate investment trust (REIT) exists that can pass through income and capital gains to investors without paying corporation tax, so providing a purer form of real estate investment. These type of structures could reach the UK soon, which would boost the publicly listed property securities dramatically and change the fund landscape. Property ETFs will likely follow. In fact, you can already get European (ex-UK) property exposure through an ETF.

Route 2: Funds that invest directly in property

This is a rapidly growing field that you may wish to consider, with onshore and offshore funds, authorised and non-authorised funds and minimums that range from a few thousand pounds to millions. You will need to work out what is suitable.

These funds invest directly in properties, which they own and manage for the investors in the fund, or may in some cases invest in other property funds as well. The parameters within which they invest tend to be wide, so it is worth making sure that you know what they are investing in. Diversification, home markets, reasonable fees and a good fund management firm are as good a starting point as any. Look out for usurious fees and brokerage commissions and performance fees that eat into your returns. Costs generally in this industry remain high and it is often difficult to calculate their true effect on your money. Keep your eyes and ears open, as this is a rapidly developing space.

Route 3: Own property yourself with the attendant hassle

The final option is to hold property directly, which has become popular in the UK in terms of buy-to-let residential property or placing commercial property into personal pension plans. Direct ownership comes with the hassle and costs of finding tenants, repair, upkeep, insurance and financing. Always make sure that you can cover your outgoings for at least six months or more without tenants, if you choose this route.

Tips on having property in your portfolio

- Hold property for the long-term returns and inflation protection it will provide you, not short-term capital gains.
- It provides some protection against equity market trauma and is a useful smoother of portfolio returns.
- Expect unleveraged real returns somewhere between bonds and equities depending on the type of investment strategy you choose, in the region of 3 per cent to 4 per cent.
- Decide carefully what it is that you want property to do for you and choose which structural route is best for you to get this exposure.
- Do your best to work out all the costs. The industry generally charges high fees, so find out what they are.

17.3 Hedge funds – are they all they are cracked up to be?

You have probably read or heard some of the hype surrounding the hedge fund world, predominantly that smart investors are delivering skill-based returns that are absolute (positive) in nature and have strong diversifying benefits for traditional portfolios. Other stories make more gripping news;

managers living jet-set lifestyles and buying New York apartments purely to hang newly acquired masterpieces in, being paid over a billion dollars in a single year in one case and, of course, funds that go spectacularly bust. It's hard to tell fact from fiction in this industry.

A growing band of investors obviously believes some of the above because money has poured into the industry in the early 2000s. By the start of 2005, assets stood at around $1.2 trillion globally, in around 10,000 funds, of which about 1,000 are funds of hedge funds (Tass, 2005). That's almost three times the value of the entire UK unit trust industry! The most valuable thing we can do in this short section is to explore some of the claims being made, which appear to contradict all of the evidence about the zero-sum game, market efficiency and the broad lack of performance persistence across the traditional investment industry. You really need to tackle these philosophical issues before you can hope to make a decision about whether to pursue hedge funds as a suitable portfolio building block.

What are hedge funds?

It's hard to get a handle on what hedge funds are because they can be almost whatever the hedge fund manager wants them to be, although they tend to get lumped into broad categories with exotic names such as *convertible arbitrage*, *global macro* and *equity market neutral*. It is worth remembering that within these categories, the strategies used vary widely. Hedge fund

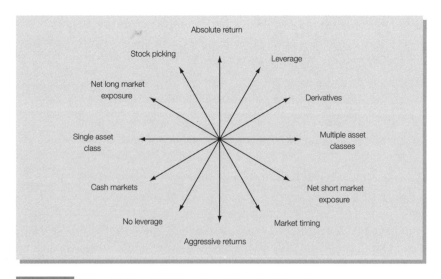

figure 17.6 Every hedge fund's web pattern is different

managers have the scope and the freedom more or less to do what they want with your money, adopting almost any strategy that they think will work. One thing they all have in common is that they have some form of participation in the upside of your money, sometimes known as *carried interest*. These performance fees usually take 20 per cent of all gains above a certain level and this is on top of annual management fees of 2 per cent or so. Figure 17.6 provides a 'spider's web' grid for describing the parameters of hedge funds. Every fund will have its unique pattern.

One point worth noting is that they are not in themselves a new asset class, but merely strategies that use existing asset classes (i.e. building blocks) to generate returns. As a very sweeping generalisation, strategies fall into two broad categories: those seeking to deliver *absolute returns,* being the preservation of capital at all times and the expectation of cash-beating returns (rather than returns measured relative to specific market indices, which is the way of the traditional active management industry) and those who are going aggressively for out-and-out returns, taking big bets with high levels of leverage. This chapter focuses on the first group.

If you want some definitions on different hedge fund strategies, a good place to start is looking at the CSFB/Tremont definitions on *www.hedgeindex.com*, where you can also download index data free, for personal use.

Claims of hedge fund managers

Let's take a look at the implicit claims that are being made by hedge fund industry as a whole, which you need to challenge before you take them at face value:

■ The hedge fund industry contains above-average skills in aggregate, as many of the best and brightest fund managers and bank traders have entered the industry.

■ These exceptional skills can and will deliver absolute returns to investors.

■ These returns will be uncorrelated with traditional bond and equity portfolios because they are based on skill and not markets.

■ To date, industry returns indicate that this is so.

■ It is worth paying 2 per cent on your assets every year and giving up 20 per cent of your upside for getting access to these skill-based absolute returns.

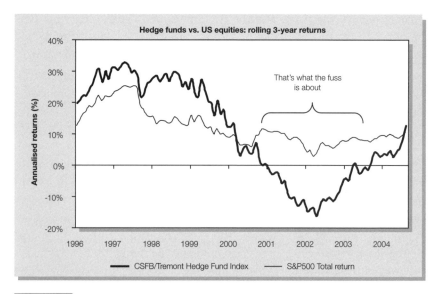

figure 17.7 **Absolute returns from hedge funds**

Source: Hedge funds © CSFB/Tremont, all rights reserved; S&P500, Standard & Poor's

These are big claims to make, which challenge the nature of the investment industry itself. They suggest that a $1.2 trillion industry can beat the market, after usurious fees and unbelievably high turnover, in aggregate, despite the fact that the traditional industry hasn't done so, that patsies are hard to find and that the bulk of managers came from, or are still at, traditional investment management firms anyway. Call me a sceptic if you like. Charts like Figure 17.7 illustrate the foundation of the industry's claims and are a driver in interest and action on the part of investors.

You can see why, at first glance, there is so much interest in them, given the apparent way that they resisted the fall in equity markets. There may be some real value to be had from hedge funds but, as you will see below, not necessarily for the reasons claimed.

Unravelling the reality

The central claim of the industry that exceptional skills are driving returns is simply not credible, in aggregate. While I'm sure a few exceptional managers exist, who through their superior skill and insight can generate persistent skill-based returns, I find it hard to believe that the industry, as a whole, is the winner in the zero-sum game.

Suspending the zero-sum game for hedge fund managers? I don't think so!

Sure, the wider parameters that hedge fund managers give themselves provide more scope to make returns and magnify them with leverage; but you and I know that generating skill-based returns through market timing and security selection is a substantially-less-than-zero-sum game, particularly after the high costs of the industry. Yet, just because the playing field is wider, it does not mean that the basic rules of the game have changed. Even if the markets that some hedge fund managers operate in are less efficient, costs tend to be higher and the zero-sum game still applies. If returns are truly skill-based, then someone has to pay for a hedge fund manager's skill-based returns. So who is the patsy?

As you know, institutional investors, who represent the bulk of actively managed assets, have failed to generate skill-based returns as a group over time, indicating that patsies are hard to find. As we previously explored, even the most likely candidates, being individuals trading their own brokerage accounts, turn out to make market returns as a group, before costs, so it's not them either. It begs the question of just who is going to fund the promised skill-based returns of the $1.2 trillion hedge fund industry. Either someone is taking a severe investment beating, or something else is going on.

A sceptic might be inclined to believe that the incredibly high failure rate of hedge funds points to the patsies being some of the less skilled or unlucky hedge fund managers themselves. They have a longer leash on which to roam the markets for opportunities and leverage their positions but this also provides greater opportunity to lose. It is estimated that more than 3,000 funds have disappeared since the start of 2000, with an attrition rate of around 10 per cent of funds in 2004 alone, as many failed to make decent returns, fell prey to operational issues, or closed for other reasons. Accurate numbers are hard to obtain, as some funds don't even get recorded before failing. It seems that around 30 per cent of funds don't even make their third birthday (Brooks and Kat, 2002).

Perhaps there's another explanation

Perhaps returns of hedge funds are not purely skill-based and are more market-driven than is acknowledged. This school of thought is rapidly growing. It appears that many funds are delivering market exposure to less familiar asset classes, rather than delivering skill-based returns. Not in itself a bad thing, though, if you are seeking diversification of the exposures and risks in your portfolio.

A recent study (Gehin and Vaissie, 2005) separated out the returns generated from markets, those from market timing (active switching between markets, which is skill-based) and finally, those derived from picking securities (also skill-based). The results indicate that if, let's say, returns were 10 per cent in one year, then picking stocks only contributed 0.4 per cent of this return, market timing deducted about 0.4 per cent, and the underlying market exposures contributed 9.99 per cent. This varies by strategy, and will vary by fund too, but the underlying message is clear: a strong case can be made that market factors seem to drive hedge fund returns in aggregate, not skill. These market factors include traditional equity and bond risks, but also other market exposures such as volatility, liquidity, value and default risk, which investors may not have been exposure to. Think of these as additional and unusual building blocks.

Times of poor returns across hedge funds, such as in early 2005, would suggest that this is the case as skill-based returns should not result in collective weakness in performance across the board. These finding would also imply that hedge funds returns are likely to be *cyclical* and not *absolute* in nature. If you accept the premise above, *absolute returns* come from the diversification of various sources of market exposure – which brings us back to the development of a sensible long-term mix of building blocks, which is the basic premise of this book. All roads lead to diversification! Perhaps hedge funds should be regarded as very expensive ways of obtaining alternative market exposure, as opposed to sources of skill-based returns. That in itself is not a bad thing, but it is not what it purports to be and it is questionable, if this is the case, whether current fee scales are either justified or sustainable.

Industry numbers mask reality

Perhaps in an attempt to simplify our investment decision-making, we are prone to overlook the quality of the data series that we can use. Without care, hedge fund data can be very misleading. There is only a decade of spotty industry data, which is a lot shorter, and far less clean, than the century of data we have for traditional asset classes, such as bonds and equities. Hedge fund industry data may not be telling us the whole truth.

Industry return numbers may well be significantly overstated due to a number of well-recorded biases: self-selected universes; survivorship bias where only surviving funds' data is included; the fact that some funds fail before ever getting into an index; and others that enter the universe back-fill their good data. All in all, data biases could overstate returns by 6 per cent to 8 per cent a year according to Professor Harry Kat, a leading voice of commonsense on the hedge fund scene (Davis, 2004).

Industry risk numbers are probably understated. Some hedge fund strategies generate returns that do not have a bell-shaped distribution but more of a 'that's good, that's nice, that's great ... what the hell happened there?' profile of returns. Maybe some funds haven't hit their 'what the hell happened there?' moment yet, but that does not mean that they won't. Nicholas Taleb, in *Fooled by Randomness*, elaborates on a mindset referred to as 'black swans', where traders (and people in all walks of life) disassociate profits they make from the potential catastrophic losses that may be lurking around the corner (Taleb, 2004). Just because you have never seen a black swan does not mean that they don't exist.

Correlations with traditional investments are probably understated. Stale pricing, where asset are only re-priced periodically, is common and can result in significant understatement of true price volatility and overstate the beneficial risk reduction they appear to bring to an investor's portfolio, particularly in an industry where many strategies invest in exotic and less liquid securities. It is also worth bearing in mind that in extreme market conditions, just when you need the low correlations, most strategies will be affected in one way or another: liquidity invariably dries up, credit spreads widen, and irrational investor withdrawals exacerbate the difficulties of managing the portfolio through these periods, particularly in illiquid holdings.

Fund of funds – paying someone to tackle the issues for you

Let's assume that you have decided that the benefits of owning access to skill-based returns, or more likely exposure to alternative sources of market exposure, is appealing, despite the fees. You now have the unenviable task of finding the right hedge fund investment to make. Unless you are exceptionally wealthy and sophisticated financially, your strategy should be to pick a fund of hedge funds (or one of the alternatives) that provides you with the building-block characteristics you are looking for – preferably equity-like returns, with less than equity risk and a low correlation to bonds and equities.

A good hedge fund of funds manager performs a number of roles: it selects funds after good due diligence, constructs a portfolio with a range of strategies and managers to create favourable portfolio characteristics; and

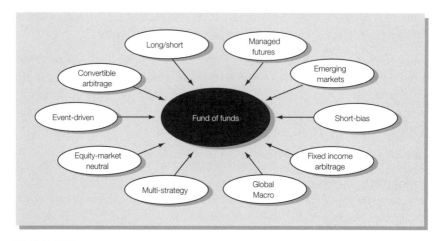

figure 17.8 A carefully constructed portfolio can have appealing characteristics

handles the monitoring and management of the portfolio of funds. This comes at a price: commonly, a hedge fund of funds fees are 1 per cent a year plus 10 per cent of the upside and that's on top of the 2 per cent and 20 per cent that each fund manager takes on average. Figure 17.8 provides a generic representation of a fund of funds. Don't be too concerned about what each of the strategies is – what you should be interested in are the characteristics of the hedge fund of fund's portfolio of strategies and the diversification it will bring to your portfolio.

Selecting the right fund of funds

Private banks and other gatekeepers have been bringing out new products rapidly to provide their clients with access to this new world. A word of caution: like managers themselves, fund of funds also show a wide variety of strategies and return dispersion. You have more than 1,000 to choose from.

Seek out reputable managers and try and understand how their fund is expected to behave, how many managers it has and how combined together they will produce these characteristics. You would be well advised to make sure you understand what a fund of fund is trying to achieve and that it has a well thought out plan for achieving its goals. Research has shown that the average fund of funds generated returns of 3 per cent less than funds of funds made up of funds selected at random (Kat, 2002), so it's not an easy, infallible or a cheap option. Many investors simply go with the product suggested by their advisor, as any other route consumes time and effort. Investing by default is a weak strategy; best not to invest than invest badly.

Developments that provide access to hedge fund characteristics

This is a fast moving space, as firms try and deliver products that get around the considerable practical issues that investors, like you, face when trying to access the beneficial characteristics that hedge funds may deliver.

Investable indices: a passive approach to investing

A number of organisations have begun to develop indices of *investable* hedge funds, where the index constitutes a number of hedge funds, of various strategies, assembled according to some predefined criteria. Examples include the MSCI Hedge Invest Index and the CSFB/Tremont Investable Hedge Fund Index. Products based on these pools of managers avoid the layer of fees associated with fund of fund managers, which is a start, and they provide a broad multi-strategy approach. This may be the way forward for some and is an area worth having on your radar screen. Critics of this approach claim that only desperate managers open themselves up to these programmes! The jury is still out.

Access sources of market exposure, not manager skill

Some innovative firms, particularly in the USA, are developing interesting products that concur with the proposition above that hedge fund returns are largely driven by exposure to a variety of well known, and sometimes less well-known, market exposures. While individual funds are different, and exposures vary over time, their aggregate exposures across the industry are relatively stable. These firms recreate such market exposures to replicate hedge funds in general and at significantly lower costs, because you don't have to give up 20 per cent of your upside. Keep an eye out for developments that could be a good way to get such building-block exposure.

A final word of caution

Bill Gross, managing director of PIMCO, one of the most highly respected active management companies, has said of hedge funds (2004):

'Hedge funds in reality are just unregulated banks, operating on a poorly disclosed amount of equity capital and taking the spread between their cost of funds and their riskier and longer dated assets ... to my thinking it's leverage, not the investment acumen of 7,000 fund managers that makes this mare go.'

There are a few talented managers who will generate good absolute returns that are down to skill and not luck; but they are hard to find. You have to decide whether it is worth trying.

Guidelines for using hedge funds

I am not saying don't invest in hedge funds, but do take care and effort in deciding what you want to achieve and how you propose to achieve it. It takes far more than just investment in a fund. Here are some guidelines to help with this decision.

Guideline 1
Ask yourself why you are thinking of investing in hedge funds. If it is to diversify the risk in your portfolio, have you pursued all the other options using less esoteric investments such as real estate funds and commodity-based exchange-traded fund? If not, then maybe take a look there first. Look to see whether you can replicate the characteristics by using traditional asset classes first. What about holding a little more in bonds?

Guideline 2
Treat any industry generalisations with scepticism and make allowances for the overstatement of returns and the understatement of volatility and correlations.

Guideline 3
Decide what it is that you want your hedge fund of funds to do for you and focus on finding a fund with these attributes and a convincing pitch as to how and why it will deliver.

Guideline 4
Evidently, this game is about picking individual managers. Ask yourself just how many managers will actually deliver consistently positive returns over your investment timeframe and who will still be around when you need them in twenty years' time. You have to find a way of selecting your fund of funds managers who will generate consistent skill-based returns, over time. If you don't have a process then ask yourself whether you can afford to get manager selection choices wrong and whether you should be playing this game at all.

Guideline 5
Perhaps consider using an investable index product where your money is

invested in a pool of managers that constitute an investable index. At least take some time to research them. The benefits are that you do not have to select managers yourself or choose a fund of funds manager and pay a second layer of substantial fees. Keep looking for new products.

Guideline 6

Finally, be prepared to be disappointed. Hedge fund investing is not alchemy and most managers have not yet seen a financial market crisis such as the Russian bond crisis that brought down Long Term Capital in 1998. At the very least accept that absolute return orientated hedge funds are an unproven option.

17.4 Commodities

Commodities are the raw materials that get used in the manufacturing economies around the world. Investing in commodities has been peripheral to most investors for some time, probably due to periods of lacklustre performance because innovation in technology to exploit natural resources had increased supply and prices were on a downward trend in real terms. But the demand for commodities has been growing as emerging economies that tend to use a high level of commodities have entered a period of strong growth. Some of these economies, such as China, India and Brazil are huge and the world's population grows by one hundred million people a year. In 2003, China alone used half of the world's supply of cement and a third of the world's production of steel and coal, yet car ownership is only equivalent to that in the USA in 1910 at around eight cars per thousand people compared with nine hundred cars per thousand in the USA today (Burgin, 2005).

This demand for oil, gas, metals, minerals, timber and foodstuffs continues to rise. Yet, you should not be tempted into market-timing plays but should consider the beneficial long-term characteristics that commodities can bring to your portfolio. To some extent that depends on how you get exposure to them.

Different routes to exposure

To make life more complicated, there are three main ways of getting exposure to commodities. The first is to own physical commodities and gain exposure directly to changes in commodity prices, although I'm not sure where you would store all the oil and pork bellies! This may work for gold, but by and large this is not a practical method.

The second way is indirect exposure, where you own shares in resource-orientated firms extracting and processing commodities, probably via a fund. Your return in this case comes from the change in share price and dividends, which you could expect to have a reasonable correlation to commodity prices in the longer term.

The third way is to invest in a fund or ETF that invests in commodity futures. This needs a little explanation. In its simplest sense, a producer of physical commodities, such as a farmer or a mining company, may want to hedge themselves against falls in prices and thus be able to protect their future revenue. They are willing to pay a premium for this protection. The other side of the contract takes this premium in return for accepting this price uncertainty – that's the side you will be on. Because futures contracts are traded on margin (i.e. you only have to put down small proportion of the face value of the contract) the bulk of the money sits in short-dated, low-risk government securities, earning a low return. The combination of the two is what you end up with. You hope that the premium covers you when prices fall – on occasion it may not be enough and you will make losses. In effect, you are being rewarded for insuring others against commodity price volatility, not just from upward directional movements in commodity price changes.

You need to decide which route to take. The few index funds and ETFs that exist are based on baskets of commodity futures. Actively managed funds focus on listed securities that are correlated to prices. Both tend to have high correlations to inflation.

Going down the commodity futures route

As a building block, commodity futures have a good medium to long-term record in protecting investors from inflation. The premium for investing in commodities from 1959–2004 was around 3.5 per cent above US government bonds, similar to that of equities, but are uncorrelated with them or bonds and are positively correlated with inflation, unexpected inflation and changes in expected inflation (Gorton and Rouwenhorst, 2004). Although, as ever in investing, there is no certainty that this pattern will continue over the period you will be investing, there is a sound argument that with increased supply around the world and increased demand, where the marginal demand is from emerging countries with more volatile economies, price volatility is likely to be high. Figure 17.9 gives the annual real returns from commodity futures in US$. This does not reflect the movement in exchange rates between the USA and the UK.

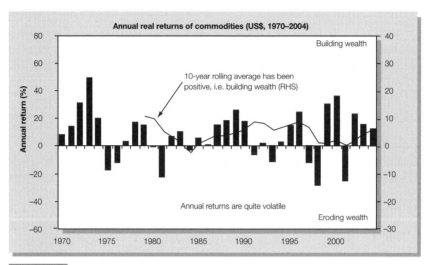

figure 17.9 **Commodity futures provide a good hedge against inflation**

Source: Goldman Sachs Commodity Index (Thomson Datastream)

You can see that real returns have been volatile with some large downturns; in fact over this period they were about as volatile as equities. Over this period as a whole, real returns have been strong at around 7 per cent in sterling terms.

Adding commodity futures to a portfolio

While the volatility of commodity futures is high and comparable to that of equities, because they have a low to negative correlation with other building blocks their effect on a portfolio with a bias towards equities will be to dampen volatility, if taken from your equity allocation – Markovitz's free lunch at work again. If, on the other hand, you have a shorter time horizon, or are withdrawing an income from your portfolio, you might do better to avoid adding a building block with high volatility, despite its low correlations, or only make small allocations to it.

Perhaps interesting to note, if you are invested in a fund that replicates the FTSE All-Share index, you will already have some indirect exposure to commodities, in particular oil, through holding companies such as Shell and BP. In a global equity benchmark, such as the MSCI World Index, energy, raw materials and mining stocks, the latter being a proxy for commodities, represent about 12 per cent.

Commodity futures the easy way

Fortunately, an ETF that tracks the Goldman Sachs Commodity Index has been issued, which trades in euros on the Deutsche Börse. This gives cheap access to a basket of commodities, made up of four sectors: energy, about 77 per cent (e.g. Brent and natural gas); metals about eight per cent (precious and industrial); agriculture about 10 per cent (e.g. corn and coffee); and livestock about 4 per cent (live cattle and lean hogs).

Active funds investing in stocks

Actively managed funds and investment trusts are another option, some of which have been around for some time (or have teams that have been). Firms offering these funds include JP Morgan, First State and Merrill Lynch. I'm not recommending them, just offering examples! These funds invest in companies involved in resource extraction and, in some cases, processing. The only advice I can give is to look for a fund with a good spread of commodity exposure, a reputable manager and reasonable fees. The same principles established previously apply – people and process are key.

Structured notes may be applicable in some cases

A number of structured notes that in some cases provide a guarantee of your nominal capital back after five years and the opportunity for say 200 per cent of the upside of a basket of commodity futures. While I am not personally that keen on structured notes for the long-term investor, because it is hard to see how much you are paying for the privilege and you should be focused on the longer-term diversification benefits of commodities, they may have a place to play for investors approaching the transition point at which they need cash. These notes may be a gamble worth playing, in moderation, in such a case.

17.5 International equities

International equities in this context refers to the equity markets of developed nations outside your domestic market. For the UK, these are USA and Canada, the twelve big EU countries (ex-UK), Finland, Norway and Switzerland, Japan, Hong Kong, Singapore, Australia and New Zealand.

Misconceptions about international equities

Investors often make three elementary mistakes when they think about investing in international equities: first, they think that because stepping away from home shores feels riskier, it must be riskier, thereby delivering higher returns; second, they tend to believe that they are obtaining substantial levels of diversification when the truth is that it is somewhat limited and apparently ever more so; and third, many forget that owning foreign equities means that you will own foreign currency exposure as well, adding another dimension of risk. Let's tackle these one by one.

Investing in the USA may seem riskier to a UK-based investor and vice versa, but in themselves the markets have similar levels of risk and return. In the long run, the rates of real growth of developed economies are much the same as the UK, so you would expect returns to be comparable, long term, from the equity markets of large, developed nations, where the earnings generated actually flow through to investors. Sure, from an active manager's perspective, the return opportunities are greater as the choice of markets is greater, but that does not imply that returns will be higher – that depends where you stand on the active against index debate.

The second mistake is believing that you have gained a high level of diversification from your domestic equity exposure. In fact, while you do get some benefits, as economies may be at different stages of their economic cycles, or have different local factors affecting their performance, these are limited. Periods may occur when there are prolonged differences either in your favour or against you, which may be due to the markets and/or the exchange rate movements between countries. Also, it is increasingly observed that when one big market falls, so do most around the globe. Figure 17.10 shows that the direction of market movements is similar between UK and international equities.

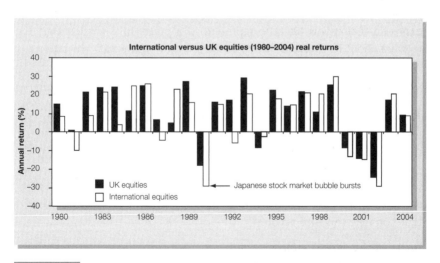

figure 17.10 Real returns of UK and international equities (1980–2004)

Source: *UK Equities – DMS Global Data (Ibbotson) © 2006 E Dimson, P Marsh and M Staunton; International Equities – MSCI World ex-UK Index*

Over the twenty-five-year period of Figure 17.10, UK equities returned around 9.5 per cent and international equities around 7.5 per cent. The difference between the two is largely due to the fact that the stock market bubble in Japan burst, with dire and continuing consequences for the Japanese economy. It is a salutary lesson in the longevity of some market crashes, where even fifteen years later, the market still languished at around 25 per cent of its previous high. By all means use international equities to diversify your domestic equity market risk, just remember not to place too much store in the diversification benefit. On this basis, one could question why big UK pension funds hold around 45 per cent in UK equities and 25 per cent in international equities and holding so few other return smoothers such as commodities and property, that should provide better return-smoothing.

Third, currency exposure comes with international investing. For example, when the pound is strong, it cuts returns made from overseas investments. Imagine that you own the US stock market and it goes up by 10 per cent, but sterling strengthens against the dollar by 15 per cent: when you convert your US holdings back into sterling, you will have lost 5 per cent or so. As with all markets, the direction and longevity of currency movements is not easy to predict and many long-term investors remain unhedged, i.e. they accept this inherent currency exposure in investing overseas, maintaining a stance that they hope will even out in the long term. Equity market risk and currency are comparable in magnitude and currency exposure may provide limited diversification benefits. However, given the relatively small exposure that this is likely to represent in a portfolio, I wouldn't get too worried about it – a maximum of 20 per cent of your equity allocation.

Getting exposure to international equities

There are two ways to implement an international equity allocation. The first is to buy a fund; that replicates a particular international equity index; the second is to buy one that is actively managed to try and beat the market. As ever, the same arguments and rules apply in choosing which way to go. Some funds may be global rather than international in nature, the difference being that the former usually include the UK, so make sure that you take this into account.

International/global indices usually are put together based on the market capitalisation of different stock markets around the world; yet earlier we assumed that returns would be more or less equivalent over time between markets. The result is that you end up with a portfolio skewed by market

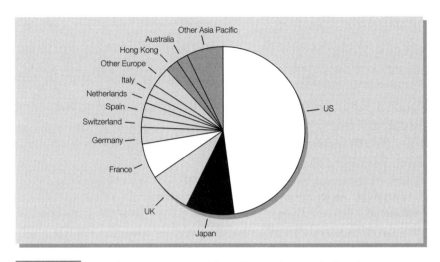

figure 17.11 The US dominates world equity market capitalisation

Source: FIBV

capitalisation rather than one that is most effectively spread between markets and regions. To illustrate the point, US investors looking for international equity exposure in 1989 would have seen a market-cap-weighted allocation to Japan of over half, which left them exposed to the crash that followed. Global market capitalisations are illustrated in Figure 17.11.

The UK represents around 8 per cent of global equity market capitalisation, but the USA dominates, in part because it has the most developed capital markets. In an international equity allocation, this would be more than half. Germany and France have historically had less of an equity orientation and pack a punch below their economic clout. A few indices use gross domestic product (GDP) weightings, but these are rarely the base for retail products.

An argument can be made for building international exposure using regional building blocks that spread out your exposure a little more evenly. You could reasonably allocate your international equity exposure as 35 per cent to the USA, 35 per cent to Europe, 20 per cent to Japan and 10 per cent to the Far East, ex-Japan, for example. A wide number of index funds, ETFs and active funds exist.

Again, moderation is the key word.

References

Brooks, C. and Kat, H. (2002) *The statistical properties of hedge fund index returns and their implications for investors.* Cass Business School, Working Paper # 0004. Available from: http://www.cass.city.ac.uk

Burgin, P. (2005). It's time to look towards alternative fuel sources. *Investment Week Natural Resources Supplement,* November.

Davis, P. (2004) Academic raises doubts about hedge fund returns, *Financial Times,* (FT*fn*) issue no. 133, p. 2.

Gehin, W. and Vaissie, M. (2005) *The right place for alternative beta in hedge fund portfolios: An answer to the capacity effect fantasy.* Edhec-Risk Asset Management Research Centre. Available from: http:// www.edhec-risk.com

Gompers, P. and Lerner, J. (2001) Private equity and asset allocation: Clues to a puzzle. *Private Equity Research Initiative 2001*, Salomon Smith Barney, vol. 1., no. III.

Gorton, G. and Rouwenhorst, K. G. (2004) Fact and fantasies about commodities futures. *NBER Working Paper Series*, Working Paper 10595, National Bureau of Economic Research, p.16.

Gross, W. (2004) *Investment outlook.* PIMCO, August 10.

Kat, H. M. and Lu, S. (2002) *An excursion into the statistical properties of individual hedge fund returns.* Cass Business School working paper # 0016. Available from: http://www.cass.city.ac.uk

Taleb, N. N. (2004) *Fooled By randomness: The hidden role of chance in life and in the markets.* 2nd ed. New York: Texere, p. 110.

Tass Research (2005) *Slower flows for fourth quarter; hedge funds mark another record growth year in 2004.* White Plains, NY: Lipper HedgeWorld. Available from: http://www.hedgeworld.com

18

Spotlight on return enhancers

Having found ways to make smooth out returns using *return smoothers*, you might find that where you have added building blocks with lower long-term returns and lower risk, your overall portfolio returns have been reduced. In response, you may wish to include some *returns enhancers* to boost returns. The problem you face is that there is no sure fire way of doing so, as each return-enhancing building block has its own theoretical as well as practical nuances that you need to feel comfortable with before throwing your money on the table. Here you can find a balanced insight into each of the blocks.

We will focus on three Level 2 building blocks: the equities of smaller companies; the equities of companies that appear to be valued for less than they are really worth (value stocks); and those of companies in countries that are aspiring to become developed markets.

Remember that with all investing, additional returns always come with additional risk, of one sort or another. You rarely get something for nothing.

18.1 Smaller companies – higher returns?

According to the manual of investing sound bites, the equities of smaller companies (small-cap stocks) will outperform those of larger companies, over time. As a consequence, small caps may provide an opportunity to enhance returns relative to the market as a whole, which comprises predominantly larger companies. Small-cap stocks exhibit a higher level of return volatility than the market as a whole, which accounts for some of the additional returns, but does not explain everything. A premium, the small-cap (or size) premium as it is known, is paid to investors for the additional risks that they take relative to larger company stocks, both in terms of additional volatility and risks that cannot be diversified away. Some investors try and capture this premium by adding additional exposure to smaller companies. It is not guaranteed to succeed and you need to make your own mind up.

Looking deeper into the data and arguments behind the small-cap premium will allow you to decide for yourself whether you want to include an additional exposure to them.

What do the data tell us?

In the USA, the outperformance of small-cap stocks over large-cap stocks over the past eighty years or so has been around 2 per cent a year on average, but there have been times when this has not been the case. It would appear that either there is a reward for taking some kind of non-market risk, or that this is an anomaly in the data series; more on that later.

Looking at the UK, where we can use the Hoare Govett Smaller Company Index, which represents the bottom 10 per cent of the market's capitalisation, you can see that a small-cap premium appears to exist (Figure 18.1). This index has data going back only to 1955. Figure 18.1 illustrates the cumulative difference in real returns over the data series.

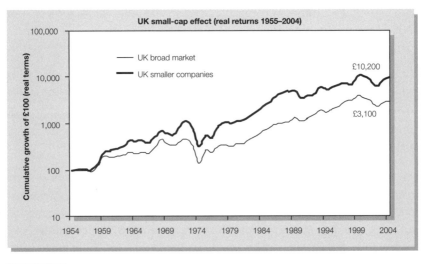

figure 18.1 UK small-cap stocks have outperformed the market as a whole

Source: DMS Global Data (Ibbotson) © 2006 E Dimson, P Marsh and M Staunton; Small Cap, HGSC Index

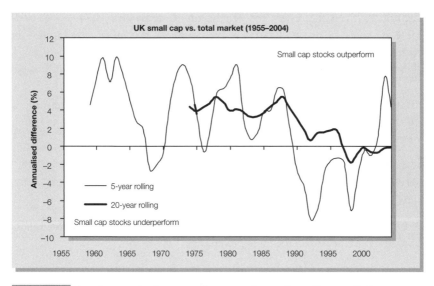

figure 18.2 **Small-cap stocks sometimes underperform the market**

Source: DMS Global Data (Ibbotson) © 2006 E Dimson, P Marsh and M Staunton; Small Cap, HGSC Index

The *small-cap effect* over this period was around 2.5 per cent a year. The academics who compiled the data series also suggest from their work that from 1900 to 1955 a small but positive size premium may have existed (Dimson et al., 2002). However, you would be wise to remember that such averages mask periods, sometimes as long as twenty years, over which you would not have received this premium, but the reverse (Figure 18.2).

The swings between periods of outperformance and underperformance of small cap stocks relative to the market may tempt you into trying to time your entry and exit into small cap stocks to capture the periods of outperformance and avoid periods of underperformance. Pick up the money section of any Sunday paper to see how much pressure there is on you to time markets. Don't be tempted because even the most astute professionals find this hard to do. Being a contrarian is not a route to an emotionally easy life!

Why does the small-cap premium exist?

Now we get to the crux of the debate. I wish I could answer this question, but I can't. In fact, when you review the discussions and ideas of academics and practitioners in the industry, you see that their views are varied and inconclusive. This should be a warning to you that owning small-cap stocks is not a sure thing. However, there does appear to be some form of risk that cannot be diversified away, for which you are apparently being rewarded. Here are some of the explanations from some of the most astute investors in the business.

Burton Malkiel (1999):

'The higher returns for smaller companies may simply be the requisite reward owed to investors for assuming a greater risk of disappointment in the investment returns they expect.'

'The small-cap effect found in some studies is simply a result of what is called "survivorship bias" ... Today's list of companies include only small firms that have survived – not the small firms that later went bankrupt.'

An interview with Eugene Fama by Peter Tanous (1997a) about the small-cap effect included the following exchange:

Fama: 'The risk in my terms can't be explained by the market. It means that because they move together, there is something about these small stocks that creates an undiversifiable risk. The undiversifiable risk is what you get paid for.'

Tanous: 'What causes that risk?'

Fama: 'You know, that's an embarrassing question because I don't know.'

John Bogle, founder of the Vanguard Group (2002):

'We see that the long period is punctuated by a whole series of reversion to the mean. Virtually the entire small-cap advantage [in the USA] took place in the first 18 years ... On balance these to-and-fro reversions have cancelled each other out, and since 1945 the returns of large-cap stocks and small-cap stocks have been virtually identical ... So ask yourself whether the evidence to justify the claim that small-cap superiority isn't too fragile a foundation on which to base a long-term strategy.'

As an investor with additional allocations to small-cap stocks, you could suffer significant periods of underperformance compared with large caps and will in all likelihood have increased the volatility of your portfolio. On the other hand, there is the potential to increase your return and ultimate purchasing power if you hold a higher than market proportion of small cap stocks in your portfolio – if you are lucky. There is no clear-cut answer. You have to go with what you feel comfortable. My advice would be to make any bets away from the total market with moderation. Remember that in a broad market index such as the FTSE All-Share, you already own about 6 per cent in small cap stocks.

18.2 Value and growth: what's that all about?

Investing in stocks with certain characteristics, rather than capitalisation as we saw above (e.g. small and large), is known as *style investing*. The two main styles are defined as *value* and *growth*. While style investing is in its infancy in the UK, it is very much mainstream in the USA. Over time, it will become more commonplace in the UK.

The value versus growth debate, like that of the small-cap premium, focuses on the fact that historic data appears to show that a basket of stocks with *value* characteristics appear to deliver a premium over stocks of companies that exhibit *growth* characteristics, in the long run. This is summed up in the sound bite used in the industry that 'value stocks beat growth stocks'. If you believe that the value premium exists and is here to stay, then you may wish to use value stocks to capture this premium for your portfolio. Remember here that you already own these value stocks in your broad based equity market allocation and you should be considering whether you wish to tilt your portfolio further towards value. Around 30 per cent of FTSE All-Share companies are classified as value stocks.

Defining value and growth

A sensible place to start this discussion is to make sure that we are all on the same page in terms of what we mean by value and growth. There are no standard definitions but common threads exist.

Value stocks defined

These are often described as stocks that are cheap or undervalued. Perhaps a more apt term for value stocks is distressed stocks. Value stocks are often categorised as weak or under-performing companies, whose stock prices have been written down by the market as a consequence, possibly to below their true or intrinsic value. Financial measures that are frequently applied to value stocks are:

- Low market value vs book value (i.e. the underlying value of a company's net assets) usually described as low price-to-book value.
- Low price relative to earnings (low P/E ratio) or in other words, the amount that an investor is willing to pay for each pound of future earnings that the company generates.
- High dividend yield, which reflects the payout of cash today as opposed to reinvestment in the business.

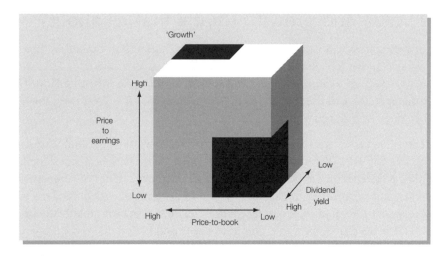

figure 18.3 **Growth and value style generalisations**

As a generalisation, value stocks are sometimes characterised by low earnings growth rates, low return on equity and high debt to capital ratios.

Growth stocks defined

On the other hand, growth stocks are companies whose earnings are growing rapidly and appear to have the ability to grow further. Even if growth rates are already high, that will not put off some investors, provided that they believe the market consensus is wrong. In a growth investor's view, earnings growth drives stock price performance and performance is largely independent of the stocks value today. This earnings growth will increase book value and if the ratio of price-to-book remains constant, then the share price of the company will rise. Financial measures that are frequently applied to growth stocks include: high P/E ratios, high price-to-book ratios, low dividend yield (and high corporate reinvestment rates), low debt to capital and high earnings growth rates. The generalised differences between the two are set out in Figure 18.3.

In reality, it's not so clear cut

While the industry often portrays these two styles of investing as mutually exclusive and some investment managers live or die by their belief in one or the other, the reality is that assessing the fundamental value of a company needs to take into account all aspects of its business. This quote from Warren Buffett (1992) perhaps reminds us to beware of labels assigned to companies that appear to hold different characteristics.

'Most analysts feel that they must choose between two approaches customarily thought to be in opposition "value" and "growth". Indeed, many investment professionals see any mixing of the two terms as a form of intellectual cross-dressing. We view this as fuzzy thinking (in which, it must be confessed, I myself engaged some years ago). In our opinion, the two approaches are joined at the hip: growth is always a component in the calculation of value, constituting a variable whose importance can range from negligible to enormous and whose impact can be negative as well as positive. In addition, we think that the very term "value investing" is redundant. What is "investing" if it is not the act of seeking value at least sufficient to justify the amount paid?'

At face value, value wins

Much of the academic work relating to the value premium is from the USA: from the data, it appears that a substantial premium exists for investing in value stocks compared with growth stocks. Between 1928 and 2004, value stocks in the USA outperformed growth stocks by around 3.5 per cent a year, on average, with a volatility of around 28 per cent for the former and 21 per cent for the latter (Ibbotson, 2004).

This is consistent from a UK perspective

UK research is scarce in comparison, although the recent advent of better data has improved the potential for research, although it is a shame that it is not freely available. In the UK (and other international markets) a value premium appears to exist too. In the UK, the annualised value-growth premium was 2.7 per cent a year on average from 1900–2000 (Dimson et al., 2002).

But there are no guarantees

Figure 18.4 identifies considerable periods of time in the USA over which value stocks have underperformed growth stocks. This creates a dilemma: do you try and obtain the value premium by holding more value stocks in your portfolio? If so, are you prepared to sit out what could be lengthy and painful periods of underperformance and hope to be rewarded? It's not recommended that you try and time when to be in value stocks and when to be in growth stocks. As ever with market-timing decisions, the longevity with which value and growth styles can seem seriously out of kilter, combined with rapidity and magnitude of turnarounds makes this a really tough game to play.

Using UK data you can see that the same patterns emerge (Figure 18.5). Over shorter and longer periods of time, value sometimes will and some-

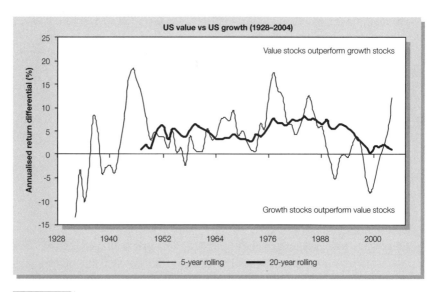

figure 18.4 Value appears to win in the long run

Source: Ibbotson Associates

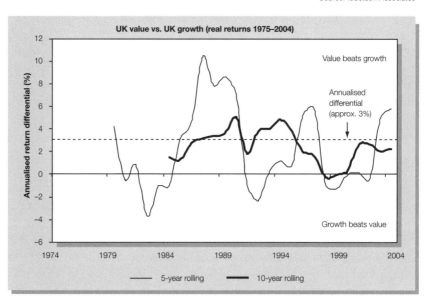

figure 18.5 Value stocks generally, but not always, outperform growth stocks

Source: MSCI

times won't outperform growth stocks. So, to make an additional allocation to value stocks requires you to feel confident that this premium is actually a reward for taking more risk, not just a data anomaly.

Why have value stocks outperformed growth stocks?

Again, like the small-cap debate, there is no clear winner in terms of explanations, although the debaters fall into a couple of camps. Rex Sinquefield is an investment academic and chairman of Dimensional Fund Advisors, a firm that specialises in providing index products with the ability to tilt portfolios using capitalisation and style classifications. He states (Tanous, 1997b):

'On average, they're going to have future earnings problems. That's a source of risk. The market doesn't like that. So, small stocks and value stocks seem to be associated with higher rates of return. But it's really a cost of capital question. The value companies are struggling, and because they have this kind of risk they have to pay more for equity capital. The high cost of capital for the firm means a high rate of return for the investor.'

Eugene Fama reinforces this view (Tanous, 1997a):

'To me, stock prices are just the prices that produce the expected returns that people require to hold them. If they are growth companies, people are willing to hold them at a lower expected return ... Value stocks may continue to take their knocks. Their prices reflect the fact that they are in poor times. As a result, because people don't want to hold them – in our view because they are riskier – they have higher expected returns.'

John Bogle (2002) provides his own thoughts based largely around his belief in a return-to-mean for markets over time:

'Place me squarely in the camp of the contrarians who don't accept the inherent superiority of value strategies over growth strategies.'

At the end of the day, I don't think either you or I are any the wiser. The only thing worth remembering is that the market, for whatever reason, requires that perceived risks are rewarded. If you wish for the higher returns than value stocks, or for that matter small-cap stocks, potentially provide, you will be taking on more risk, and this risk in the widest sense will not just be measured by volatility of returns. Place your bets in moderation.

18.3 Emerging market equities make sense in theory

The term 'emerging markets' usually refers to low or middle-income economies based on per capita gross national income below the World Bank's high-income threshold in 2002 of around $9,000 a head (Toyat,

2004). The story behind investing in emerging market equities is simple in theory, although in the limited time that they have been widely tracked (since 1987) the jury is still out on whether they deliver the benefits that you would expect to investors. As such, any allocation needs to be based on your confidence, or otherwise, that the story will pay off over your investment period. Conviction is needed otherwise when things go badly (as they may well do) you will be tempted to cut your losses and run – the classic buy-high-sell-low strategy.

The theoretical case for including them in your mix

Individual emerging markets frequently exhibit very wide swings in returns, an example being the Thai stock market that was up over 100 per cent in 1993 but subsequently fell by over 80 per cent, so owning a basket of different countries is essential to reduces this volatility, but it is still substantial.

The higher risks that accompany such investment should be rewarded or why would investors bother to put money into these markets? Remember that investing in emerging economies leaves you open to the vagaries of less-developed markets, including the political (coups, despots, anti-capitalists, etc), economic, social and legal risks that can affect your money. For example, in Malaysia during the Asian crisis, the government effectively stopped investors from repatriating their money by imposing draconian penalties on anyone who wanted to liquidate their portfolios.

In theory too, investing in dynamic, growing economies, such as India, China and Brazil where the long-term rate of real growth is higher than that in developed nations such as the UK and the USA, should generate higher levels of return; although that presupposes that profits made actually flow through to shareholders either as dividends or earnings growth that results in capital gains. Poor governance, corruption, family holdings and poor accounting practices may hinder this. As these economic, legal and governance environments improve, this argument may hold more water. It is always worth remembering that the USA and Japan were once emerging market economies and that Greece and Portugal made the transition from the MSCI Emerging Markets Index to the developed MSCI EAFE (i.e. global ex-US) Index in 1997 and 2001 respectively (Tokat, 2004).

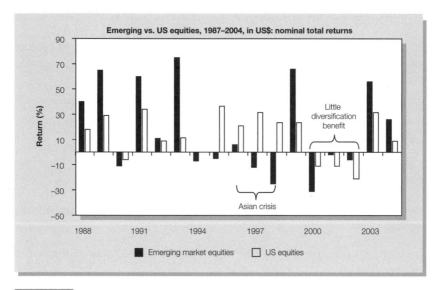

figure 18.6 **Theory and reality are not always the same**

Source: Emerging Market, MSCI

The empirical case is less clear cut

From 1987 to 2004, emerging market equities only beat US equities by 1 per cent returning just over 13 per cent a year, but with around twice the level of volatility (35 per cent to 18 per cent). Not a very encouraging result given the risks you are taking.

Figure 18.6 reveals the volatility of emerging market equities. You can see that the patterns of returns are not perfectly correlated and some would argue that they provide a strong diversification benefit. I'm not so sure in practice how valuable this will be, particularly as the smoothing effect tends to fail when developed markets are in turmoil, and the amounts you add need to be small given the high volatility that they represent. Over the period from 1999 to 2003, rolling three-year correlations were as high as 0.8, although in most of the 1990s it ranged from 0.2 to 0.6. This book uses 0.6 as the correlation for emerging market equities, which may be generous.

The data available is far from ideal. First, it only starts in 1988 and second it has a range of biases that probably overstate returns. These include the fact that only companies and countries with relatively successful histories are covered, known as survivorship bias. From an empirical standpoint the story looks unconvincing. So what should you do?

Tips for investing in emerging market equities

If you are keen on the theory of investing in emerging markets to capture the extra returns that come with additional risk and potentially to capture the growth of such economies, then here are some tips:

■ do so in moderation;

■ own a diversified pool of markets, rather than putting all your eggs in one basket, such as China, despite what the Sunday papers may say;

■ be prepared for the times when returns diverge substantially from UK and developed markets on the downside;

■ don't be overly optimistic about the degree to which a free lunch is on offer.

View emerging market equity investments as a leveraged play on developed market equities.

The old argument as to whether you should index in these less efficient markets or choose an active manager exists. As ever, the costs of exchange-traded funds and index funds, which provide access to a broad basket of companies and countries, are less than those of active managers. Turnover costs tend to be higher in these markets, so turnover will erode returns. An ETF does exist in the UK and is a reasonable solution. There is a limited number of specialist, actively managed emerging market funds. Less than half of active funds beat the index in the three and five years to 2003.

Alternatively, the FTSE All-World Index (as opposed to the FTSE World Index) has a higher exposure to emerging markets. You will also find that some actively managed international equity funds will have some emerging market exposure – read the prospectus and look at the fund fact sheets to find out.

In any case, limit emerging market exposure generally to around 5 per cent of your portfolio, if you include it. More, and the volatility increases quickly, as does the likely effect of downside divergence effects on your portfolio; less, and your allocation becomes irrelevant.

References

Bogle, J. C. (2002) *The telltale chart*. Bogle Financial Markets Research Center. Available from: http://www.vanguard.com.

Buffett, W. (1992) *Chairman's Letter to Shareholders 1991*. Berkshire Hathaway Inc.

Dimson, E., Marsh, P. R. and Staunton, M. (2002) *Triumph of the optimists: 101 years of global investment data*. Princeton, NJ: Princeton University Press, p. 145.

Ibbotson Associates (2005) *Stocks, bonds, bills, inflation (SBBI) – 2005 yearbook*. Chicago: Ibbotson Associates.

Malkiel, B. G. (1999) *A random walk down Wall Street*. 7th ed. New York: W.W. Norton, p. 251.

MSCI. UK value and growth stocks 1974–2004. Available from: www.mscidata.com

Tanous, P. J. (1997a) *An interview with Eugene Fama – Investment gurus* [online]. Available from: http://library.dfaus.com/reprints/interview_fama_tanous.

Tanous, P. J. (1997b) *An interview with Rex Sinquefield – Investment gurus* [online]. Available from: http://library.dfaus.com/reprints/interview_sinquefield_tanous/

Tokat, Y. (2004) *International equity investing: Investing in emerging markets*. Vanguard Investment Counseling & Research. Available from: www.vanguard.com.

Conclusion

This book has, I hope, been useful to you both in getting you into a smarter investing mindset and in allowing you to decide what type of portfolio makes sense and how you can put this into practice. If you take anything away from this book, then let it be these six points:

1 Getting the mix of investment building blocks right is the most critical factor. Remember that diversification makes good sense and is the only free lunch that investing provides you. Spread your portfolio into a number of building blocks to create a portfolio that will help you through the seasons.

2 Remember that risk and return go hand in hand with few if any exceptions. If it looks too good to be true, it probably is.

3 Make a pact with yourself only to make investment choices that increase your chances of being successful. Remember that you are always aiming to lose the fewest points relative to the market, which means controlling all costs at every point of the process.

4 Stick with your chosen mix at all times, but rebalance your portfolio if the proportions move significantly out of line using cash flows from the portfolio or additional contributions wherever possible.

5 Implement the portfolio using low-cost index funds (or exchange-traded funds) as the default vehicle to give yourself the greatest chance of capturing the bulk of the market returns that each of your portfolio building blocks delivers. Use active managers if index funds or equivalent are not available or where they can truly convince you, on terms that you set, that they have the people, process and commitment to deliver market-beating returns for you in the future. If you're not sure, don't risk it.

6 Try your hardest to control your emotions: avoid feeling covetous of building blocks doing better than your own; don't be tempted by greed or paralysed by fear. If you have been diligent in establishing your investment portfolio (1–4 above), then, when times get tough, as they will, choose to do nothing as your default strategy!

Finally, be confident that you are now a *smarter investor* than most and enjoy your investing and the wealth it brings you, with any luck!

Bibliography

The following resources are well worth taking a look at. They have been a considerable source of information, wisdom and thought-provoking debate for me in writing this book.

Websites

These websites are in addition to the sites already referenced in Chapter 12.

www.vanguard.com is excellent if you want basic education on investing. While the site is US-orientated, its basic ideas and principles still apply. Especially read the speeches given by John C. Bogle, which can be found via the link to the 'Bogle Financial Markets Research Centre'.

www.indexinvestor.com where you can find excellent articles and analysis on the efficacy of index investing. Much of this is free and an annual subscription to the rest is good value at $25 a year.

www.dfaus.com is the public website of a leading index firm which has Eugene Fama and Kenneth French as directors, both leading investment academics. There is a link to a library that has an assortment of articles, research and video clips.

Insightful books

The books below have influenced my thinking over the years and I thank the authors for putting their knowledge and ideas on to paper for all of us to share. It is worth noting that these are all US-focused books, a point not lost on me and my decision to write a book for UK investors. The concepts and ideas apply across borders, but the evidence tends to come from US data.

***Winning the Loser's Game*, Charles D. Ellis, McGraw-Hill** (ISBN 0–07–138767–6).

This is an excellent book that I read in 1994, and wished I had done sooner. It is Charles Ellis' insight into the *'losing-the-fewest points'* strategy that underpins the philosophy that we developed. An easy and entertaining read.

***Common Sense on Mutual Funds*, John C. Bogle, John Wiley & Sons, Inc.** (ISBN 0–471–29543–4). An insightful and valuable book from one of the true visionaries of the industry, a frequent thorn in the side of the active investment management industry, and a true champion of investors. I owe a considerable amount to his insight, wisdom and integrity.

***Pioneering Portfolio Management*, David F. Swensen, The Free Press**

(ISBN 0–684–86443–6). David Swensen is the Chief Investment Officer at Yale University in the USA and is responsible for the management of the University's endowment fund. He is one of the most progressive thinkers in the business, with a clear philosophy of where his team can and cannot add value. Yale has been at the forefront in the move into alternative investment products such as private equity and absolute return strategies (hedge funds). An excellent read for those of you who want to see what a leading investment team are doing.

The Index Fund Solution, **Richard E. Evans and Burton G. Malkiel**. (ISBN0–684–85250–0). This book establishes sound arguments for why most investors should invest in index funds. It also provides some straight-talking guidelines for establishing an investment plan for you. US orientated.

Fooled by Randomness: Nassim Nicholas Taleb, TEXERE Thompson (ISBN1–59799–184–5). This is a wonderfully written book, the focus of which is best described in its full title: *Fooled by Randomness, The Hidden Role of Chance in Life and in the Markets*. A stimulating read.

Data-orientated books

Stocks, Bonds, Bills and Inflation (SBBI)– Yearbook, **Ibbotson Associates**. (ISBN 1–882864–012–3). This book provides the definitive data that is used widely throughout the investment management world for US data. It goes back to 1926, and is the cleanest data available. The book also contains some interesting commentary and observations on the long-term data series. It is an annual publication.

Triumph of the Optimists, **E. Dimson, P. Marsh and M. Staunton, Princeton University Press** (ISBN 0–691–09194–3). This book provides the best UK data available for equities bonds and cash, and data on 15 other countries. However, unlike the SBBI above it does not provide you with the underlying data, which can only be purchased via Ibbotson. It is a useful book though. The analysis in my book is derived from the underlying data, which I purchased. I thank them for what must have been an unenviable task.

Asset allocation software

Portfolio Pathfinder: One of the only packages that focuses on the real risk that investors face, which is that of not being able to meet their purchasing power obligations, needs and goals during their lifetimes. It uses mean-variance optimisation to find efficient portfolios and helps you, via a series of educational and decision-making graphs to decide which portfolio structure is likely to meet your purchasing power goals most effectively. It uses Monte Carlo simulations to do so. It is a reasonably straightforward piece of software that most advisors and reasonably interested investors can use. At the moment it is a US-orientated model that needs a bit of fiddling around to use for other investors. Well worth a look at the website and a call to Dick Purcell, the driving force behind it. *www.planscan.net*

MC Retire: This software is from Efficient Solutions and can be found at *www.effisols.com.* It uses a Monte Carlo simulation to help you to evaluate the chances of success of different investment and withdrawal strategies. At less than $30 it is worth a look. Playing with it provides you an insight into the issues that you face in the distribution phase of your investing. You can also buy a simple optimiser programme relatively cheaply if you want to play around with one.

Additional sources

Bernstein, W. (2001) *The four pillars of investing.* New York: McGraw-Hill.

Bogle, J. C. (1994) *Bogle on mutual funds: New perspectives for the intelligent investor.* New York: Dell.

Brennan, J. (2002) *Straight talk on investing: What you need to know.* New York: Wiley.

Isaacman, M. (2000) *How to be an index investor.* New York: McGraw-Hill.

Markovitz, H. (1952) Portfolio selection, *Journal of Finance,* vol. VII, no.1.

Nofsinger, J. R. (2001) *Investment madness: How psychology affects your investing ... and what to do about it.* Upper Saddle River, NJ: Financial Times Prentice Hall.

Shiller, R. J. (2001) *Irrational exuberance.* Woodstock, UK: Princeton University Press.

Index